Information
and
Capital Markets

Norman Strong and Martin Walker

Basil Blackwell

First published 1987
First published in paperback 1989

Basil Blackwell Ltd
108 Cowley Road, Oxford, OX4 1JF, UK

Basil Blackwell Inc.
432 Park Avenue South, Suite 1503
New York, NY 10016, USA

British Library Cataloguing in Publication Data

Strong, Norman
Information and capital markets.
1. Information theory in economics
I. Title   II. Walker, Martin, 1953–
330.1   HB133

ISBN 0-631-13834-X
0-631-16887-7

Library of Congress Cataloging in Publication Data

Strong, Norman, 1954–
Information and capital markets.
Bibliography: p.
Includes index.
1. Capital market.   2. Uncertainty.   3. Rational
expectations (Economic theory)
I. Walker, Martin, 1953–   . II. Title.
HG4523.S77   1987   332′.041   86-31721

ISBN 0-631-13834-X
0-631-16887-7

Phototypeset in 10 on 11½ pt Times
by Dobbie Typesetting Service, Plymouth Devon
Printed in Great Britain by Billing & Sons Limited, Worcester

Contents

Contents

Contents

Preface

Potential readers of this book are confronted by an information choice problem. They know the book contains information but in deciding whether to invest real resources in reading it (i.e., the opportunity cost of the reader's time and possibly the purchase price) they need to know whether the benefits to be derived from the content are likely to exceed the expected costs.

On the cost side, potential purchasers will already know the purchase price or the fine of an overdue library book. As for the opportunity cost of the reader's time, we have tried to keep the analysis in the book as simple as possible, subject to presenting an intellectually interesting treatment of each topic. In particular, the level of mathematical sophistication is no higher than that demanded of second year undergraduates in accounting, economics or finance.

On the benefits side, there are several reasons why we think the reader will find the following chapters worthy of attention. First, we hope the reader will find the content intellectually stimulating. Information economics is a fascinating area which, in a puzzle solving sense, can give many hours of innocent pleasure.

Second, financial economics is one of the few areas where advances in theoretical knowledge are rapidly impounded into practice. Theories of capital asset pricing, option pricing, and the hypothesis of informational efficiency have already exerted a considerable influence on the financial sector. It is our belief that many of the ideas discussed below will also prove to be of considerable practical importance.

Third, this is the first attempt to pull together the vast literature on information and capital markets into a single text. We have attempted to devise a unifying theoretical framework and a common notation which allows the contributions of individual journal articles to be placed into a wider context. All too often the insights of information economics as they relate to the theory of finance are relegated to footnotes or, at best, treated as minor extensions of the main theme. This is due, in part, to the apparently fragmented nature of the information economics literature. A major purpose of this text is to demonstrate the logical coherence of the information economics literature as it relates to modern finance. We hope to show that information economics provides a complete and logically consistent theoretical foundation for modern finance.

We owe a debt to the writings of others. We are grateful to all the authors referenced in the bibliography for lighting our way. In particular we would like to thank Amin Amershi for allowing us to use some unpublished work. We are also grateful to Mark Casson and the publishers Basil Blackwell for encouraging this project; Michael Bromwich and three referees for their detailed comments; and Christopher Napier who made helpful comments on the early chapters. Secretarial assistance was ably provided by Vivien Hope, Mandy Smith, Claudine Chouchan, and Marriane Tappas. Any remaining errors are entirely the authors' responsibility.

N. Strong
M. Walker

Introduction

The main purpose of this text is to review the implications of the economics of information for our understanding of how capital markets function. In addition the text will discuss the nature and role of information in stock market economies.

The purpose of this introduction is to preview the main themes of the text and to explain our basic methodological approach. Section 0.1 outlines the main themes with which we shall be concerned. Section 0.2 explains the basic methodological principles underlying the rest of the text. Section 0.3 provides a guided tour of the remaining chapters. Section 0.4 notes three limitations to the scope of the text.

0.1 MAIN THEMES

The first major question with which we shall be concerned is the nature of information. For the purposes of this text information is broadly defined as any device that helps to reduce uncertainty. We represent uncertainty by assuming that, at any point in time, the economy can be in one of several possible states of the world. Information is then represented as any device that helps one either to detect the current state of the world or to forecast the future state of the world. For example, consider the decision problem of a farmer as set out below:

	Wet summer	Dry summer
Plant barley	£10,000	£50,000
Plant potatoes	£30,000	£20,000

At the start of the year the farmer must decide whether to plant barley or potatoes. The profit he derives from his crop depends on whether the summer is wet or dry[1]. The figures in the above table show the farmer's profit for each possible weather/crop combination.

Suppose the farmer believes that there is an equal probability of a wet or dry summer and suppose he wishes to maximize his expected profit. Then he will choose to plant barley since his expected profit from producing barley is £30,000 compared with only £25,000 if he plants potatoes.

Now suppose that the farmer can purchase a perfect weather forecast before making his crop decision. In this case he will plant barley if the forecast is 'dry' yielding a conditionally certain profit of £50,000 and potatoes if the weather forecast is 'wet' yielding a conditionally certain profit of £30,000. Prior to receiving the forecast, which he expects to be wet or dry with equal probability, his overall expected profit will be £40,000, £10,000 more than his expected profit in the absence of the forecast.

In this example the state of the world is represented by the state of the weather and information is represented by the weather forecast. Chapter 1 broadens this example to allow for situations that involve more than two possible states of the world and for situations where the state forecast is less than perfect.

The above example also assumed that the farmer could somehow attach probabilities to the various possible states and that he could rank alternative decisions in terms of their expected profit. Chapter 1 provides a more general treatment of rational behaviour under uncertainty. In particular it focuses on the expected utility approach to decision making under uncertainty. For the special case where the outcomes of the decision maker's action choice can be represented along a single 'monetary' dimension this theory predicts that rational individuals will rank alternative actions according to their expected utility where the expected utility of an action is defined as follows:

$$EU(a) = \sum_s U(C(a, s)) \; \phi(s). \tag{0.1}$$

where $C(a, s)$ is the monetary payoff the individual receives in state s if he chooses action a; $U(\cdot)$ is the utility function of the individual defined over monetary outcomes; and $\phi(s)$ is the probability assigned by the individual to state s.

In the previous example the farmer was assumed to rank alternative crops according to their expected profitability. This can be represented in the form (0.1) by defining the farmer's utility function as follows:

$$U(C) = C \tag{0.2}$$

That is, the farmer's utility is equal to the amount of money he receives.

In reality experience shows that the utility function (0.2) leads to rankings of alternative monetary gambles which conflict with the rankings exhibited by most individuals. In particular (0.2) implies that an individual would be indifferent between a certain payoff, X, and any monetary gamble with an expected payoff equal to X. However, most individuals in most situations prefer a certain sum to a risky gamble with the same expected payoff, that is, most individuals exhibit a degree of risk aversion. Chapter 1 shows how risk aversion can be captured mathematically by adopting a functional form for $U(\cdot)$ which is increasing and strictly concave in monetary payoff. Individuals with utility functions of this type are referred to as strictly risk-averse individuals. Individuals with utility functions of the form (0.2) are referred to as risk-neutral individuals.

Following Chapter 1 the remainder of the text focuses on economies in which two or more individuals interact with each other. Moving to multiperson economies leads to two major themes that do not arise in single-person economies. The first of these is the issue of efficient risk sharing. The second is concerned with issues relating to the distribution of information between individuals. The remainder of this section considers each of these new themes in turn.

To appreciate the basic ideas behind the issue of efficient risk sharing consider an economy involving two farmers. Farmer 1 has land that does well in dry summers whilst farmer 2 has land that does well in wet summers. Both farmers believe that wet and dry summers are equally likely. The profits of the two farmers are described as follows:

	Dry summer	Wet summer
Farmer 1	£20,000	£4,000
Farmer 2	£4,000	£20,000

Notice that the profits of the two farmers sum to £24,000 in both dry and wet summers. If both farmers are risk-averse they can make themselves better off by devising some means of sharing the total profits equally.

Chapters 2 and 3 focus on the contractual devices that allow such risk-sharing arrangements to take place. Special attention is paid to the role of various types of securities in risk sharing.

Chapter 2 focuses on two major types of securities: simple contingent claims and complex contingent claims. Simple contingent claims are securities for which the seller agrees to pay one unit of purchasing power to the buyer if and only if one particular state occurs. In our example involving the two farmers there are just two possible simple contingent claims, claims to 'dry' purchasing power and claims to 'wet' purchasing power. Complex contingent claims are securities for which the seller agrees to pay a varying amount to the buyer depending on the state of the world. In fact a simple contingent claim is a special case of a complex contingent claim with a particularly simple payoff pattern.

We show that it will always be possible to achieve fully efficient risk sharing if trade takes place in a *complete* set of simple contingent claims. In other words if claims to purchasing power in one state can be exchanged against claims to purchasing power in any other state then fully efficient risk sharing is possible. Thus, for example, our two farmers can achieve fully efficient risk sharing if farmer 1 exchanges 8,000 claims to 'dry' purchasing power for 8,000 claims to 'wet' purchasing power from farmer 2.

Chapter 2 also shows that fully efficient risk sharing can be achieved via trade in complex claims provided there is sufficient 'variety' in the payoff patterns of the traded claims. For example, consider an arrangement whereby farmer 1 agrees to sell half of his profits in exchange for half the profits of farmer 2. In other words farmer 1 exchanges a complex claim yielding £10,000 in dry summers and £2,000 in wet summers for a complex claim yielding £2,000 in dry summers and £10,000 in wet summers. This arrangement achieves exactly the same risk-sharing arrangement as is achieved via trade in simple contingent claims.

Chapter 3 examines some of the issues that arise for the efficiency of risk sharing when the set of primary tradable contingent claims is less than complete. We begin by noting that incompleteness in the set of tradable claims can lead to socially inefficient outcomes in the sense that the conditions for fully efficient risk sharing may no longer be satisfied. We then go on to consider whether there are any conditions under which fully efficient risk sharing can be achieved with a less than complete set of primary tradable securities. In general there are two, complementary, approaches here. On the one hand various kinds of derivative securities such as options on the original set of tradable securities can be introduced into the market. Under certain circumstances the introduction of such derivative securities makes an otherwise incomplete securities market complete. On the other hand some authors have shown that by placing certain restrictions on the characteristics of individuals in the economy, fully efficient risk sharing can be achieved despite an incomplete set of tradable securities.

The remaining chapters focus on the effects of information in multiperson economies. Chapter 4 focuses on the social value of public information. In particular it concentrates on the effect that introducing public information into an economy has on the welfare of the agents in that economy. The chapter shows that there are three main ways by which the introduction of public information can affect the welfare of society.

First, as in single-person decision problems, public information will be socially beneficial if it leads to improved production decisions: for example, if the economy can substitute potatoes for barley in wet summers. Second, public information may be beneficial if it leads to an expansion in the scope for risk sharing. For example, if improved public information leads to an increase in the set of tradable securities this may in turn lead to improved risk sharing. The third potential source of benefit from public information stems from the possibility that in multiperson economies individuals may differ in their access to information. Chapter 4 establishes the general point that many of the difficulties arising from information asymmetry can be eliminated if the information observed asymmetrically *ex ante* can be observed publicly *ex post*.[2]

The possibility that information is not distributed equally across individuals gives rise to a number of complex issues that are explored in the remaining chapters of the text. Chapter 5 concentrates on the implications for equilibrium in the economy of investors having differential access to information. Chapter 6 considers the concept of informational efficiency – the extent to which security prices reflect information.

Chapters 7 and 8 focus on some of the issues arising from the possibility that those who run a firm may have access to information that is not observed by those who invest in the firm.

In summary this book has three main themes. The first is the nature and value of information in single-person and multiperson economies. The second is the issue of optimum risk sharing and the effects of information on the risk-sharing efficiency of the economy. The third is the implications of information asymmetry for our understanding of the functioning of stock market economies.

0.2 INDIVIDUALISM, RATIONALITY AND EQUILIBRIUM

In terms of the major schools of economic thought this text is avowedly neoclassical. All the models reviewed below are based on the following core postulates of the neoclassical school:

1 *Individualism:* economic phenomena can be explained in terms of the choice behaviour of individual agents.
2 *Rationality:* theories of individual choice behaviour can be based on axioms of rationality.
3 *Equilibrium:* in explaining the behaviour of groups of individuals who interact with each other attention can be focused, at least in the first instance, on equilibrium states.

Not all social scientists accept individualism as a core postulate. As a general rule acceptance of individualism tends to depend on one's ideological position. Economists of the Austrian school, for example, are strongly committed to individualism whilst the Marxist school rejects individualism because it has no place for concepts such as social class. Neoclassical economists subscribe to individualism because they believe that it leads to fruitful explanations of economic phenomena (Hahn, 1984).

All neoclassical models assume that economic agents behave as if to maximize some well-defined objective function subject to an appropriately defined set of constraints which describe the agent's opportunity set. For example, in the theory of general competitive equilibrium the representative consumer is assumed to maximize his utility subject to a budget constraint. This approach provides a representation of individual behaviour that is analytically manageable and is often found to be consistent with the observed choice behaviour of individuals. Nevertheless the rationality postulate is not without its critics. Some critics have shown that the spontaneous behaviour of individuals in practice is often inconsistent with the strict tenets of rationality. Others have argued that individuals may be forced to adopt suboptimal choices because of the computational complexities involved in identifying optimal choices. However, despite such objections, neoclassical economics has, for the most part, continued to adhere to strong rationality postulates.

The reluctance of neoclassical economists to abandon the rationality postulate stems in part from the strong complementarity between the rationality postulate and the equilibrium postulate. Indeed we would argue that the theoretical power of the neoclassical approach stems from the unique combination of these two postulates. Equilibrium economics would not be altogether impossible without the rationality postulate but its theoretical appeal would be considerably reduced.

With regard to the equilibrium postulate the reader should note that we interpret the term quite broadly to mean any position in which the intended choices of individuals are consistent and can be implemented (see Hahn, 1973, for a useful discussion of the equilibrium postulate). This interpretation subsumes the narrower concept of general competitive equilibrium. The economics of information applies a variety of equilibrium concepts including not only the concept of general competitive equilibrium but also sophisticated equilibrium concepts derived from the theory of games. In particular, when modelling economies in which individuals have unequal access to information, some of the most fruitful equilibrium concepts are those associated with the theory of games of incomplete information (see, for example, Harsanyi, 1968).

Chapter 1 develops the particular axioms of individual rationality that underlie the rest of the text and discusses the most important implication of these axioms, namely, the expected utility hypothesis. Chapters 2 to 4 are largely concerned with models of general competitive equilibrium under uncertainty. More sophisticated equilibrium concepts are discussed in chapters 5 to 8 inclusive.

0.3 A TOUR OF CHAPTERS 1 TO 8

Chapters 1 and 2 provide a theoretical foundation for the rest of the text. Chapter 1 is concerned with rational choice behaviour in single-person decision problems involving uncertainty. The chapter begins by outlining the expected utility approach to decision making under uncertainty. This is followed by a discussion of the nature and role of information in single-person choice problems.

Chapter 2 provides an introduction to the state preference approach to the theory of markets under uncertainty. It introduces a simple two-period model which provides a convenient unifying framework for chapters 2 to 6 inclusive. Chapter 2 also provides a review of the basic concepts of Paretian welfare economics and a characterization of Pareto efficient resource allocations. The concept of Pareto efficiency provides a benchmark against which the efficiency of the allocations generated by alternative regimes of markets can be compared. The remainder of chapter 2 introduces the concept of a contingent claim and draws an important distinction between complex and simple contingent claims. The analysis shows that market-generated allocations will be fully Pareto efficient if trade takes place in a complete set of simple claims or if the set of tradable claims is such that any simple claim can be replicated by holding appropriate proportions of the tradable claims.

Chapter 3 focuses on some of the issues that arise when the original set of tradable securities is incomplete. Special attention is focused on the possibility that it may be possible to complete a market by issuing various kinds of derivative securities such as put and call options. The chapter goes on to consider the possibility of achieving fully efficient risk sharing in an incomplete market when restrictions are placed on individuals' characteristics. The chapter also considers conditions under which a market can be effectively made complete by increasing the frequency of trading in securities rather than supplementing the set of securities directly. The chapter concludes with a brief discussion of the theory of the firm under incomplete markets.

Chapter 4 extends the analysis of chapters 2 and 3 to consider the effects of information on resource allocation and social welfare. The analysis focuses mainly on the effects of an improvement in information that is observed by all individuals, that is, public information. The analysis identifies three major sources of potential social benefit from the provision of improved public information and discusses the ability of alternative regimes of markets to achieve Pareto efficiency in the presence of public information.

Chapter 5 focuses on the implications of allowing some investors access to information that is not observed by other investors. We show that a new equilibrium concept is needed to handle such situations rigorously. The novel feature of this new concept is that it takes into account the possibility that investors may use the equilibrium prices themselves as a source of information. This new equilibrium concept is that of a *rational expectations equilibrium*.

Chapter 6 discusses the concept of *informational efficiency*. This concept is commonly referred to as 'market efficiency' in the finance literature. The analysis concentrates on issues relating to the definition and meaning of informational efficiency. The chapter makes no attempt to survey the vast empirical literature on informational efficiency.

Chapters 7 and 8 are concerned with the various issues that arise when the individuals who manage a firm have access to information that is not observed by those who invest in the firm. Chapter 7 provides an introduction to signalling and screening models and discusses applications of these models in the theory of finance. Chapter 8 provides an introduction to agency theory and discusses some of its implications for mainstream finance.

0.4   OMITTED THEMES

Because of size limitations and in the interest of keeping the book as self-contained as possible a number of important themes have been excluded from the text. First, as explained in section 0.2, the text focuses entirely on neoclassical economic models. Second, the text is entirely theoretical and contains few references to the empirical literature which is both vast and worthy of a separate text. Finally, in our discussions relating to capital structure and dividend policy, we have made no attempt to include tax considerations in the analysis.

1

Information and Choice
under Uncertainty

As explained in the introduction this text will adopt strong assumptions about the rationality of individuals. Under these assumptions individuals rank alternative actions according to the expected utility of the state-contingent payoffs associated with their actions. The first task of this chapter is to discuss the assumptions underlying the expected utility approach.

assume

An important determinant of an individual's behaviour in situations involving uncertainty is his willingness to accept risk. The second section introduces the concept of risk aversion in a context where the outcomes of an individual's actions can be represented along a single, monetary, dimension.

The remainder of the chapter focuses on the nature and role of information in single-person decision problems. Section 1.3 introduces the important concept of an information function and shows how rational individuals can exploit information to improve their decisions. The final section focuses on the issue of choice between alternative information functions and includes a statement and discussion of two important theorems concerned with the comparison of information functions. The first of these theorems is known as Blackwell's theorem. The second is known as the fineness theorem.

1.1 DECISION MAKING UNDER UNCERTAINTY –
THE EXPECTED UTILITY APPROACH

Actions, States and Consequences

Under the expected utility approach to decision making under uncertainty the decision problem of an individual is represented by first assuming that the individual must choose a single action from a given set of alternative actions. Uncertainty is represented by assuming that the consequence of a particular action depends upon which one of a set of possible states of the world actually occurs. For example, suppose the choice is between planting potatoes or planting barley (see table 1.1). Planting barley produces a good crop if the state of the world is 'dry' and a poor crop if the state of the world is 'wet'. Potatoes, on the other hand, do well in 'wet' conditions and poorly in 'dry' conditions.

Table 1.1 States, actions and consequences for a simple decision problem

Set of states Set of actions	Wet s_1	Dry s_2
Plant barley a_1	Poor crop	Good crop
Plant potatoes a_2	Good crop	Poor crop

More generally let S stand for the set of all possible states of the world and let C stand for the set of consequences. The model assumes that the individual has no influence whatsoever over which of the set of states will actually occur, and the description of consequences is assumed to incorporate all aspects of the results of the individual's action that could possibly affect his personal sense of well-being. An action is represented as a mapping from the set S into the set C, that is, an action associates one and only one consequence with each state of the world. If A represents the set of all possible actions it follows that the relationship between consequences, actions and states can be expressed as a mapping from $A \times S$ (the cartesian product of A and S) into C, that is,

$$C = C(a, s) \qquad \text{for all } a, s \qquad (1.1)$$

where $C(a, s)$ represents the consequence of action a in state s.

The Expected Utility Theorem

Having provided a formal representation of the single-person decision problem the next step involves introducing a set of axioms concerned with the logical consistency of an individual's preference ranking over the set of alternative actions. The basic motivation for this approach is the hope that a small number of plausible axioms may be sufficient to provide a precise characterization of rational choice under uncertainty. The central result of this approach is the expected utility theorem which states that under a plausible set of axioms an individual will choose his action as if to maximize an objective function of the form

$$EU(a) = \sum_{s \in S} U(C(a, s)) \cdot \phi(s) \qquad (1.2)$$

where $EU(a)$ is the expected utility to the individual of action a; $C(a, s)$ is the consequence associated with action a under state s; $U(C(a, s))$ is the utility of the consequence which occurs under action a if state s occurs; and $\phi(s)$ is the individual's subjective probability of state s.

It is important to note that the utility function of the individual is not unique. Any positive linear transformation of $U(\cdot)$ will preserve the same ranking of actions according to expected utility.[1]

Assumptions that Imply the Expected Utility Hypothesis

There are a number of alternative but similar sets of assumptions that generate the expected utility hypothesis as an implication. The particular assumptions discussed below are those adopted by Marschak and Radner (1972).

The first two assumptions guarantee a minimal degree of consistency in individual choice behaviour. Together they imply that the individual is able to rank the set of alternative actions according to preference. These assumptions are:

Assumption 1: Completeness.
For any two actions, a_1 and a_2, the individual knows whether he prefers a_1 to a_2 or a_2 to a_1.

Assumption 2: Transitivity.
For any three alternatives a_1, a_2 and a_3, if a_1 is preferred to a_2 and a_2 is preferred to a_3 then a_1 must be preferred to a_3.

The third assumption is called the axiom of conditional preference and can be illustrated by reference to the example below:

	s_1	s_2	s_3
a_1	Misery	Bliss	X
a_2	Sadness	Happiness	X

In this example both actions yield the same unspecified payoff, X, in state 3. The axiom of conditional preference requires the individual's ranking of a_1 and a_2 to be independent of the particular value of X.

To see the rationale behind this axiom it is important to remember that the three states are mutually exclusive so that if either s_1 or s_2 occurs s_3 cannot occur. It would seem illogical to allow the choice between two actions, the consequences of which differ only under s_1 and s_2, to depend on the value of a consequence in a state that cannot occur if either s_1 or s_2 occur. This assumption can be stated more formally as follows:

Assumption 3: The Axiom of Conditional Preference.
Let S_0 be a proper subset of S. Now consider any four actions a', a'', b' and b'' for which the following conditions are true:

$$\left. \begin{array}{l} C(a', s) = C(b', s) \\ C(a'', s) = C(b'', s) \end{array} \right\} \text{ for all } s \text{ not in } S_0$$

and

$$\left. \begin{array}{l} C(a'', s) = C(a', s) \\ C(b'', s) = C(b', s) \end{array} \right\} \text{ for all } s \text{ in } S_0$$

Then b' is preferred to a' if and only if b'' is preferred to a''.

The assumptions introduced so far (together with certain technical continuity requirements) are sufficient to allow the expected utility of an action to be expressed by a function of the form

$$EU(a) = \sum_s V(C(a, s), s) \tag{1.3}$$

Further assumptions are required to write the function V in (1.3) in the multiplicatively separable form

$$V(C, s) = U(C).\phi(s) \tag{1.4}$$

that is, as some function $U(.)$ which depends only on the consequence, and some function $\phi(.)$ which depends only on the state.

The following two assumptions are sufficient for this purpose.

Assumption 4: Tastes are Independent of Beliefs.
The individual's conditional ordering of consequences given s is independent of s.

This assumption establishes the existence of a unique preference ordering over consequences which may be interpreted as the ordering of consequences under uncertainty.

Assumption 5: Beliefs are Independent of Tastes.
To illustrate this assumption consider the example below:

	W	W^c		Z	Z^c
a	1000	0	b	1000	0
a'	500	300	b'	500	300

In this example both W and Z are events, that is, subsets of S. The set W^c, the complement of event W is the set of states that are not included in W. Similarly Z^c is the complement of event Z. The actions a, a', b and b' give rise to monetary payoffs and the individual is assumed to prefer more money to less in all states of the world. Assumption 5 requires action a to be preferred to action b if and only if action a' is preferred to action b'.

To understand the strength of this assumption, first note that the individual's rankings over alternative actions can in some cases be interpreted as providing implicit rankings of events according to their likelihood. Thus in the above example, if the individual ranks a above b this suggests that the individual rates event W was more likely than event Z. Assumption 5 ensures the validity of this interpretation by requiring the implicit likelihood rankings of events induced by the rankings of alternative pairs of actions to be consistent. Moreover, the assumption establishes the existence of a subjective ordering of events according to probability.

A Critique of Expected Utility

The main advantage of the expected utility approach is that it provides a precise and convenient mathematical representation of the objective function of an individual faced by a decision problem involving uncertainty. Moreover this precision is achieved as an implication of five basic assumptions which most people would agree are intuitively appealing at least in the sense that they would like to think that their own choice behaviour would satisfy the assumptions. Nevertheless the theory has been subjected to serious criticism.

First there have been numerous studies which show that the spontaneous behaviour of individuals in practice often fails to satisfy the five assumptions (see in particular, Kahneman and Tversky, 1979). Moreover several writers, notably Allais (1953), have presented example decision problems where the violation of the axiom of conditional preference appears to be rational. Dreze (1974) contains a useful review of these criticisms.

A second line of criticism points out that the formalization of some decision problems (especially sequential decision problems) produces a problem that cannot be solved even by today's most powerful computers. This casts doubt on theories that assume that individuals behave as if they can solve such problems.

Against the first line of criticism one can argue that since the role of a theory is to abstract from non-systematic elements such as mistakes and the precise numerical structure of the problem, casual evidence of random deviations from the precise predictions of the theory cannot be accepted as grounds for its rejection. Sufficient grounds for rejection would be an alternative theory which consistently outpredicted the expected utility theory.

A similar response can be made to the second line of criticism. Even though it may be impossible for decision makers to behave 'perfectly' because of computation costs, this provides no grounds for believing that the decisions from the predictions of the theory will be anything other than non-systematic. Again it is possible that some other theory might be derived yielding consistently superior predictions, but no such alternative has yet appeared in the literature.[2]

1.2   MONETARY CONSEQUENCES AND RISK AVERSION

In most of the models reviewed below the consequence of an action can be represented along a single dimension which can be interpreted as money income or wealth, and an individual's utility function can be represented as a function of the amount of money he receives as a result of his action choice. Three such utility functions are illustrated in figure 1.1.

Figure 1.1(a) presents an example of a linear utility for money function. Figure 1.1(b) presents a strictly concave utility function and (c) presents a strictly convex utility function. Now consider a decision problem in which individuals with these utility functions are faced with a choice between an action, a_0, which guarantees a payoff of x, and an alternative action, a_1, which promises a 50 per cent probability of producing a payoff of $x+\theta$ and a 50 per cent probability of producing a payoff of $x-\theta$. Note that a_1 is a fair gamble with respect to a_0. According to the expected utility theorem an individual will prefer the gamble a_1 to the certain sum if and only if

$$EU(a_1) = U(x+\theta).\tfrac{1}{2} + U(x-\theta).\tfrac{1}{2} > U(x) = EU(a_0) \qquad (1.5)$$

Figure 1.1 shows that individuals with linear utility functions will be

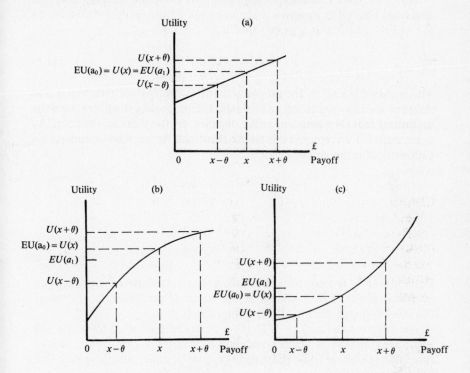

Figure 1.1 Shape of utility functions under uncertainty

indifferent between the certain payoff of x and the fair gamble, individuals with strictly concave utility functions will prefer x with certainty to the gamble, and individuals with strictly convex utility functions will prefer the fair gamble to the certain sum. This example suggests that it might be possible to describe the attitude of an individual to risk by reference to the degree of concavity/convexity of his utility function. It seems reasonable to label an individual 'risk-averse' if he has a strictly concave utility function since this implies that he will prefer a certain sum to a fair bet. Similarly it seems reasonable to label an individual 'risk-preferring' if his utility function is strictly convex. Finally, since an individual represented by fig 1.1(a) is indifferent between the certain payoff x and a fair gamble with respect to x it seems reasonable to label an individual 'risk-neutral' if he has a linear utility function.

Information and Choice under Uncertainty

This basic idea underlies various attempts to define a measure of risk aversion. One such measure is the negative of the second derivative of the utility function at a point, that is,

$$R(x) = -U''(x) \tag{1.6}$$

This measure possesses the property that it is positive for risk-averse and negative for risk-preferring individuals. Unfortunately it suffers from the limitation that its numerical value depends on the units in which utility is measured. To overcome this defect Pratt and Arrow have advanced the following alternative measures:

$$R_A(x) = -\frac{U''(x)}{U'(x)} \tag{1.7}$$

$$R_R(x) = -x\frac{U''(x)}{U'(x)} \tag{1.8}$$

Equation (1.7) is known as the Arrow–Pratt measure of absolute risk aversion, whilst (1.8) is known as the Arrow–Pratt measure of relative risk aversion (see Arrow, 1971; Pratt, 1964).

The function defined by $1/R_A(x)$ is commonly referred to as the risk tolerance function. An important class of utility functions is the class of functions exhibiting linear risk tolerance, that is, utility functions such that

$$-\frac{U'(x)}{U''(x)} = \mu + \lambda x$$

Well-known special cases of the linear risk tolerance class are:

Exponential	$U(x) = -\exp^{(-x/\mu)}$	$(\lambda = 0)$
Logarithmic	$U(x) = \ln(x + \mu)$	$(\lambda = 1)$
Quadratic	$U(x) = -2(\mu - x)^2$	$(\lambda = -1)$

1.3 INFORMATION IN SINGLE-PERSON DECISION PROBLEMS

Expected Utility under Perfect Information

Consider the single-person decision problem shown below where the numbers in the state/action matrix represent utilities, that is, $U(C(a, s))$.

States	s_1	s_2	s_3	Expected utility
Probabilities	1/3	1/3	1/3	$EU(a)$
a_1	9	4	9	22/3
a_2	7	7	7	21/3
a_3	5	5	10	20/3

In the absence of any information the optimum action choice will be a_1 with an expected utility of 22/3.

Now suppose the individual has access to some sort of early warning system that tells him which state is going to occur before he needs to select his action. Then in this case his rational strategy will be to allow his action choice to be contingent on the information he receives. In particular he should adopt a_1 if he knows s_1 is going to occur, a_2 if he knows s_2 is going to occur, and a_3 if he knows s_3 is going to occur. This strategy will yield an overall expected utility of 26/3. This represents the expected utility of perfect information. In general it can be calculated by the formula

$$EU(\text{perfect information}) = \sum_s \max_a U(a, s) . \phi(s)$$

where $\max_a U(a, s)$ is the utility level yielded by the best action if state s is certain to occur.

An Example Involving Imperfect Information

In more realistic situations the individual's early warning system will give less than perfect information. Suppose, for example, it tells him only whether s_3 will or will not occur, that is, it cannot distinguish between s_1 and s_2. In this case the individual's optimum action will still be a_3 if s_3 is going to occur. Alternatively if he knows s_3 is not going to occur then he knows that either s_1 or s_2 will occur and it seems reasonable for him to assume that they will be equally likely (given that they were equally likely before he received the signal). This results in the revised decision problem shown below.

	s_1	s_2	
Revised probabilities	½	½	$EU(a)$
a_1	9	4	13/2
a_2	7	7	14/2
a_3	5	5	10/2

The final column shows that the optimum action is a_2 with an expected utility of 14/2. To summarize, the individual's optimum action strategy is to choose a_3 if s_3 is going to occur and a_2 if s_3 is not going to occur. The overall expected utility of this strategy is 24/3 which is better than the expected utility achievable with no information but not so good as the expected utility achievable with perfect information. It is calculated by the formula

Expected utility if a_3 is selected and state 3 occurs $\times$ probability of state 3

\+

Expected utility if a_2 is selected and
state 3 does not occur $\times$ (1 – probability of state 3).

Information Functions

In handling more complicated early warning systems it is convenient to introduce the concept of an information function. An information function is simply a mapping from the set of states to a set of signals, Y. For example, the perfect information system referred to above can be represented as follows:

$$\eta_p(s_1) = y_1$$
$$\eta_p(s_2) = y_2$$
$$\eta_p(s_3) = y_3$$

where $\eta_p(.)$ is the perfect information function, and y_1, y_2 and y_3 are all elements of Y. Null information can be represented by a constant function:

$$\eta_0(s_1) = y_1$$
$$\eta_0(s_2) = y_1$$
$$\eta_0(s_3) = y_1$$

Finally the imperfect information function discussed in the previous example can be represented as

$$\eta_I(s_1) = y_1$$
$$\eta_I(s_2) = y_1$$
$$\eta_I(s_3) = y_2$$

Expected Utility in the Presence of Information – the General Case

In the absence of information the individual must choose a single action to maximize expected utility. In the presence of information the individual must choose not a single action but an action strategy relating his action choice to the signal received. An action strategy can be represented as a mapping from the set of signals into the set of actions.[3]

Given a particular information function η and a particular action strategy $a(.)$ the expected utility of an individual can be calculated directly as follows:

$$EU(\eta, a(.)) = \sum_{s} U(a(\eta(s)),s). \; \phi(s) \qquad (1.9)$$

where $EU(\eta, a(.))$ is the expected utility of the individual with information function η and action strategy $a(.)$ and $U(a(\eta(s)),s)$ is the utility payoff received in state s when the individual receives signal $\eta(s)$ and chooses action $a(\eta(s))$.

In principle, the optimum action strategy, and its associated expected utility, could be found by evaluating (1.9) for all possible action strategies. This approach is computationally burdensome. Fortunately, there is an alternative approach which produces the same end result with considerably fewer computations. To explain this alternative approach we need to introduce two new probability concepts. First for any information function, η, the probability of any particular signal occurring can be calculated as follows:

$$\phi(y/\eta) = \sum_{s \in \eta^{-1}(y)} \phi(s) \qquad (1.10)$$

where $\eta^{-1}(y)$ represents the set of states under which signal y occurs. In words, (1.10) states that the probability of signal y occurring is equal to the sum of the probabilities of the states which give rise to y. For example, in our imperfect information function $\eta_I^{-1}(y_1) = \{s_1, s_2\}$ whilst $\eta_I^{-1}(y_2) = \{s_3\}$ so

$$\phi(y_1/\eta_I) = \phi(s_1) + \phi(s_2) = 2/3$$

and

$$\phi(y_2/\eta_I) = \phi(s_3) = 1/3$$

Second, the revised probability of state s given the occurrence of signal y can be calculated as follows:

$$\phi(s/y) = 0 \text{ if } s \text{ is not an element of } \eta^{-1}(y)$$
$$\phi(s/y) = \phi(s)/\phi(y/\eta) \text{ if } s \text{ is an element of } \eta^{-1}(y) \qquad (1.11)$$

For example, the imperfect information function η_I yields:

$$\phi(s_1/y_1) = \phi(s_2/y_1) = \tfrac{1}{2} \qquad \text{and} \qquad \phi(s_3/y_1) = 0$$

Using these two definitions the right hand side of (1.9) can be alternatively expressed as

$$EU(\eta, a(.)) = \sum_y \left[\sum_{s\epsilon\eta^{-1}(y)} U(a(y),s). \ \phi(s/y) \right]. \ \phi(y/\eta) \qquad (1.12)$$

where $a(y)$ is the action chosen if signal y occurs.

The term inside the square brackets is the expected utility of action $a(y)$ calculated on the basis of the revised probabilities given by (1.11). The overall expected utility is calculated by multiplying the expected utility if signal y occurs by the probability of signal y and summing over all y.

Equation (1.12) provides a foundation for the following approach to deriving the optimum action strategy and its associated expected utility. The approach involves four steps:

Step 1   For each signal calculate $\phi(y/\eta)$ using (1.10).
Step 2   For each signal and each state calculate $\phi(s/y)$ using (1.11).
Step 3   For each signal find an action $a^*(y)$ that maximizes the term in square brackets in (1.12). That is, find $a^*(y)\epsilon A$ such that

$$\sum_{s\epsilon\eta^{-1}(y)} U(a^*(y),s).\phi(s/y) \ge \sum_{s\epsilon\eta^{-1}(y)} U(a, s).\phi(s/y) \text{ for all } a\epsilon A \qquad (1.13)$$

Step 4   The overall expected utility can then be calculated as

$$EU(a^*(.), \eta) = \sum_y \left[\sum_{s\epsilon\eta^{-1}(y)} U(a^*(y),s). \ \phi(s/y) \right]. \ \phi(y/\eta)$$

Examples of the General Approach

This approach can best be understood by working through two examples.

In our previous imperfect information example, step 3 yielded $a^*(y_1) = a_2$ and $a^*(y_2) = a_3$. The overall expected utility would be calculated according to step 4 as $(14/2 \times 2/3) + (10 \times 1/3) = 24/3$.

For a second example consider the utility payoff matrix below.

	s_1	s_2	s_3	s_4	$EU(a)$
$\phi(s)$	1/4	1/3	1/6	1/4	
a_1	4	9	6	8	7
a_2	8	6	9	4	6.5
a_3	4	3	12	6	5.5
a_4	6	6	6	10	7

In the absence of information, actions a_1 and a_4 are both optimal actions yielding an expected utility of 7. Now consider the information function η_2:

$$\eta_2(s_1) = y_1$$
$$\eta_2(s_2) = y_2$$
$$\eta_2(s_3) = y_2$$
$$\eta_2(s_4) = y_1$$

This gives $\eta_2^{-1}(y_1) = \{s_1, s_4\}$ and $\eta_2^{-1}(y_2) = \{s_2, s_3\}$.

By step 1

$$\phi(y_1/\eta_2) = 1/2 \text{ and } \phi(y_2/\eta_2) = 1/2$$

By step 2

$\phi(s_1/y_1) = 1/2$	$\phi(s_1/y_2) = 0$
$\phi(s_2/y_1) = 0$	$\phi(s_2/y_2) = 2/3$
$\phi(s_3/y_1) = 0$	$\phi(s_3/y_2) = 1/3$
$\phi(s_4/y_1) = 1/2$	$\phi(s_4/y_2) = 0$

By step 3 the optimum action under y_1 is a_4, that is, $a^*(y_1) = a_4$. This yields an expected utility (conditional on y_1) of 16/2. Similarly $a^*(y_2) = a_1$ yielding a conditional expected utility of 24/3.

By step 4 the overall expected utility is

$$(16/2 \times 1/2) + (24/3 \times 1/2) = 8$$

A Necessary Condition for Information to be Valuable

Before ending this section it is worth noting that in the context of the single-person decision problem of this chapter an information function can only increase expected utility if the optimum action in the absence of information is a suboptimal action conditional on the receipt of at least one signal. In other words the value of information stems from the ability of the individual to revise his action choice in the light of his revised probabilities. Information received after the individual has made a binding action choice is of no value.

Note also that an individual's expected utility with information is always at least as great as his expected utility without information. This follows because an individual can always choose to ignore the information and adopt the action he would have chosen in the absence of information.

1.4 RANKING INFORMATION FUNCTIONS – BLACKWELL'S THEOREM

For various reasons it may be desirable to rank alternative information functions by expected utility without having to calculate the individual's expected utility under each information alternative. This may be desirable because the calculations become rather tedious where the number of alternative actions and/or the number of signals is large. It may also be desirable from the viewpoint of an outside observer who does not have access to the subjective beliefs and the utility function of the decision maker. Several writers have identified criteria that allow the ranking of information functions without precise knowledge of the decision maker's prior beliefs and utility function. The most important result in this respect is Blackwell's theorem. As background for our discussion of this theorem we will now introduce several new set-theoretic concepts.

Payoff Adequate Partitions

First let S stand for the set of states. A *partition* of S is a set of subsets of S such that every element of S belongs to one and only one of these subsets. A partition G of S is said to be *finer* than a partition H of S if every element of G is a subset of one of the elements of H.[4]

$$\text{Example:} \quad \text{let } S = \{s_1, s_2, s_3, s_4, s_5\}$$
$$G = \{\{s_1, s_2\}, \{s_3\}, \{s_4, s_5\}\}$$
$$H = \{\{s_1, s_2, s_3\}, \{s_4, s_5\}\}$$

Then H and G are both partitions of S, and G is finer than H.

A partition G of S is said to be *payoff-adequate* if for every $g \epsilon G$, and for any action, the payoff from that action is constant across the states of the world contained in g. This is illustrated by the example below:

	s_1	s_2	s_3	s_4	s_5
a_1	1	1	1	3	3
a_2	2	2	2	2	2
a_3	3	3	4	1	1

Let $G = \{\{s_1, s_2\}, \{s_3\}, \{s_4, s_5\}\}$ and $H = \{\{s_1, s_2, s_3\}, \{s_4, s_5\}\}$

The partition G is payoff-adequate but partition H is not payoff-adequate.

The least fine payoff-adequate partition will be referred to henceforth as the minimum payoff-adequate partition. The elements of this partition will be referred to as the payoff-relevant events. In the previous example G is the minimum payoff-adequate partition and the elements of G are the payoff-relevant events. Notice that anyone who could forecast which payoff-relevant event was going to occur would effectively have perfect information.

The Partition Induced by an Information Function

The partition concept provides an alternative representation of an information function. Recall from section 1.3 that $\eta^{-1}(y)$ was defined as the subset of S that generates signal y under information function η. Clearly the collection of subsets $\eta^{-1}(y)$ generated by all possible signals constitutes a partition of S. This partition is referred to as the partition induced by η. For example, consider the following set of states.

$$S = \{s_1, s_2, s_3, s_4, s_5, s_6\}$$

Suppose under the information function R

s_1 and s_2 give rise to y_1, s_3 and s_4 give rise to y_2, and s_5 and s_6 give rise to y_3.

Then the partition associated with R is

$$\{\{s_1, s_2\}, \{s_3, s_4\}, \{s_5, s_6\}\}.$$

Noisy v. Noiseless Information Functions

The concept of the minimum payoff-adequate partition allows us to introduce a distinction between noisy and noiseless information functions. A noiseless information function is one that associates one and only one signal with each payoff-relevant event though the same signal may be associated with more than one payoff-relevant event. A noisy information function is one that is not noiseless. The distinction can be best illustrated by an example. In table 1.2 E_1, E_2 and E_3 are the payoff-relevant events. The information system that associates y_1 with s_1 to s_4, and y_2 with s_5 and s_6 is noiseless. The information function defined by the partition $\{\{s_1\}, \{s_2, s_3\}, \{s_4\}, \{s_5, s_6\}\}$ is noisy since the payoff-relevant events E_1 and E_2 each give rise to two signals.

Table 1.2   Matrix of payoff relevant events

	E_1		E_2		E_3	
	s_1	s_2	s_3	s_4	s_5	s_6
a_1	1	1	2	2	3	3
a_2	2	2	1	1	3	3

The Likelihood Matrix of an Information Function

The concept of a payoff-relevant event is also useful because it allows one to define the *likelihood matrix of an information function*. This matrix is often a very convenient device for representing an information function. Let N be the number of signals associated with an information function η, and let k be the number of payoff-relevant events.

Define $\phi(y/g)$ as the probability of signal y given payoff-relevant event g. The likelihood matrix of η, normally denoted $\Lambda(\eta)$ is defined as the $k \times N$ matrix with generic element $\phi(y_i/g_j)$. That is, the conditional probability of signal i given payoff-relevant event j is the element appearing in row j and column i of $\Lambda(\eta)$.

In order to calculate $\Lambda(\eta)$ we need a formula for calculating the revised probabilities of signals conditional on each payoff-relevant event, that is $\phi(y/g)$. The theoretical basis for the formula we employ below is known as Bayes theorem:

Let S be a set of states and G be a partition of S. Let A be any subset of S. Then for any $g \ \epsilon G$

$$\phi(A/g) = \frac{\phi(A).\phi(g/A)}{\phi(g)}$$

Equation (1.11), in fact, was just the special case of Bayes theorem with A equated with s and y equated with g. This text assumes throughout that individuals revise their subjective probabilities in the light of new information in accordance with Bayes theorem.

For present purposes we can employ Bayes theorem to calculate $\phi(y/g)$ as:

$$\phi(y/g) = \frac{\phi(y).\phi(g/y)}{\phi(g)} \qquad (1.14)$$

Notice that $\phi(y/g)$ will always be either zero or one if the information function is a noiseless one.

For example, consider again table 1.2 and consider the noisy information function defined by the partition $\{\{s_1\}, \{s_2, s_3\}, \{s_4\}, \{s_5, s_6\}\}$. This partition includes four subsets of S corresponding respectively to signals y_1 to y_4. There are three payoff-relevant events and so the likelihood matrix will have three rows and four columns. If we assume that the six states are equally likely the likelihood matrix becomes that shown below:

	y_1	y_2	y_3	y_4
E_1	1/2	1/2	0	0
E_2	0	1/2	1/2	0
E_3	0	0	0	1

Notice that the elements of each row of the likelihood matrix sum to 1.

The Fineness Theorem and Blackwell's Theorem

We are now in a position to state two important results on the comparison of information functions. The first result, know as *the fineness theorem*, is completely general and applies to the comparison of all information functions associated with a given S.

The Fineness Theorem

Let η and η' be two distinct information functions. Then η will be preferred to η' for any utility function and any set of prior beliefs if and only if the partition induced by η is finer than the partition induced by η'.

The if part of this theorem is fairly obvious since if η is finer than η' it follows that any individual with access to η can always choose to behave as if he had access to η'. The 'only if' part of the theorem is proved in Marschak and Radner (1972) p. 55. This part of the theorem is particularly important because it implies that, unless η is finer than η' or η' is finer than η there will always exist some utility function/subjective beliefs pairs which rank η above η' and some utility function/subjective beliefs pairs which rank η' above η.

A more precise result can be proved if the payoff-adequate partition is the same for all the utility function/subjective belief pairs for which the comparison of information functions is required. This result is referred to as Blackwell's Theorem (Blackwell 1953):

Blackwell's Theorem

For a fixed payoff-adequate partition, G, information function η will be weakly preferred to information function η' for any utility function and any set of prior beliefs for which G is payoff-adequate if and only if there exists an $N \times N'$ Markov matrix M such that[5]

$$\Lambda(\eta') = \Lambda(\eta).M \qquad (1.15)$$

Blackwell's theorem can be explained by means of the simple example below:

Information and Choice under Uncertainty

G	$\Lambda(\eta)$		M		$\Lambda(\eta')$	
	y_1	y_2	p_1	p_2	y_1'	y_2'
g_1	0.9	0.1	0.6	0.4	0.56	0.44
g_2	0.3	0.7	0.2	0.8	0.32	0.68

This shows the likelihood matrices of two information functions η and η' and a Markov matrix M such that $\Lambda(\eta') = \Lambda(\eta).M$.

Suppose an individual with access to η decides that, if he receives signal y_1, he will throw a ten-sided dice and act as if y_1' had occurred under η' if the value of the dice falls between 1 and 6 (inclusive), and act as if y_2' had occurred if the dice falls between 7 and 10. Similarly, if y_2 occurs he will act as if y_1' had occurred if the dice falls between 1 and 2, and as if y_2' had occurred for values between 3 and 10. In this way the individual can exactly simulate information function η' by simply subjecting the signals received under η to random noise.

The reader may find it helpful to see (1.15) expressed in summation form as follows:

$$\phi(y_i'/g_j) = \sum_i \phi(y_i/g_j).p_{ij} \qquad \text{for all } y_i' \text{and all } g_j$$

where p_{ij} is the element in the ith row and jth column of the matrix M. Expressing (1.15) in this form clearly shows that each signal from η' is just a probabilistic transformation of the signals from η if the Markov condition holds.

What Blackwell's theorem tells us is that if for a given pair of information functions, η and η', $\Lambda(\eta')$ can be derived from $\Lambda(\eta)$ by the application of a 'noise matrix', then η must be at least as valuable (in the sense of yielding a higher expected utility) as η' for any utility function and any set of prior beliefs.

In addition the converse of this relationship also holds. If η is weakly preferred to η' for all utility functions and prior beliefs then a noise matrix will exist which satisfies the above relationship.

Blackwell's theorem establishes that it will be possible to rank information functions independently of the particular beliefs and preferences of the decision maker if and only if one information function is a 'noisier' version of the other. If η and η' cannot be linked by a Markov matrix then there will exist some utility function/prior beliefs pairs that rank η above η', and some pairs that rank η' above η.

Blackwell's theorem also establishes that all rational expected utility maximizers prefer more information to less. The expected utility approach implicitly assumes unlimited calculating ability on behalf of the decision maker and has no place for concepts such as information overload.

1.5 CONCLUDING REMARKS

This chapter has concentrated entirely on single-person decision problems. Its main purpose has been to produce a characterization of rational individual behaviour under uncertainty. The characterization has three main features.

First, individuals choose actions as if to maximize their expected utility. Second, in choosing between alternative monetary gambles, individuals may differ in their rankings of alternative gambles according to their risk attitudes. Third, rational individuals with access to an information system revise their subjective probabilities in a Bayesian fashion in the light of signals received.

Subsequent chapters extend the analysis to consider the effects of information on the behaviour and welfare of groups of individuals in the context of stock market economies. The analysis will be conducted under the assumption that all individuals are rational expected utility maximizers who are risk-averse with respect to monetary gambles (we will occasionally assume some individuals are risk-neutral).

2

Models of Complete Markets under Uncertainty

The previous chapter examined the value of information in a single-person context. Chapters 4 to 8 will examine various aspects of information in a multiperson context, where special attention will be paid to the effects of information on security markets. But in considering the effects of information in a market setting it is sensible to consider first, models in which individuals have no information, and then to introduce gradually the various complications that arise when individuals do have information. In this way the effects of information can be seen most clearly. The purpose of this and the following chapter, therefore, is to provide an introduction to the theory of markets under uncertainty, under the assumption that individuals have no information other than that implicit in their exogenously given prior beliefs.

The analysis of this chapter will be conducted within the confines of a model economy which is assumed to last for two time periods and in which there is a single consumption/investment good. This model economy or a variant of it will be used later to illuminate the analysis of subsequent chapters.

The plan of this chapter is as follows. Section 2.1 describes the technology and resource constraints of the model economy and also the preference structures of the individuals in the economy. Section 2.2 reviews the basic concepts of Paretian welfare economics and derives a set of conditions which are both necessary and sufficient for full Pareto efficiency. Section 2.3 begins by providing an introduction to the contingent claims model of markets under uncertainty. Under the assumption of a complete set of simple state-contingent claims (or Arrow–Debreu securities) the analysis derives the two fundamental theorems of welfare economics. As a prelude to considering stock market economies, the section goes on to consider a setting in which simple state-contingent claims are replaced by complex contingent claims. The final part of section 2.3 considers the implications of moving to a stock market economy in which trade is restricted to firm specific securities such as stocks and bonds. The analysis of section 2.3 shows that with final allocations being reached through trade either in complex contingent claims or in firm specific securities, the market will behave as if a complete set of simple contingent claims exists provided there is sufficient variety in the payoff vectors of the traded securities, in a sense to be made more precise below. Moreover if this condition on variety is satisfied, all investors will unanimously prefer production plans that maximize the net market values of firms. In addition the market value of each firm will be independent of the proportion of the firm financed by debt, that is, the Modigliani–Miller (1958) capital structure proposition will hold.

2.1 TECHNOLOGY, RESOURCE CONSTRAINTS AND UTILITY

The model we adopt assumes that the economy lasts for two periods, the current period (labelled $t=0$) and the future period (labelled $t=1$). There are two types of agent in the economy: consumers (indexed by $i=1, \ldots, I$) and firms (indexed by $j=1, \ldots, J$). There is one commodity. Let M represent the quantity of the commodity available now at $t=0$. This initial endowment can be divided between immediate consumption and investment in firms. Investment in firms produces a payoff for consumption in the future period. In general the payoff from investment in any one of the firms will be contingent on the state of the world in the future period. Let S stand for the number of possible $t=1$ states (assumed finite).

It is assumed that the technology of every firm is known to every consumer and can be represented by a production function of the form

$$y_{j0}=g_j(y_{j1}, \ldots, y_{jS}) \qquad j=1, \ldots, J \qquad (2.1)$$

where y_{j0} is the input of the current commodity required for the production plan of firm j; y_{js} is the output of firm j at $t=1$ in state s.

The function g_j describes the relationship between state-contingent output levels of the consumption good at the end of the period for firm j and the level of input or investment at the beginning of the period. It is assumed that g_j is strictly convex, differentiable and strictly increasing in all its arguments. These assumptions serve the purpose of making the treatment in this chapter more tractable by allowing the use of calculus and by ensuring that certain necessary optimality conditions derived below are also sufficient. Their economic rationale is that they guarantee well-behaved production functions. For example, strict convexity requires production to be perfectly divisible and rules out economies of scale; differentiability ensures that the relation between outputs and inputs is smooth; and the assumption that g_j is strictly increasing in all its arguments ensures that there is no free production.

Letting C_{i0} be the amount of immediate consumption by consumer i, and letting C_{is} be the amount of consumption by consumer i in state s at $t = 1$, the physical resource constraints of the economy can be expressed as follows:

$$\sum_i C_{i0} + \sum_j y_{j0} \leq M \tag{2.2}$$

and

$$\sum_i C_{is} \leq \sum_j y_{js} \qquad \text{for all } s \tag{2.3}$$

In words, (2.2) states that aggregate current consumption plus aggregate investment cannot exceed currently available resources. Similarly, (2.3) states that aggregate consumption in any state s cannot exceed the aggregate amount produced in state s.

Each individual consumer is assumed to maximize expected utility given by

$$EU_i = U_{i0}(C_{i0}) + \sum_s U_{i1}(C_{is}) \cdot \phi_{is} \tag{2.4}$$

where $U_{i0}(C_{i0})$ is the utility of current consumption by individual i; $U_{i1}(C_{is})$ is the utility of consumption in state s by individual i;[1] and ϕ_{is} is individual i's subjective probability of state s.

One further assumption has been imposed on (2.4) in addition to the normal assumptions required for the expected utility formulation. Specifically (2.4) assumes that utility is additively separable over time. None of the results of this chapter relies on this assumption. However, many of the results of subsequent chapters require this particular specification of the utility function. As separability is an often-invoked assumption and as it makes the analysis more tractable it is introduced now in order to unify the treatment in this text.[2] The analysis below also assumes that the utility functions of all consumers are strictly increasing, twice differentiable and strictly concave (that is, all consumers are strictly risk-averse). These assumptions are made to ensure that the consumer's utility maximization problem is well defined.

2.2 PARETO EFFICIENCY AND EFFICIENT RESOURCE ALLOCATION

One purpose of this text is to explore the efficiency properties of alternative market regimes. In undertaking this task it is important to be quite clear as to the meaning of the term 'efficiency'. This is especially important in the context of a book on information and capital markets because the word 'efficiency' is used in the capital markets literature in two quite distinct senses. On the one hand concepts of *allocative or Pareto efficiency* are used in assessing the welfare properties of equilibrium resource allocations (usually with reference to market economies). On the other hand the concept of *informational efficiency* crops up frequently in discussions concerned with the relationship between market prices and information. This chapter and chapters 3 and 4 are concerned solely with the allocative efficiency of market regimes. Issues relating to the informational efficiency of capital markets (including the definition of information efficiency) are discussed in chapters 5 and 6.

Pareto Efficiency

The concept of Pareto efficiency is employed in welfare economics as a benchmark against which the efficiency of the equilibrium outcomes of alternative resource allocation mechanisms can be assessed. Broadly speaking a Pareto efficient allocation of resources can be defined as a feasible allocation for which there exists no other feasible allocation that makes at least one member of the economy strictly better off while making no other member strictly worse off. To make this definition operational in the context of a particular economic model the researcher must provide precise criteria to identify the set of feasible resource allocations, and a measure of individual welfare.

For the purposes of this chapter we will adopt the following terminology. First, by an *allocation* is meant a set of I consumption vectors, one for each individual, where $C_i = (C_{i0}, C_{i1}, \ldots, C_{iS})$ is the consumption vector for individual i, and a set of J production plans one for every firm, where $y_j = (y_{j0}, y_{j1}, \ldots, y_{jS})$ is the production plan for firm j. Second, an allocation will be said to be *feasible* if it satisfies the production relationship, (2.1), for every firm and if the physical resource constraints (2.2) and (2.3) are both satisfied. The set A will be taken to represent the set of all feasible allocations. Third, throughout this text an individual's expected utility will be employed as his measure of welfare. Thus in comparing two allocations, a and b, we will say that an individual is better off under allocation a than under allocation b if and only if his expected utility under *a* is greater than his expected utility under *b*.

We are now in a position to provide a more precise definition of Pareto efficiency. An allocation, *a*, will be said to achieve *full Pareto efficiency* (FPE) if and only if

(i)   *a* is feasible;
(ii) there is no other feasible allocation, $\bar{a}$, such that at least one individual has a greater expected utility under $\bar{a}$ than under *a*, and no individual has a lower expected utility under $\bar{a}$ than under *a*.

Some explanation may be needed here as to why the word 'full' has been introduced into the above definition. The word full in this context relates to the definition of a feasible resource allocation, which describes as feasible any allocation that is physically possible. In particular, subject to the technological constraint on production and the physical resource constraints, individuals are free to vary independently the amounts of consumption in different states of the world. Some of the models reviewed in later chapters adopt more restrictive definitions of feasibility that incorporate constraints on the dimension of the subspace spanned by the production plans of firms and on the consumption vectors of individuals.[3] Concepts of Pareto efficiency that impose additional restrictions on the set of feasible allocations will be referred to under the heading of *constrained Pareto efficiency* to distinguish them from the concept of FPE considered in this chapter.

Necessary and Sufficient Conditions for Full Pareto Efficiency

Borch (1967) has provided an alternative, but equivalent, characterization of Pareto efficiency which has proved more useful for analysis. In particular Borch has shown that any allocation that solves an optimization problem of the following form will achieve FPE:

$$\underset{a\epsilon A}{\text{maximize}} \sum_i k_i.EU_i \qquad (2.5)$$

where the k_is are non-negative constants with at least one k_i strictly positive. In words, (2.5) states that any allocation that maximizes a positively weighted sum of the *I* consumers' expected utilities subject to the feasibility constraint achieves FPE. Moreover, the converse of this proposition also holds, that is, any Pareto efficient allocation can be represented as the solution to a problem of the type (2.5) given a suitable choice of the weights k_i, $i = 1, \ldots, I$.

Using this approach, the Pareto efficient allocations of our model can be characterized as the solutions to the following class of constrained optimization problems:

$$\underset{\{C_i\},\,\{y_j\}}{\text{maximize}} \ \underset{i}{\Sigma} \ k_i \left[U_{i0}(C_{i0}) + \underset{s}{\Sigma} \ U_{i1}(C_{is}) \cdot \phi_{is} \right]$$

subject to (2.1), (2.2) and (2.3), with $k_i \geq 0$ for all i and at least one $k_i > 0$. We will refer to such problems as the central planner's problem in order to distinguish them from the problem of efficiency of market economies which will be considered below.

Given strict risk aversion on behalf of all consumers, the objective function of this problem is strictly concave, and given the strict convexity of $g_j(.)$, the feasible region is convex. The problem can be solved using the Lagrange multiplier technique (see, for example, Dixit, 1976). Ignoring all non-negativity restrictions, the Lagrangean of the problem can be expressed as

$$L = \underset{i}{\Sigma} \ k_i \left[U_{i0}(C_{i0}) + \underset{s}{\Sigma} \ U_{i1}(C_{is}) \phi_{is} \right] + \lambda \left[M - \underset{i}{\Sigma} \ C_{i0} \right.$$

$$\left. - \underset{j}{\Sigma} \ g_i(y_{j1}, \ldots, y_{jS}) \right] + \underset{s}{\Sigma} \ \mu_s \left(\underset{j}{\Sigma} \ y_{js} - \underset{i}{\Sigma} \ C_{is} \right)$$

where (2.1) has been substituted into (2.2) for y_{j0}, and λ and μ_s are Lagrange multipliers.

The first-order conditions for a solution to the central planner's problem are given by differentiating L with respect to C_{i0} ($i = 1, \ldots, I$), C_{is} ($i = 1, \ldots, I; s = 1, \ldots, S$), and y_j ($j = 1, \ldots, J; s = 1, \ldots, S$), setting the derivatives equal to zero, and solving these equations along with the constraints (2.2) and (2.3) for an optimal solution. These conditions are

$$
\begin{array}{lll}
k_i U'_{i0} - \lambda = 0 & i = 1, \ldots, I & \text{(2.6a)} \\
k_i \cdot U_{i1s} \cdot \phi_{is} - \mu_s = 0 & i = 1, \ldots, I; s = 1, \ldots, S & \text{(2.6b)} \\
-\lambda \cdot g_{js} + \mu_s = 0 & j = 1, \ldots, J; s = 1, \ldots, S & \text{(2.6c)}
\end{array}
$$

plus the constraints (2.2) and (2.3). Here, U'_{i0} is the first derivative of $U_{i0}(.)$ with respect to C_{i0}. Similarly, U_{i1s} is the first partial derivative of U_{i1} with respect to C_{is}. Finally, g_{js} is the partial derivative of $g_j(.)$ with respect to y_{js}. Given the strict concavity of the objective function and the convexity of the feasible region, these conditions are both necessary and sufficient for an optimum solution.

The economic interpretation of these conditions can be seen most clearly by expressing them in a more convenient form. First note that for any pair of states (s and r) conditions (2.6b) can be expressed as

$$\frac{U_{i1s} \cdot \phi_{is}}{U_{i1r} \cdot \phi_{ir}} = \frac{\mu_s}{\mu_r} \qquad \text{for all } i \qquad (2.7a)$$

This states that the marginal rates of substitution between consumption in any two states must be the same for all individuals. If we interpret consumption in different states as different consumption goods the reader will appreciate that there is a direct analogy here with the conventional conditions for the optimal allocation of a bundle of consumption goods under conditions of certainty (see, for example, Varian, 1984, p. 204). The difference here is that the slope of an individual's indifference curve in state-contingent consumption space reflects not only the individual's utility of consumption but also his subjective beliefs as to the two states. Second, conditions (2.6a) and (2.6b) together yield

$$U_{i1s} \cdot \phi_{is} / U_{i0}' = \mu_s / \lambda \qquad \text{for all } i \qquad (2.7b)$$

Once again this condition can be given an interpretation in more familiar microeconomic terminology. It states that the marginal rates of substitution between current consumption and state s consumption should be equal across individuals. Finally, conditions (2.6c) can be used to generate the conventional conditions for efficiency in production:

$$g_{js} / g_{jr} = \mu_s / \mu_r \qquad \text{for all } j \qquad (2.7c)$$
$$g_{js} = \mu_s / \lambda \qquad \text{for all } s \text{ and all } j \qquad (2.7d)$$

Equation (2.7c) says that for any pair of states, marginal rates of transformation of output in state s for output in state r must be equal for all firms and (by (2.7a)) must be equal to the (common) marginal rate of substitution between consumption in state s and consumption in state r. Condition (2.7d) requires the marginal cost of state s output to be equal across firms, and (by (2.7b)) to equal the marginal rate of substitution between current consumption and state s consumption.

We will say that FPE obtains whenever conditions (2.7a)–(2.7d) are met. Section 2.3 will examine the ability of market economies to attain FPE. But before considering this issue we give below a diagrammatic representation of Pareto efficiency before ending this section with two numerical examples illustrating the Borch characterization of FPE for an exchange economy.

The Pareto Efficient Frontier

Closely related to the concept of Pareto efficiency is the concept of the Pareto efficient frontier. To understand this concept first note that given any particular allocation we can calculate an *I*-vector of associated expected utilities of the *I* individuals in the economy by using (2.4). Now consider an *I*-dimensional space with the expected utility of individual *i* measured along the *i*th axis. Then the set of feasible expected utility vectors can be defined as the set of *I*-vectors of expected utilities associated with the set of feasible allocations. The right upper boundary of this set of feasible expected utilities is the Pareto efficient frontier. A point on this frontier can be generated by first solving (2.5) for a particular set of the weights k_i, $i = 1, \ldots, I$, and then calculating the expected utilities associated with this efficient allocation. The complete frontier can be generated by solving (2.5) repeatedly for all possible choices of the k_i.

The Pareto efficient frontier for a two-person economy with the two consumers denoted *A* and *B* is illustrated in figure 2.1. The shaded area in the figure represents the set of feasible expected utility vectors. The right upper boundary of this set is the Pareto efficient frontier. So, for example, the points *P* and *Q* correspond to values of $k_A = 0$ and $k_B = 0$ respectively while other points on the frontier are found by allowing k_A and k_B to vary. All expected utility pairs above and to the right of the Pareto efficient frontier are infeasible. Distinct points along the frontier are Pareto non-comparable since movement along the curve always results

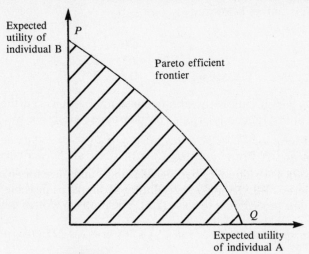

FIGURE 2.1:

in one individual being made worse off. However, for any point to the left of the frontier there will exist some feasible reallocation of resources achieved by shifting resources between firms, between consumers, or from current consumption to current investment (or some combination of these alternatives) which will result in both individuals being made strictly better off in expected utility terms.

Illustration of Full Pareto Efficiency in an Exchange Economy

It is instructive to consider two numerical examples that illustrate the Borch characterization of FPE. These two examples also serve to illustrate two important results that will be used in chapter 3. To use the simplest setting possible, assume that firms' production decisions have been specified exogenously. This essentially means that we are working within an exchange economy with given future period state-contingent aggregate production levels. Also, we shall ignore the initial ($t = 0$) consumption decision in order to concentrate on the efficient allocation of future period output levels among consumers. Assume there are two consumers in the economy, denoted A and B.

Example 2.1 For our first example, assume that uncertainty is captured by three states of the world, that aggregate output (or total market wealth) levels are 1.75, 2.5 and 2.5 consumption units in states s_1, s_2 and s_3 respectively, and that A and B believe homogeneously that states s_1 and s_3 are equally likely to occur and each twice as likely to occur as s_2. We can set this out as below.

	s_1	s_2	s_3
C_M	1.75	2.5	2.5
ϕ_A, ϕ_B	2/5	1/5	2/5

where C_M denotes market wealth in consumption units. Further assume that the utility functions of our two consumers are given by

$$U_A(C_s) = \ln C_s \quad \text{and} \quad U_B(C_s) = 7C_s - 2C_s^2$$

At this stage we introduce our central planner and solve for an allocation that achieves FPE. To make the solution as simple as possible let us set $k_A = k_B$. The procedure is to solve (2.5). The problem written out in full is

$$\underset{\{C_{As}, C_{Bs}\}}{\text{maximize}} \ 2/5.\ln C_{A1} + 1/5.\ln C_{A2} + 2/5.\ln C_{A3} + 2/5.(7C_{B1} - 2C_{B1}^2)$$
$$+ 1/5.(7C_{B2} - 2C_{B2}^2) + 2/5.(7C_{B3} - 2C_{B3}^2)$$

subject to $C_{A1} + C_{B1} = 1.75$
$$C_{A2} + C_{B2} = 2.5$$
$$C_{A3} + C_{B3} = 2.5$$

The optimality conditions are given by equations (2.6b). These can be solved by equating the marginal utilities in each state for consumers A and B and then introducing the corresponding resource constraint. The reader should check that this gives the pairs of equations

$$2/5C_{A1} = 2/5. (7 - 4C_{B1}); \quad C_{A1} + C_{B1} = 1.75$$
$$1/5C_{A2} = 1/5. (7 - 4C_{B2}); \quad C_{A2} + C_{B2} = 2.5$$
$$2/5C_{A3} = 2/5. (7 - 4C_{B3}); \quad C_{A3} + C_{B3} = 2.5$$

for states s_1, s_2 and s_3. Solving these equations gives the optimal allocation below:

	s_1	s_2	s_3
C_A	1/2	1	1
C_B	5/4	3/2	3/2
C_M	1.75	2.5	2.5

This example illustrates the result that, in general, FPE requires consumer allocations to be variable across states in which market wealth levels vary. For example, market wealth levels here vary across states s_1 and s_2 (or s_3). For this market risk to be efficiently shared between A and B requires that the proportions of total market wealth given to each consumer vary across these states. So consumer A receives two-sevenths of the total market wealth if s_1 occurs and two-fifths if s_2 occurs. On the other hand, where beliefs are homogeneous and market wealth levels are constant, as illustrated by states s_2 and s_3, then there is no market risk to be shared and FPE could be achieved with the allocations depending only upon the event $\{s_2, s_3\}$, consumer A receiving two-fifths and consumer B receiving three-fifths of total market wealth in either state.

Example 2.2 For our second example assume that there are three states of the world and that market wealth levels are constant across the states at 3 consumption units; but now assume that beliefs are heterogeneous. Specifically, we have the setting below:

	s_1	s_2	s_3
C_1	3	3	3
ϕ_A	1/4	1/2	1/4
ϕ_B	1/6	1/3	1/2

In order to simplify the calculations, assume that consumers A and B have identical logarithmic utility functions

$$U_A(C_s) = U_B(C_s) = \ln C_s$$

Following an identical solution procedure to our first example gives the FPE allocation (for $k_A = k_B$) below.

	s_1	s_2	s_3
C_A	9/5	9/5	1
C_B	6/5	6/5	2
C_M	3	3	3

This example illustrates a second general result. This is that for FPE to be achieved, consumer allocations must be variable across events for which beliefs conditional on the events differ. Note that this does not require allocations to be variable across all states for which prior beliefs differ. So, in this example, consumers A and B differ in their prior beliefs across all three states. But the conditional beliefs given the possible non-degenerate events are as below.

	s_1	s_2	s_3
$\phi_A(s/\{s_1, s_2\})$	1/3	2/3	0
$\phi_B(s/\{s_1, s_2\})$	1/3	2/3	0
$\phi_A(s/\{s_1, s_3\})$	1/2	0	1/2
$\phi_B(s/\{s_1, s_3\})$	1/4	0	3/4
$\phi_A(s/\{s_2, s_3\})$	0	2/3	1/3
$\phi_B(s/\{s_2, s_3\})$	0	2/5	3/5

From this we see that conditional on the event $\{s_1, s_2\}$ beliefs are homogeneous. This means that FPE requires that consumer allocations in states s_1 and s_2 depend only upon the event $\{s_1, s_2\}$, with A and B receiving the same share of total market wealth in each member state of the event. However, FPE for this example requires that allocations be independently variable across the pairs of states (s_1, s_3) and (s_2, s_3).

Both of the results illustrated by these two examples are discussed further in the following chapter.

2.3 MARKETS UNDER UNCERTAINTY

The starting point of the modern literature on markets under uncertainty is the contingent claims model of Arrow (1964) and Debreu (1959). These authors showed how considerations of uncertainty can be formally incorporated into the conventional neoclassical model of general equilibrium by an ingenious choice of definition of the concept of a commodity. In particular they advanced the idea that commodities can be distinguished according to the state of the world in which they are delivered in addition to their other descriptive characteristics (such as time of delivery).

Within the context of the present single-good economy we can distinguish several different types of commodities. There are claims to immediate consumption and claims to consumption at the end of the period. Moreover, different types of claims to future period consumption can be distinguished according to the state of the world in which delivery occurs. A claim to consumption that is contingent on the occurrence of one and only one state of the world will be referred to as a *simple state-contingent claim*. Hence, in the present context, there are potentially S different types of simple state-contingent claim, one for each state of the world. One can also conceive of more complicated claims that pay off varying quantities of the consumption good in different states of the world. Such claims will be referred to below as *complex contingent claims*.

The previous section defined the concept of FPE and showed how the necessary and sufficient conditions for FPE can be represented as a solution to the decision problem of a central planner who is assumed to know all the production technologies, utility functions and resource constraints in the economy and who allocates resources in order to maximize a weighted sum of consumers' expected utilities. The purpose of this section is to consider whether, and under what conditions, some form of market mechanism will be able to achieve equilibrium allocations that are fully Pareto efficient. The distinguishing characteristic of a market economy is that the equilibrium allocation is realized through a decentralized price mechanism. The section begins by considering the equilibrium allocations yielded by a market mechanism in which there is unrestricted trade in a complete set of simple contingent claims as well as in claims to immediate consumption. The existence of a complete set of simple state-contingent claims means that individuals can purchase claims to consumption contingent on all S distinct states of the world. Having analysed the efficiency properties of this market mechanism, the efficiency properties of markets in which trade is restricted to complex contingent claims will be considered. This serves as a useful precursor to the consideration of stock market economies in which equilibrium allocations are attained indirectly through trade in the securities of firms.

Market Equilibrium with a Complete Set of
Simple State-Contingent Claims

We start our analysis of market equilibrium by deriving a set of conditions that characterizes equilibrium resource allocations in a market economy in the presence of a complete set of simple state-contingent claims. These conditions are then shown to correspond to the conditions derived in the previous section for Pareto efficient allocations. In particular, the analysis shows that all equilibrium allocations achieve FPE, and that any allocation that achieves FPE can be realized as an equilibrium allocation given a suitable distribution of initial endowments.

To begin the analysis let us assume that consumers come into the world with given initial endowments of the current commodity and given proportional holdings in the J firms. Let $\bar{C}_{i0}$ represent the current consumption endowment of consumer i, and let $\bar{x}_{ij}$ represent the endowment proportion of firm j owned by consumer i. Then we have

$$\sum_i \bar{C}_{i0} = M \tag{2.8a}$$

$$\sum_i \bar{x}_{ij} = 1 \qquad \text{for all } j \tag{2.8b}$$

In words, all currently available resources are initially distributed in some way among the individuals in the economy, either through their endowment of current consumption claims (equation (2.8a)) or through their proportional ownership of firms (equation (2.8b)); and for any one firm the sum of shareholders' proportional ownership must sum to unity (equation (2.8b)). Now letting p_s be the market price of a claim to one unit of consumption in state s, and letting p_0 be the price of current consumption (the usual practice in the literature is to let $p_0 = 1$, that is, current consumption becomes the numeraire commodity), we can consider the choice problem of a single consumer, represented formally as follows:

$$\underset{\{C_i\}}{\text{maximize}} \; U_{i0}(C_{i0}) + \sum U_{i1}(C_{is}) \cdot \phi_{is} \tag{2.9}$$

subject to

$$p_0 \cdot C_{i0} + \sum_s p_s \cdot C_{is} \le p_0 \cdot \bar{C}_{i0} + \sum_j \bar{x}_{ij} \left(\sum_s p_s \cdot y_{js} - p_0 \cdot y_{j0} \right) \tag{2.10}$$

Equation (2.9) states that the consumer is an expected utility maximizer, while (2.10) is the budget constraint. The left hand side of (2.10) represents the value of the consumer's final holding of state claims plus the value of current consumption. This must be less than or equal to the right hand side which is the value of the initial endowment of current consumption plus the value of ownership interests in the J firms. The term in parentheses is the net market value of firm j, of which the ith consumer receives the proportion $\bar{x}_{ij}$.

Assuming the consumer acts as a price taker, the first-order conditions for a solution to the above problem are (2.10) plus

$$U'_{i0} = p_0 . \theta_i \qquad (2.11a)$$

$$U_{i1s} . \phi_{is} = p_s . \theta_i \qquad \text{for all } s \qquad (2.11b)$$

where θ_i is the Lagrange multiplier on (2.10).

Now consider the decision problem of the firm. Before this can be represented as a simple maximization problem, it is necessary to specify an objective function for the firm. Moreover, this objective function must reflect the wishes of the firm's owners. In fact, given complete markets, the appropriate specification of a firm's objective function can be inferred directly from the consumer's choice problem if it is assumed that each firm exerts no perceptible influence on the prices of contingent claims. In this case the firm's choice of production plan only affects the welfare of its owners via its influence on the value of their initial holdings. As a result, each owner will prefer the firm to maximize its net market value; that is, the objective function of firm j will be

$$\underset{\{y_j\}}{\text{maximize}} \ \sum_s p_s . y_{js} - p_0 . y_{j0} \qquad (2.12)$$

The only constraint facing the firm is its production function, (2.1). Substituting this into (2.12) gives

$$\underset{\{y_j\}}{\text{maximize}} \ \sum_s p_s . y_{js} - p_0 . g_j(.)$$

which yields the following first-order conditions for an optimum production plan for firm j:

$$g_{js} = p_s / p_0 \qquad \text{for all } s \qquad (2.13a)$$

We emphasize again here that in this market economy firms exist only to produce future period state-contingent consumption claims. Consumer allocations are achieved by direct trading in simple state-contingent consumption claims, as should be clear from the specification in (2.9) and (2.10). We also have the standard result that for given prices there is no uncertainty over the value of any firm, which is therefore known at time 0.

Finally, we know that in equilibrium, demand must equal supply for every good, which implies the market clearing conditions

$$\sum_i C_{is} = \sum_j y_{js} \qquad \text{for all } s \qquad (2.13b)$$

$$\sum_i C_{i0} + \sum_j y_{j0} = \sum_i \bar{C}_{i0} \qquad (2.13c)$$

Equations (2.10) and (2.11) provide just enough equations to determine $C_{i0}, \ldots, C_{is}$ and θ_i for a given price vector. Similarly (2.13a) provides enough equations to determine the jth firm's production plan. Equations (2.13b) and (2.13c) provide $S+1$ additional equations and there are $S+1$ unknown prices, p_0 to p_s. As is well known, only relative prices matter in determining an equilibrium. But if we set p_0 equal to 1 we can dispense with equation (2.13c) because with $p_0 = 1$, so that current consumption becomes numeraire, and with (2.10) satisfied for all consumers and (2.13b) satisfied for all s, then by summing (2.10) across consumers it is easy to show that (2.13c) must also be satisfied. (This is Walras's law applied to our model economy.) Using (2.8) and comparing (2.13b) and (2.13c) with (2.2) and (2.3) it can be seen that any equilibrium allocation must be feasible. The question then is, will it also be Pareto efficient?

To answer this question consider the central planner's problem in which k_i is set equal to $1/\theta_i$, for all i, where θ_i is the optimum value of the Lagrange multiplier on consumer i's budget constraint under a given equilibrium price vector. Now set λ in (2.6) equal to the equilibrium value of p_0, and set μ_s in (2.6) equal to the equilibrium value of p_s. The reader can verify that the equilibrium conditions (2.11a), (2.11b) and (2.13a) become equivalent to (2.6a), (2.6b) and (2.6c). This means that any competitive market equilibrium satisfies the conditions for a solution to a central planner's problem of the form (2.5). Since Borch has shown that any allocation that solves a problem of the form (2.5) is fully Pareto efficient it follows that any competitive market equilibrium with trade in a complete set of simple state–contingent claims achieves FPE. This establishes the *First Theorem of Welfare Economics* for our simple economy, that is, every perfectly competitive equilibrium allocation is Pareto efficient. The converse of this proposition is called the *Second Theorem of Welfare Economics*. This theorem states that any Pareto efficient allocation can be achieved as a perfectly competitive equilibrium given a suitable initial distribution of endowments. To see that the second theorem holds for our simple economy, consider any Pareto efficient allocation satisfying (2.2), (2.3) and (2.6). Let λ^* and μ_s^*, $(s = 1, \ldots, S)$, be the optimum values of the $S+1$ Lagrange multipliers in the central planner's problem associated with this Pareto efficient allocation. Let $(C_{i0}^*, \ldots, C_{iS}^*)$ be the ith consumer's consumption vector. Now consider a market allocation with $p_0 = \lambda^*$, $p_s = \mu_s^* (s = 1, \ldots, S)$, and initial endowments as follows:

$$\bar{C}_{i0} = (SV_i / \sum_i SV_i)M \qquad (2.14a)$$

$$\bar{x}_{ij} = (SV_i / \sum_i SV_i) \qquad (2.14b)$$

where

$$SV_i = \lambda^* C_{i0}^* + \sum_s \mu_s^* C_{is}^* \qquad (2.14c)$$

Here SV_i is the 'shadow value' of the ith consumer's consumption vector where the Lagrange multipliers are used as the shadow prices.

The reader can check that with endowments defined by (2.14a) to (2.14c) and with market prices set equal to the Lagrange multipliers associated with the Pareto efficient allocation, the perfectly competitive equilibrium will be the Pareto efficient allocation itself. Hence any Pareto efficient allocation can be achieved as a perfectly competitive equilibrium.

Illustration of Market Equilibrium

A simple numerical illustration might help in the understanding of this section.

Example 2.3   We will take an economy comprising a single firm, X, and two individuals, A and B. We will again assume that the production plan of the firm is given and ignore the first period problem to concentrate on the market allocation of risk. The state-contingent output levels of the firm and the beliefs of the two individuals are given as below:

	s_1	s_2	s_3
X	2	3	3
ϕ_A	1/6	1/3	1/2
ϕ_B	1/2	1/4	1/4

We will assume that individual A is endowed with a 60 per cent ownership of firm X, individual B owning the remaining 40 per cent.

The competitive market equilibrium is solved for in two stages:

(a) each individual's decision problem (corresponding to (2.9) and (2.10)) is solved for state-contingent consumption demands as functions of the (as yet unknown) equilibrium prices; and

(b) aggregate demands are equated with aggregate supplies (as given by (2.13b)) and the system is solved for equilibrium prices.

To ease the computations we shall assume that both individuals have logarithmic utility functions specified as $U(C_s) = \ln C_s$. Individual A's decision problem can then be written as:

$$\underset{\{C_{Ai}\}}{\text{maximize}} \; \frac{1}{6} \ln C_{A1} + \frac{1}{3} \ln C_{A2} + \frac{1}{2} \ln C_{A3}$$

subject to

$$C_{A1} + p_2 C_{A2} + p_3 C_{A3} = 0.6(2 + 3p_2 + 3p_3)$$

where we have taken consumption in state 1 to be numeraire ($p_1 = 1$). Note that in this case individual A's wealth is given as 60 per cent of the total market value of the firm since we are ignoring the first-period consumption–investment problem. Using the standard procedure of forming the Lagrangean function and differentiating partially with respect to the arguments of A's objective function gives the three equations

$$C_{A1} = \frac{1}{6\theta}; \qquad p_2 C_{A2} = \frac{1}{3\theta}; \qquad p_3 C_{A3} = \frac{1}{2\theta}$$

where θ is the multiplier on A's budget constraint. Substitution into the budget constraint yields

$$1/\theta = W_A$$

where W_A ($= 0.6(2 + 3p_2 + 3p_3)$) is the value of A's endowment. A's demands as functions of equilibrium prices are therefore

$$C_{A1} = W_A/6; \qquad C_{A2} = W_A/3p_2; \qquad C_{A3} = W_A/2p_3.$$

A similar procedure gives B's demands as

$$C_{B1} = W_B/2; \qquad C_{B2} = W_B/4p_2; \qquad C_{B3} = W_B/4p_3.$$

where W_B ($= 0.4(2 + 3p_2 + 3p_3)$) is the value of B's endowment.

All that remains is to equate total demands with total supplies and to solve for equilibrium prices. Equating demands and supplies gives

$$3(2 + 3p_2 + 3p_3)/10 = 2$$
$$3(2 + 3p_2 + 3p_3)/10p_2 = 3$$
$$3(2 + 3p_2 + 3p_3)/10p_3 = 3$$

These three equations give a set of two linearly independent equations in two unknowns which can be solved for (two) relative prices:

$$(p_1, p_2, p_3) = (1, 2/3, 8/9)$$

The corresponding equilibrium allocations are as below:

	s_1	s_2	s_3
C_A	2/3	2	9/4
C_B	4/3	1	3/4
X	2	3	3

The reader can check that this competitive market allocation corresponds to a central planner's economy with $k_B = 2/3.k_A$. Similarly the FPE allocation corresponding to the central planner's weights (k_A, k_B) is given by setting the initial ownership endowments as

$$\bar{x}_A = k_A/(k_A + k_B) \qquad \text{and} \qquad \bar{x}_B = k_B/(k_A + k_B)$$

Complex Contingent Claims

The analysis so far has been conducted under the assumption that trade takes place in a complete set of simple state-contingent claims. In other words we assumed that prices existed for claims to consumption contingent on each distinct state of the world and that trade took place direct in (infinitely divisible) simple state-contingent claims. This meant that, for example, if an individual maximized expected utility by consuming 5.2 units of consumption in state s then 5.2 state-s-contingent claims were purchased. However, the restriction to simple contingent claims is not essential to the analysis. Exactly the same results will obtain in an economy where trade is restricted to take place in a set of complex contingent claims provided there is sufficient variety in the set of tradable claims. To make this condition more precise, suppose there are R different types of tradable complex contingent claims and let $C_r = (C_{r1}, \ldots, C_{rS})$ be the state-contingent payoff vector corresponding to the rth complex contingent claim. Let C be an $R \times S$ matrix with C_r as its rth row. (We will refer to C as the 'state–security' payoff matrix.) Then the set of tradable claims is said to be *complete* if the rank of C is equal to S, and *incomplete* if the rank of C is less than S. In other words if there are as many linearly independent complex contingent claims as there are states of the world then the set of tradable claims is complete.

To give an example, assume that uncertainty is captured by three states of the world that can occur at $t = 1$. Assume there are four tradable securities in the economy with the state-contingent payoffs below.

p		s_1	s_2	s_3
2.45	C_1	3	4	3
2.0	C_2	2	2	4
3.15	C_3	3	5	5
2.25	C_4	1	1	7

Here the column headed p gives the current price or market value of the four securities and the state–security payoff matrix is given by the last three columns. By trade being restricted to complex contingent claims we mean that individuals can hold a claim to any proportion of the payoff of any security; but, for example, if the final allocation has an individual holding the proportion x_1 of security 1, then the individual receives the proportion x_1 of whatever is the state-contingent payoff of security 1. In particular, the proportion x_1 is not allowed to vary across the states of the world. The reader can note that the state-contingent payoffs corresponding to a complete set of simple contingent claims, or Arrow–Debreu securities, would be represented by the identity state–security matrix.

From the table above the reader can check that the rank of the (4×3) payoff matrix is 3 and so the set of tradable claims is complete. If the fourth security was eliminated and the payoff from C_3 in state 1 changed to 4 then the set of tradable securities would become incomplete since the rank of the payoff matrix would be 2. (In this case the third security payoff equals the first security payoff plus half the second security payoff whatever the state of the world.)

The economic importance of the completeness condition is that it means that any economy with a complete set of complex contingent claims can achieve exactly the same equilibrium allocations (in terms of production and consumption vectors) as the economy with a complete set of simple state-contingent claims. This follows from a simple result in linear algebra that any set of S linearly independent rows of C forms a basis for the simple state-contingent payoff space. In terms of economics this result means that all S simple state-contingent claims can be artificially created by a suitable combination of the S linearly independent complex contingent claims. Hence any pattern of state-contingent consumption can be replicated by a suitable weighted sum of the S linearly independent complex contingent claims. Moreover, if the set of tradable claims is complete then even though there are no explicit prices for simple contingent claims there will exist a set of prices for simple state-contingent claims implicit in the prices of the traded securities. In particular the implicit prices of simple state-contingent claims can be derived as

$$p_s = C_s^{-1} \cdot p$$

where p_s is a vector of implicit prices for the S simple state-contingent claims; p is a vector of prices of S linearly independent traded securities; and C_s^{-1} is the inverse of the payoff matrix formed by the S linearly independent securities.

For the example of the table above, the vector of implicit prices is $p_s = (0.3, 0.2, 0.25)$. This can be established for whichever three securities are selected for the matrix C_s. Also, in the absence of arbitrage opportunities (and *a fortiori* in equilibrium), the fourth security is necessarily priced to be consistent with this vector of implicit prices.

If the market in complex contingent claims is complete then the previous analysis of market equilibrium with a complete set of simple state-contingent securities continues to hold. The only difference is in the means of resource allocation where a simple contingent claim will now correspond to a particular linear combination of complex contingent claims. For example, from the table above, a state-1-contingent claim corresponds to purchasing one unit of C_1, half a unit of C_2, and short selling one unit of C_3.[4]

Stock Market Economies and Firm-Specific Securities

The possibility that a complete set of complex claims can achieve exactly the same allocations as a complete set of simple state-contingent claims is particularly interesting in the context of a book on stock market economies because most of the securities traded in such economies are complex contingent claims. Consider, for example, a firm with limited liability that issues a single type of (possibly risky) debt and a single type of equity. Debt financing can be represented in a single future period model as a promise to pay a fixed amount, D_j, if the output of the firm exceeds D_j, and the whole of the firm's output if this is less than D_j. The equity of the company is a claim to whatever remains after the debtholders have been paid, that is, zero if $y_{js} < D_j$ or $(y_{js} - D_j)$ otherwise.

Formally, we can express this as follows:

$$y_{js} = \min[D, y_{js}] + \max[y_{js} - D, 0]$$

where $\min[D, y_{js}]$ is the payment to debtholders; and $\max[y_{js} - D, 0]$ is the payment to shareholders.

In general, both debt and equity securities will be complex contingent claims and, if trade is confined to the securities of firms, there may be no explicit prices for simple state claims. However, as in the previous subsection, a complete set of prices for simple state-contingent claims will be implicit in the prices of the securities of firms provided the number of linearly independent firm-specific securities is equal to S.

Earlier in this section the analysis showed that all shareholders will wish their firms to choose value-maximizing production plans in the presence of a complete set of simple state-contingent claims markets. Under the assumption that there is a complete set of firm-specific securities and assuming that firms act competitively in taking security prices as given, a similar proposition can be proved in the case where trade is restricted to the securities of firms. The completeness assumption is sufficient to allow each consumer's decision problem to be represented as if there is a complete set of simple state claims as in (2.9) and (2.10). The competitivity assumption ensures that the prices of simple state-contingent claims, which are implicit in the prices of the tradable claims, will be independent of the actions of any particular firm. Hence the only perceptible effect of a firm's decisions on the welfare of its owners will be the effect of those decisions on the market value of their equity, that is, on the right hand side of (2.10). Since for a given set of simple state-contingent prices, all consumers prefer more wealth to less it follows that all consumers will unanimously prefer value-maximizing production plans.

Therefore, with firms pursuing value-maximizing production plans and with trade restricted to a complete set of firm-specific securities, a stock market economy will achieve FPE.

The Modigliani–Miller Capital Structure Proposition

A central proposition of the modern theory of corporate finance is the capital structure proposition of Modigliani and Miller (1958). This proposition establishes that, under certain sets of circumstances, the value of a firm will be independent of its debt policy. One particular set of circumstances where the Modigliani–Miller theorem holds is where the market for firm-specific securities is both perfect and complete.

To see this, note first that the market value of a firm after all financing and production decisions have been made is given as follows:

$$\bar{P}_j = P_j + B_j \tag{2.15}$$

where P_j is the market value of equity; and B_j is the market value of debt.

Given the assumption of a perfect market any security issued by a firm can be replicated by an appropriate weighted sum of the securities of other firms. Hence, if there are to be no riskless arbitrage opportunities, the value of any particular security must be equal to V, where V is defined as follows:

$$V = \sum_{s=1}^{S} p_s . x_s \tag{2.16}$$

where p_s is the implicit market price of a simple state-s-contingent claim and x_s is the payoff from the security in state s.

In words, (2.16) states that the value of a security must be equal to the sum of the values of the simple state-contingent payoffs generated by that security. Now since the sum of the payoffs on the debt and equity of the firm is equal to y_{js} in all states of the world, it follows that

$$P_j + B_j = \sum_s p_s . y_{js}$$

Substituting this result for $P_j + B_j$ in (2.15) shows that $\bar{P}_j$ is always equal to the market value of the firm's production plan whatever the value of B_j. Hence $\bar{P}_j$ is independent of B_j, that is, the Modigliani–Miller proposition holds.

2.4   CONCLUDING REMARKS

The main purpose of this chapter has been to examine the efficiency properties of markets under uncertainty. The analysis was conducted in the context of a simple two-period model. The main finding of this chapter is that a market regime can achieve full Pareto efficiency under conditions of uncertainty provided that the set of tradable securities is complete. The crucial requirement is that individuals must be able to trade claims to consumption contingent on each state of the world. However, trade in a complete set of simple state claims is not strictly necessary for full Pareto efficiency. What matters is that the state-contingent payoff patterns of the set of tradable securities must exhibit sufficient variety. In particular, a market regime in which trade is restricted to firm-specific securities will be able to achieve FPE provided the set of tradable securities is complete.

This chapter also examined the implications of the completeness assumption for the theory of the firm. Given completeness and a competitivity assumption, it can be shown that a firm's shareholders will unanimously prefer value-maximizing production plans. In addition, for any given production plan, the market value of the firm will be independent of the proportion of the firm that is financed by debt.

The analysis so far has been conducted under the assumption that the set of tradable securities is complete and that consumers have no information other than that implicit in their prior beliefs. The next two chapters focus on some of the issues that arise when these two assumptions are relaxed. Chapter 3 focuses on the implications of incompleteness for our understanding of the efficiency properties of markets and considers an important distinction between institutional and informational incompleteness. Chapter 4 focuses on the value and effects of information in the context of stock market economies.

3

Models of Incomplete Markets
under Uncertainty

The previous chapter has shown that a market with a complete set of state-contingent claims will attain FPE for any configuration of endowments, preferences and beliefs of the individuals in the economy. But the existence of a complete set of state-contingent claims is rather a stiff requirement, particularly if a multiperiod trading model is considered and it is remembered that a state involves a description of the entire history of the economy. The natural question that has been addressed in the literature is whether there are circumstances in which the requirement can be relaxed. Much of the literature has posed this question within a pure exchange model in which production decisions are given exogenously. Two main approaches can be distinguished. The first has been to consider whether an incomplete set of primary securities can be made complete by augmenting them with a set of associated derivative securities. Primary securities refer to those that are in positive net supply, equity shares being the standard example. Derivative securities are defined here as having payoffs that depend in some way on the payoffs from the primary securities. They are created by traders themselves and in their most common form are in zero net supply. Options and futures are typical though special examples. The second approach has been to consider whether there are any simple conditions on individuals' characteristics that will allow an incomplete set of state-contingent claims to achieve FPE. The initial attempt at this approach in fact considered whether satisfaction of the conditions would allow a simpler set of derivative securities to augment the set of primary securities in facilitating FPE. More recently, the relationship between the two approaches has been spelt out.

These issues are considered in the first four sections of this chapter. We begin in section 3.1 by giving both a diagrammatic and a numerical

illustration of how the conditions for FPE can break down when the set
of state-contingent claims is incomplete. Section 3.2 examines a market
economy where the primary set of complex contingent claims is incomplete
and considers whether the introduction of options written on the primary
securities can complete the market. In section 3.3 we consider the
implications of assuming some degree of homogeneity of investor beliefs
for the set of securities required to attain FPE. More importantly we
consider an issue that is crucial in examining the role of information in
market economies; this issue concerns the types of securities that are
potentially tradable in a market economy. In section 3.4 we add an extra
degree of complexity to the previous analysis by explicitly considering a
multiperiod economy. The section then discusses more specialized models
that are well known in the literature and impose additional simplifying
assumptions beyond those imposed in previous sections.

   A more recent approach to the issue of the number of securities required
to complete a market has considered whether frequency of trading can
serve as a substitute for numbers of securities in providing the required
risk allocation opportunities. Depending upon how uncertainty is resolved
over time, allowing frequent trading in a few long-lived securities may
effectively complete the market even if there is a large number of different
states of the world at the time horizon. This approach is considered in
section 3.5.

   A further important issue in an incomplete stock market economy is
the role of the firm. In a complete market, the firm's role is clearly spelt
out. It should maximize its net market value. The unambiguous (and only)
effect of this is to expand shareholders' opportunity sets. But with an
incomplete stock market, the firm's objective is not so obvious. This issue
is explored briefly in section 3.6.

3.1   INCOMPLETE MARKETS AND ALLOCATIVE EFFICIENCY

The basic difficulty raised by incompleteness can be demonstrated by
reference to a simple economy involving just two individuals and two states
of the world. Suppose the only tradable security is a riskless asset with
a gross payoff of 100 in either state. Assume that individual A believes
state 2 is twice as likely to occur as state 1 while individual B reverses these
probabilities. Figure 3.1 illustrates the difficulty raised by incompleteness.

   Figure 3.1 shows an Edgeworth box diagram where the two goods to
be shared are claims to consumption in alternative states of the world.
The origin for individual A is at the bottom left hand corner of the box,
while the origin for individual B is at the top right hand corner of the

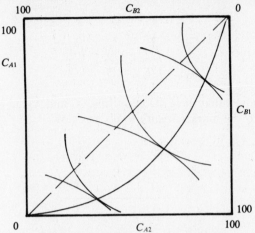

Figure 3.1 Edgeworth box diagram

box. C_{is} is the consumption by individual i in state s, and the box is 100 units square. The set of efficient allocations (the contract curve) is the unbroken line joining points of tangency between the (convex) indifference curves of the two individuals. Under uncertainty, the shape of the indifference curves reflects not only the preferences of individuals but also their subjective beliefs. This is why, when viewed from their respective origins and maintaining the assumption of state-independent utilities, individual A's indifference curves have a steep slope reflecting the belief that state 2 is twice as likely as state 1, whereas individual B's indifference curves have a shallow slope reflecting the reverse beliefs. When markets are complete any point along the contract curve can be achieved given a suitable choice of initial endowments. With incomplete markets only the allocations lying along the broken diagonal of the box can be achieved through holdings of the risk-free security. In the terminology of linear algebra, figure 3.1 shows that the market allocations are restricted to a subspace of the commodity space. In this case the commodity space is two-dimensional whilst the market allocation space is one-dimensional.

Although there is no total market risk to be shared in this example, divergent beliefs requires that side-betting on the state of the world be possible if FPE is to be achieved. But with only a risk-free security available for trade this is not possible. The only feasible allocations are those in which $C_{A1} = C_{A2}$ and $C_{B1} = C_{B2}$. We can show the same general result by extending example 2.2 of chapter 2.

Example 3.1 In example 2.2 the aggregate market wealth levels and beliefs of the two individuals, A and B, were given as below:

	s_1	s_2	s_3
C_M	3	3	3
ϕ_A	1/4	1/2	1/4
ϕ_B	1/6	1/3	1/2

Let us assume now that there are two firms, X_1 and X_2, in this economy contributing to the market wealth levels as below.

	s_1	s_2	s_3
X_1	3	0	0
X_2	0	3	3
C_M	3	3	3

Assuming trade is restricted to claims to the entire output vectors of these two firms then the attainable allocations are as below.

	s_1	s_2	s_3
A	$3x_1$	$3x_2$	$3x_2$
B	$3(1-x_1)$	$3(1-x_2)$	$3(1-x_2)$

Here x_i is individual A's ownership share of the output of firm i. Maintaining the assumption of logarithmic utilities, the central planner's problem for this economy (for $k_A = k_B$) can be set out as

$$\text{maximize } \frac{1}{4}\ln 3x_1 + \frac{3}{4}\ln 3x_2 + \frac{1}{6}\ln 3(1-x_1) + \frac{5}{6}\ln 3(1-x_2)$$

This objective function is unconstrained since the restrictions on the set of feasible allocations imposed by assuming a stock market economy are already taken into account in the specification of the state-contingent consumption levels. The solution gives the ownership shares $x_1 = 3/5$ and $x_2 = 9/19$ with the corresponding allocation below:

	s_1	s_2	s_3
A	9/5	27/19	27/19
B	6/5	30/19	30/19

The reader can check that this allocation leaves both individuals A and B with lower levels of utility than with the FPE allocation of example 2.2. The allocation here is constrained Pareto efficient. That is, within the constrained set of feasible allocations, no alternative allocation to the competitive equilibrium allocation results in any individual having a greater expected utility with no reduction in the other individual's expected utility. The constraint that prevents FPE from being attained is that consumption in states s_2 and s_3 cannot be independently varied. Although the economy contains two linearly independent firm securities, this linear independence is between states s_1 and s_2 (or s_3) whereas we know from example 2.2 that individuals A and B need to be able to allocate consumption levels independently across states s_2 and s_3 if FPE is to be attained.

By restricting the analysis to exchange economies, it is possible to repeat the previous chapter's analysis of Pareto efficiency and apply it to incomplete markets. In particular, it is possible to show that equilibrium in a competitive market economy trading in an incomplete set of state-contingent claims will result in constrained Pareto efficiency (CPE) being attained. Moreover, for any set of weights that the central planner might assign to individuals in determining a constrained Pareto efficient allocation of resources there corresponds a competitive market equilibrium with a suitable choice of endowments which achieves that constrained Pareto efficient allocation.

3.2 COMPLETING THE MARKET WITH OPTIONS

It should be clear that, in general, FPE will not obtain where markets are incomplete. For example, in a stock market economy, with trade constrained to an incomplete set of given firm-specific securities, the competitive equilibrium will ensure that individuals are as well off as possible (in the Paretian sense) given the constraint. But the resulting allocation will be constrained Pareto efficient. At the same time, the analysis of the previous chapter shows that if individuals consider transactions other than exchanging company shares and/or debt then it may be possible to achieve a Pareto preferred allocation. In particular, if individuals create the correct number and type of Arrow–Debreu securities to complete the market, then FPE will be attained. In practice, individuals do not create pure Arrow–Debreu securities, but something similar to this artificial creation of trading instruments has taken place. The purpose of the present section is to review an important contribution that focuses on the idea that it may be possible to complete a market economy by allowing trade in a particular form of derivative security in addition to the original primary complex contingent claims. We begin by considering the case where trade restricted to proportional ownership of the entire state-contingent payoff vector of complex securities results in an incomplete market. We then investigate whether the introduction of *options* can complete the market and thus allow FPE to be attained for any set of endowments, preferences and beliefs of individuals. If the reader prefers, the set of primary securities can be considered throughout this section as being the securities of all-equity financed firms, with the derivative securities corresponding to share options. At the end of the section we consider the special case of the firm creating its own options by issuing debt securities.

The first insight that a complete set of markets could still be attained despite an incomplete set of primary securities is due to Ross (1976). Ross proves a series of results that show the power of ordinary options written on the primary securities to complete the market. Some simple numerical examples best illustrate Ross's results.

Consider the market illustrated below:

	s_1	s_2	s_3
X_1	4	3	1

Here, uncertainty is captured by three states of the world, but with only one primary security, X_1, available, the market is clearly incomplete. A complete market in primary securities would require three linearly independent securities. However, the introduction of two ordinary call options[1] on X_1 with exercise prices of 1 and 2 respectively gives the revised payoff structure shown below:

	s_1	s_2	s_3
X_1	4	3	1
$C(X_1; 1)$	3	2	0
$C(X_1; 2)$	2	1	0

So, for example, a call option on X_1 with an exercise price of 2 gives a payoff in s_2 of $(3-2) = 1$. The reader should check that the introduction of these two derivative securities completes the market – investors can now achieve any desired combination of state-contingent payoffs. Unfortunately, the power of options to complete markets will not always be satisfied so easily. A simple way to see this is to alter the payoffs from X_1 so that the payoff in s_1 becomes 3. Now, no option written on X_1 can possibly distinguish between states s_1 and s_2 and the market cannot be completed. This illustrates a necessary condition for ordinary options to be able to complete the market, which is that the set of primary securities must have payoffs that can distinguish between states. However, this condition is not sufficient to guarantee the result. Ross provides the example below where the necessary condition is not sufficient.

	s_1	s_2	s_3	s_4
X_1	1	1	2	2
X_2	1	2	1	2

Here there are two primary securities which between them allow each state to be distinguished since no two columns of the array are identical. Augmenting the primary securities with ordinary call options written on each individual security with common exercise price of 1, gives the set of payoffs below:

	s_1	s_2	s_3	s_4
X_1	1	1	2	2
X_2	1	2	1	2
$C(X_1; 1)$	0	0	1	1
$C(X_2; 1)$	0	1	0	1

In this example, the two primary securities are linearly independent. Security X_1 and its derivative option are also linearly independent, as are X_2 and its derivative option. But the four securities together are linearly dependent and span a subspace of dimension 3. The fact that the addition of the first and fourth columns gives the same answer as the addition of the second and third columns means that traders would be constrained to receiving the same aggregate state-contingent payoffs for states s_1 and s_4 together as for states s_2 and s_3 together. For example, the reader will find it impossible to achieve the state-contingent payoff vector (1, 2, 1, 3) no matter what combination of primary and derivative securities are chosen.

But this does not mean that the power of options to complete a market is ended here. Ross proves a still more powerful result which in practice might be taken to illustrate the efficiency properties of an option written on an index of securities. Specifically, Ross proves that the previous condition that primary securities must have payoffs that can distinguish each state is both necessary and sufficient for there to exist a portfolio of the primary securities on which options can then be written which will complete the market.

To see this, consider a portfolio comprising two units of X_1 and one unit of X_2, the two securities in the previous illustration. This gives a portfolio with a state-contingent payoff vector (3, 4, 5, 6). The reader can check that call options on this portfolio with exercise prices of 3 and 4, together with the two primary securities give a complete market. Thus, as long as the primary securities allow each state to be distinguished, a portfolio can be constructed whose payoffs alone distinguish each state. Ordinary options on the portfolio will then complete the market, and FPE will be guaranteed for any set of investor beliefs.

Finally consider the example below:

	s_1	s_2	s_1
X_1	1	0	1
X_2	0	1	1
X_3	0	0	1

Here we assume securities X_2 and X_3 are the debt and equity instruments respectively of a single firm. If this firm had issued only equity, its payoff vector would have been $(0, 1, 2)$ and the market would have been incomplete. By issuing debt, the firm completes the market. In effect, the equity instrument is a kind of call option on the market value of the firm with an exercise price of 1. The debt instrument, on the other hand, is equivalent to a combination of a risk-free debt instrument with a guaranteed payoff of 1 plus a put option[2] written on the end-of-period value of the firm with an exercise price of 1. Thus if state s_1 occurs and the firm has a zero cash flow it declares insolvency and 'puts' the empty shell of the firm onto the debtholders. The exercise price here exactly cancels the guaranteed debt payoff. The example also illustrates a situation where, with trading restricted to the entire vectors of cash flows, X_i, the firm's financial policy does affect its value. This is because the firm has market power over the implicit prices of simple contingent claims. By issuing debt, the firm alters the set of feasible trades available to individuals in the economy; the Modigliani–Miller capital structure proposition theorem fails to hold. We will return to this example in the following section.

3.3   CONDITIONS ON INDIVIDUALS' CHARACTERISTICS

Ross's contribution imposes no restrictions on the characteristics of investors. His analysis shows that, in general, quite complicated derivative securities will be necessary to complete the market. Subsequent research has examined the implications of imposing restrictions on the heterogeneity of investors' beliefs for the complexity of the derivative securities required to sustain FPE. This research has also addressed the problem, alluded to at the beginning of the previous section, of which types of securities are potentially tradable in a market economy. This is an important issue when considering the introduction of new trading instruments. Addressing the issue of what securities are tradable also serves to clarify the role of information in a market economy. The problem is that the set of securities that are currently traded may be determined by an institutional incompleteness which imposes restrictions on trade over and above any restrictions on trade due to informational incompleteness. To suggest that the introduction of new trading instruments, which serve only to overcome the institutional incompleteness, will result in FPE being achieved, avoids the more fundamental issue of why the institutional restriction exists in the first instance. If efficiency considerations require the institutional restriction to be in place then completing the market with derivative securities to achieve FPE is not a feasible possibility. Of course, this is not to deny that in practice, with advances in technology, efficiency considerations may result in institutional restrictions being relaxed over time and new securities being created. But the whole issue requires careful examination.

We discuss below some work of Amershi which highlights these considerations and, as a practical example, we apply Amershi's results to the capital structure decision of the firm. But the discussion begins with a paper by Hakansson which considers the implications of introducing some degree of homogeneity of investor beliefs for the set of securities required to achieve FPE. The section ends with an appraisal of the discussion.

Hakansson's Superfund

The first detailed attempt to analyse FPE from the standpoint of restrictions on investors' beliefs is presented in Hakansson (1977). Hakansson initially considers a one-period model in which traders' utilities depend only upon end-of-period wealth levels. The setting is therefore equivalent to that of our numerical examples 2.1 to 2.3 and 3.1. Hakansson's model allows us to consider whether FPE can be attained in economies in which states of the world are characterized by descriptors that are unrelated to security payoffs. If this is the case, then no derivative security will be able to distinguish between such states and it will be impossible to artificially create simple contingent claims corresponding to these states. Within the setting that Ross assumes, individuals will be constrained to consume equal amounts in states where the security payoffs are identical. In general, constrained Pareto efficiency rather than FPE will obtain.

In this setting, Hakansson derives a remarkable condition on investor beliefs which if satisfied allows a simple set of derivative securities to achieve FPE in an incomplete market. We have already laid the foundations for this result in examples 2.1 and 2.2 of chapter 2. But it is useful to consider Hakansson's original development of the idea. Hakansson calls the novel derivative securities that he introduces, *supershares*. The idea of a supershare is best illustrated by an example as below:

	s_1	s_2	s_3	s_4	s_5
X_1	1	1	2	1	3
X_2	2	2	4	2	3
$X_1 + X_2$	3	3	6	3	6

The numbers shown here are the total payoffs from the supply of the securities X_1 and X_2 with $X_1 + X_2$ indicating market aggregate wealth levels. A superstate is any set of states in which aggregate wealth levels are equal. This gives two superstates for the above example, $\{s_1, s_2, s_4\}$ and $\{s_3, s_5\}$. A supershare is a security that pays 1 if a given superstate occurs and nothing otherwise. The two supershares, denoted Z_1 and Z_2 corresponding to this example are shown below:

	s_1	s_2	s_3	s_4	s_5
Z_1	1	1	0	1	0
Z_2	0	0	1	0	1

Hakansson proves that if investors' beliefs conditional on any superstate occurring are homogeneous, then a superfund which acquires the market and then issues supershares will allow FPE to be attained. A pair of unconditional heterogeneous beliefs that satisfy the Hakansson condition might be as below:

	s_1	s_2	s_3	s_4	s_5
ϕ_A	1/12	1/6	1/3	1/4	1/6
ϕ_B	1/9	2/9	2/9	1/3	1/9

Given the event $\{s_1, s_2, s_4\}$, the agreed conditional probabilities are (1/6, 1/3, 0, 1/2, 0), and given the event $\{s_3, s_5\}$ they are (0, 0, 2/3, 0, 1/3). Despite the fact that prior beliefs over, say, the states s_1, s_2 and s_4 are divergent, the beliefs conditional on the event $\{s_1, s_2, s_4\}$ are homogeneous. The same holds for the event $\{s_3, s_5\}$. As a result, trade in the supershares Z_1 and Z_2 achieves FPE.

In a one-period pure exchange economy, the Hakansson result on FPE follows from the satisfaction of two conditions that can be seen as facilitating the efficient allocation of risks and were illustrated in examples 2.1 and 2.2 of chapter 2. First, if the aggregate risk in the economy, as given by variations in market wealth levels, is to be efficiently shared out among investors, then the available tradable securities must be able to resolve any differences in market wealth. Second, if investors are to be able to resolve any differences in beliefs, the available tradable securities must be sufficient to accommodate side–betting on events for which investors disagree on the conditional state probabilities.

Amershi's Contribution

In his analysis of the superfund, Hakansson requires that investors' beliefs be homogeneous conditional on the superstate. In a recent paper, Amershi (1985) has identified the trading structures that achieve FPE if this assumption does not hold. Amershi's main result is that FPE obtains if and only if the publicly available information allows traders to strike contracts contingent on events that define a certain minimal partition over states of the world. The partition is that produced by a *minimal aggregate wealth sufficient statistic* (MAWSS). Amershi clearly shows that it is this concept that drives all previous results on FPE in pure exchange economies. For example, Hakansson's result on supershares holds precisely because the partition defined by tradable supershares defines a MAWSS.

To illustrate the concept of a MAWSS, consider the array below showing total payoffs from two risky securities and the associated aggregate market payoffs.

	s_1	s_2	s_3	s_4	s_5
X_1	1	2	1	2	2
X_2	2	1	1	2	2
$X_1 + X_2$	3	3	2	4	4

Now consider the three sets of beliefs below, for the two individuals in the economy.

		s_1	s_2	s_3	s_4	s_5
Case 1	ϕ_A	1/8	1/8	1/2	1/12	1/6
	ϕ_B	3/20	3/20	1/10	1/5	2/5
Case 2	ϕ_A	1/3	1/8	7/24	1/12	1/6
	ϕ_B	3/20	3/20	1/10	1/5	2/5
Case 3	ϕ_A	1/3	1/8	7/24	1/8	1/8
	ϕ_B	3/20	3/20	1/10	1/5	2/5

The partition produced by an *aggregate wealth sufficient statistic* satisfies two conditions. First, it must be at least as fine as the partition defined by the aggregate wealth levels in the economy. From the previous array this is seen to be

$$\Gamma(X_1 + X_2) = \{\{s_1, s_2\}, \{s_3\}, \{s_4, s_5\}\}$$

(Here, capital gamma, Γ, is the notation for a partition.) Second, it must be at least as fine as the partition defined by the condition that for any event in the partition, the beliefs of individuals conditional on that event must be identical. For example, for case 1 above, this requirement also defines the partition

$$\{\{s_1, s_2\}, \{s_3\}, \{s_4, s_5\}\}$$

and the reader can check that conditional beliefs are homogeneously agreed as below:

	s_1	s_2	s_3	s_4	s_5
$\phi(s/\{s_1, s_2\})$	1/2	1/2	0	0	0
$\phi(s/\{s_3\})$	0	0	1	0	0
$\phi(s/\{s_4, s_5\})$	0	0	0	1/3	2/3

Amershi suggests an easy method for deriving the partition of event-conditional belief homogeneity. For the general case of I individuals with beliefs $\phi_1(s), \ldots, \phi_I(s)$ over states of the world $s \epsilon S$, the procedure is to first calculate the expression

$$\phi(s) = \sum_{i=1}^{I} \phi_i(s)/I \qquad\qquad s = 1, \ldots, S \qquad\qquad (3.1)$$

Then for each individual calculate the ratios

$$\psi_i(s) = \phi_i(s)/\phi(s) \qquad\qquad s = 1, \ldots, S \qquad\qquad (3.2)$$

The appropriate partition is then defined by the condition that these measures be the same for each state within the event. For example, for case 1 above, (3.2) gives the result below:

	s_1	s_2	s_3	s_4	s_5
ψ_A	10/11	10/11	5/3	10/17	10/17
ψ_B	12/11	12/11	1/3	24/17	24/17

The partition of event-conditional belief homogeneity is therefore

$$\Gamma_1(\psi_A, \psi_B) = \{\{s_1, s_2\}, \{s_3\}, \{s_4, s_5\}\}$$

as we found before. With this device, the reader can check that the corresponding partitions for cases 2 and 3 are

Case 2 $\quad \Gamma_2(\psi_A, \psi_B) = \{\{s_1\}, \{s_2\}, \{s_3\}, \{s_4, s_5\}\}$
Case 3 $\quad \Gamma_3(\psi_A, \psi_B) = \{\{s_1\}, \{s_2\}, \{s_3\}, \{s_4\}, \{s_5\}\}$

Referring back to case 1, any partition that is at least as fine as $\Gamma(X_1 + X_2)$ – which equals $\Gamma_1(\psi_A, \psi_B)$ – is *aggregate wealth sufficient* (AWS) and the least fine such partition is *minimal aggregate wealth sufficient* (MAWS). Clearly here the MAWS partition is $\Gamma(X_1 + X_2)$. We can therefore say that for this case, Hakansson's market of supershares would achieve FPE.

For case 2, the MAWS partition is given by $\Gamma_2(\psi_A, \psi_B)$, since this is finer than $\Gamma(X_1 + X_2)$. Similarly, for case 3 the MAWS partition is given by $\Gamma_3(\psi_A, \psi_B)$. If beliefs were homogeneous to begin with, the MAWS partition would be given by $\Gamma(X_1 + X_2)$.

For each of these examples, if traders can strike contracts contingent on events identified by the MAWS partition, then FPE will be achieved. This is because the risks, or variations, in the aggregate wealth levels can be allocated across individuals and because the diversity of beliefs can be accommodated through side-betting on particular events. These are the general results that motivated the numerical examples 2.1 and 2.2 in chapter 2.

We now come to the informational requirements for FPE to be achieved. As we saw for case 1, Hakansson's market of supershares would achieve this. But for case 2 the market of supershares would not allow the two investors to resolve their differences of opinion between states s_1 and s_2. However, Amershi has offered an important insight that applies directly to this case. (A similar analysis would apply to the example we used in the previous subsection to illustrate Hakansson's results if beliefs conditional on the event $\{s_3, s_5\}$ had not been equal.) If we assume that all security cash flows are publicly observable, which seems a reasonable assumption to make within the present setting, then individuals should be able to make contracts contingent on the events identified by the cash flows X_1 and X_2. This partition is

$$\Gamma(X_1, X_2) = \{\{s_1\}, \{s_2\}, \{s_3\}, \{s_4, s_5\}\}$$

The market structure based on this information would contain the securities below:

	s_1	s_2	s_3	s_4	s_5
H_1	1	0	0	0	0
H_2	0	1	0	0	0
H_3	0	0	1	0	0
H_4	0	0	0	1	1

For example, H_2 would be a claim to a unit payoff if and only if the cash flow from security X_1 was 2 and the cash flow from security X_2 was 1. This market structure provides a MAWS partition and achieves FPE.

Case 3 is a situation where a full set of Arrow–Debreu securities – in other words, a complete market structure – is required to achieve FPE.

Finally, return to the example of the array on p. 58. There we had the array of securities and cash flows below.

	s_1	s_2	s_3
X_1	1	0	1
X_2	0	1	1
X_3	0	0	1

Here, securities X_2 and X_3 are interpreted as being the debt and equity instruments of a single firm. If this firm had been all equity financed the associated array of cash flows would have been

	s_1	s_2	s_3
X_1	1	0	1
X_2	0	1	2

Previously we argued that by issuing debt the firm can make the market complete. Amershi's work shows that when considering market incompleteness it is important to distinguish between institutional restrictions on trade and informational restrictions on trade. If we assume that trade is restricted to the vectors of cash flows, X_i, then this imposes an institutional restriction that is not explained within the example. This may be a reasonable short-cut to take in modelling certain types of stock market economies. But given the exogenously imposed restriction on trade, it seems artificial to suppose that the firm, by simply creating a debt instrument, can make an incomplete market complete. Why should the firm alone have the power to overcome the institutional restriction? In the absence of institutional restrictions, why should traders themselves not be able to trade on the basis of the contingency that the cash payoff from the firm is 2? On the other hand, if we consider informational restrictions alone, then even with only the securities X_1 and X_2 of the above array available, the cash flows from these securities allow each individual state to be identified. Thus, at a basic theoretical level, the Modigliani–Miller theorem on capital structure would necessarily appear to hold in a pure exchange economy in the absence of institutional restrictions on trade (Amershi, 1981); the creation of debt instruments has no effect on the set of contingencies on which individuals can trade and so the firm's value is independent of its capital structure.

Comparing Alternative Market Structures

The comparison between options and supershares when either can achieve FPE, has been made by Hakansson. One result is that if a financial intermediary or *superfund* issues the set of supershares then no short positions are required by investors. Indeed, this result holds as long as the superfund acquires a sufficiently large proportion of the aggregate wealth portfolio and trade is allowed in supershares as well as in the primary securities. Augmenting the market with options, on the other hand, would in general require that some investors go short in some securities. An additional advantage of achieving FPE through supershares over completing the market with options is that the latter alternative will typically require a larger number of new derivative securities to be created.

However, as Amershi points out, if the only restriction on trade is that caused by a lack of information then the general case for considering either options or supershares seems unclear. Assuming that individual security cash flows are publicly observed, then the only informational constraint on trading is that it is restricted, in the absence of further information, to those events in the partition identified by the security cash flows. Any additional constraint, for example of the type that investors are unable to vary the number of securities they buy across different states of the world, involves an institutional restriction that cannot be justified or explained on pure informational grounds.

Informational considerations alone therefore imply the existence of a tradable market structure already in place which is at least as powerful as a market for options or supershares. Another way of saying this is that informational considerations alone do not give rise to a demand for options or supershares. Their existence must be justified by other means, such as institutional restrictions or transactions costs.

3.4 EXTENSIONS AND SIMPLIFICATIONS

Until now the analysis of this chapter has been assuming implicitly a model with only one future period in which there is any uncertainty. In a

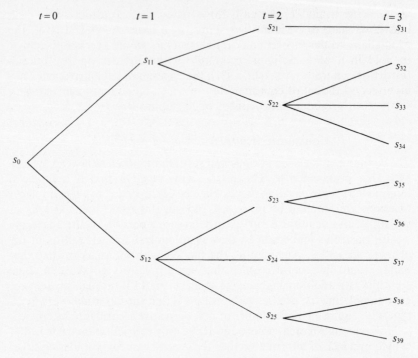

Figure 3.2   Tree structure representing uncertainty in a multiperiod model

multiperiod uncertainty model, much more information may be required if FPE is to be achieved. The reader might conceptualize uncertainty in a multiperiod model in either of two ways. First it can be represented as a tree structure as suggested by figure 3.2. Here a state of the world would be described by, say, $(s_0, s_{12}, s_{23}, s_{36})$ with any one node of the tree being an event, or subset of states of the world. Alternatively, events that can occur at time t might be given as S_t with the set of possible states of the world being given by the Cartesian product $S_0 \times S_1 \times \ldots \times S_t \times \ldots$ (with S_0 normally taken to have a single root element). This alternative model of uncertainty through time explicitly allows for events at any one date to be preceded by more than one event at the immediately previous date, although there is also nothing within the tree structure to rule this out.

In a multiperiod model a further condition must be met in order for FPE to be achieved. This is that investors must now be able to allocate wealth across different events in different time periods. The preceding analysis of the requirements for FPE in the one-period case carries over to the multiperiod case only if utility functions are additively separable over time. That is,

$$U_i(C_{i1}, \ldots, C_{iT}) = \sum_{t=1}^{T} U_i(C_{it}) \tag{3.3}$$

However, if condition (3.3) does not hold then the amount of information required to achieve FPE is vastly magnified. The information structure available at any time t must define a partition that is able to accommodate variations in aggregate wealth for all time periods $\bar{t} > t$ as well as allowing side-betting over events where the conditional state beliefs differ between agents.

The assumption of time-additive utilities, which either explicitly or implicitly has been a standard assumption made in the literature, therefore greatly eases the informational requirements for FPE. Other simplifying assumptions have played even more important roles in the literature. These assumptions have often been invoked in models with only one future period anyway so that the previous multiperiod complication has been avoided. The general motivation for introducing these strong assumptions has been to render general financial asset models tractable to comparative statics and to allow empirically testable pricing relationships to be derived.

Two-Fund Separation

The major simplifying assumption adopted in the literature has been that of homogeneous beliefs. As should be clear from the previous analysis, the tradable securities must then allow sufficient scope to accommodate variations in aggregate wealth. If we consider incompleteness brought about by informational considerations alone then Hakansson's set of supershares will be tradable. With beliefs being homogeneous to begin with, trade in the supershares will achieve FPE despite market incompleteness. However, virtually all of the early work in this area analysed a stock market economy in which trade was assumed to be restricted for institutional reasons to the entire vector of a firm's state-contingent cash payoff. Further homogeneity restrictions on investors in addition to homogeneous beliefs were then investigated to see whether FPE might still obtain with incomplete markets.

Cass and Stiglitz (1970) were the first to consider in depth, restrictions on the functional form of utility functions. Their most important result applies to a stock market economy having several risky securities and a single risk-free security. They show that if and only if all individuals possess utility functions belonging to the same linear risk tolerance class then all individuals mix the risky securities in the same way regardless of wealth levels. By utility functions belonging to the same linear risk tolerance class we mean $-U'_i(y)/U''_i(y) = \mu_i + \lambda y$, where the requirement that λ be equal across individuals is usually referred to as individuals being equally cautious (see chapter 1). As a result, two securities, one being the risk-free security, the other being the appropriate portfolio of risky securities, are sufficient to achieve the benefits of a complete market and ensure FPE. In this case two-fund separation is said to hold.

The Capital Asset Pricing Model

An even more celebrated special case of two-fund separation has formed the dominant theoretical framework in finance since the mid 1960s. This is the mean–variance capital asset pricing model (CAPM) of Sharpe (1964) and Lintner (1965). In addition to homogeneous beliefs, this model assumes that the expected utility of each individual can be expressed as a function of the mean and the variance of end-of-period income. Mean–variance analysis had been previously applied to portfolio theory by Markovitz (1959) and by Tobin (1958). Sharpe and Lintner extended this analysis to an equilibrium theory of security pricing.

Both Markovitz and Tobin had noted that mean–variance analysis can be justified either by assuming that utility functions are quadratic (see chapter 1) or by assuming that security returns have a multivariate normal distribution. The former justification has rather gone out of fashion since Arrow (1971) noted that quadratic utility functions exhibit the counter-intuitive result that risk tolerance falls as wealth increases. On the other hand, restriction to normal distributions is inherently incompatible with FPE since feasibility as defined in chapter 2 requires that all distributions be available for trade. The CAPM has one important implication in addition to two-fund separation. This is that the optimal (market) portfolio of risky securities is mean–variance efficient. By this is meant that among all portfolios with the same mean return the market portfolio minimizes the variance of return.

3.5   TRADING FREQUENCY AND LONG-LIVED SECURITIES

A further means of completing a stock market economy has received attention in recent years. Notable contributions to this area are Kreps (1982) and Duffie and Huang (1985) although the idea has its origins in the works of Arrow (1964) on the allocational role of financial securities and Black and Scholes (1973) on the pricing of options. Black and Scholes derive a formula for the price of an option in terms of only two

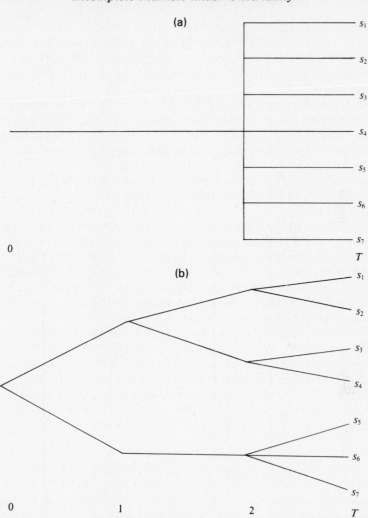

Figure 3.3   Alternative tree structures showing how uncertainty unfolds over time

securities despite there being an infinite number of states of the world. This is achieved by assuming continuous trading in the two securities throughout the life of the option, which means that the payoffs from the option can always be replicated by continuously adjusting the portfolio of the two available securities. In effect, increasing the frequency of trading in a few long-lived securities gives the same effect as increasing the number of securities but allowing only one trading round.

To appreciate the basic idea, assume a two-period (0 and T) exchange economy with consumers' utility functions defined over time T state-contingent consumption claims. Consider two possible ways in which uncertainty might unfold between time 0 and time T, as shown in figure 3.3.

For the decision tree shown in figure 3.3a no further information is learned between time 0 and time T and seven linearly independent securities would be required to span the state space (and so complete the market) no matter what the frequency of trading. But figure 3.3b depicts a situation where information is received between time 0 and time T and some uncertainty is resolved through time. In this case it may be possible for three securities to span the state space if additional trade is allowed in long-lived securities at time points 1 and 2 (Kreps, 1982, p. 211 gives the precise condition). The determination of the number 3 for this example is given by the maximum number of branches leaving any node of the decision tree. The branches leaving any node of the decision tree can be interpreted as the information signals that can be received before reaching the next node of the tree. To span the state space there must be as many securities as the maximum number of alternative signals it is possible to receive at any one time between time 0 and time T.[3]

Earlier in the chapter we compared alternative market structures in terms of the number of securities required to complete markets. This new suggestion of substituting increased frequency of trading for increased numbers of securities may seem to avoid this comparison. But as Duffie and Huang point out (1985, p. 1337), a fair comparison in terms of efficiency requires considering both the number of securities and the frequency of trading, and it is not clear at present how the trade-off resolves itself.

3.6 PRODUCTION DECISIONS IN INCOMPLETE MARKETS

Chapter 2 showed that in a market economy with a complete set of simple state-contingent claims, if firms behave competitively then shareholders prefer the firm to maximize its net market value (or equivalently, in a two-period economy, its profits), and the resulting equilibrium achieves FPE. We also showed that this result remains unaffected in moving to a stock market economy provided that the set of firm securities is complete.[4] In a stock market economy firms not only issue securities that confer ownership and so affect the distribution of wealth among consumers, but firms also have the potential to affect the prices of traded securities and to determine the marketed space of future consumption itself. But if the market is complete and firms behave competitively, then firms have neither any affect on the equilibrium price vector nor any effect on the space of marketed choices. A similar result can be shown to hold for a market economy in which trade is constrained to an incomplete set of state-contingent claims but where there is no trade in firm securities; again, given competitivity, shareholders prefer profit maximization and the resulting equilibrium achieves CPE.[5] In each of these cases the only effect any firm's decision has on individuals is to change their initial wealth. Therefore, every shareholder prefers a firm to maximize its market value, with the resulting equilibrium achieving FPE or CPE as the case may be. A more difficult problem concerns the investment policies of firms in an incomplete stock market economy.

It is important to note that the assumption of a stock market economy automatically imposes an institutional incompleteness on the economy which is not explained within the model. A more natural way to explore the decision making of firms may be to recognize explicitly the divorce between the owners of the firm and the firm's managers. This problem of agency and the accompanying problem of incentives arises whenever the firm's managers have access to information that is not available to shareholders. An assumption of information asymmetry and therefore of informational incompleteness appears to be a more primitive starting point than the assumption of institutional incompleteness in examining a stock market economy. This issue will be taken up in detail in chapters 7 and 8. However, for the moment we continue to assume that all individuals in the economy have the same information so that shareholders observe as much as managers. This effectively means that we can assume that managers act in the best interests of shareholders.

The question that has been addressed within this setting is, what objective should the managers pursue on behalf of the firm's owners? In particular, the search in the literature has been for conditions under which shareholders will unanimously agree on net market value maximization as the appropriate objective for the firm.

In an incomplete stock market economy there are three conceivable effects of a change in a firm's production plan on an initial shareholder's utility.[6] First, there can be a change in the shareholder's wealth due to the change in the net market value of the firm (this assumes the absence of technological interdependencies between firms). In other words, the change in production results in the shareholder's budget constraint (as given by equation (2.10) of chapter 2) being either tightened or loosened. This is termed the *wealth effect* in the literature. Second, there can be changes in the prices of securities purchased by shareholders in the stock market. This is the first part of what is termed the *consumption effect* in the literature. Third, there can be changes in the space of marketed contingencies, which affects the risk-sharing opportunities available to stockholders. In the literature this is referred to as the second part of the consumption effect.

Conditions that guarantee shareholder unanimity are that all shareholders agree on the directions of the wealth effect and of the consumption effect and that they agree on the relative importance of these two effects. In practice, the literature has concentrated on finding conditions that rule out any consumption effects, and that guarantee unanimity over the wealth effect.

Conditions which achieve the desired result and which usefully summarize the results of this literature are given by DeAngelo (1981). DeAngelo finds that for a standard stock market economy with no constraints on individual exchange opportunities (other than an assumption of competitive behaviour and the possible incompleteness of the market), and with no technological interdependencies between firms, two assumptions are sufficient to ensure that net market value maximization is unanimously preferred by shareholders. The first assumption states that the production decision of any firm has no effect on the marketed space of consumption claims. This is the assumption of *spanning*, so called because it amounts to assuming that any firm's production plan can be expressed as a linear combination of the production plans of other firms in the stock market. The second assumption is that the production decision of any firm is perceived as having no effect on the prices of consumption claims. This is the assumption of *competitivity*. The spanning assumption rules out the second part of the consumption effect while the addition of the competitivity assumption rules out the first part of the consumption effect. With the twin assumptions of spanning and competitivity it is possible to show that all initial shareholders in a firm will unanimously agree not only that the firm should maximize its net market value but also which production plan achieves this result. The reasoning is as follows. Where the stock market is incomplete, shareholders' marginal rates of substitution between state-contingent consumption and current consumption will not be equalized. Shareholders' implicit prices for state-contingent consumption will therefore differ, and so shareholders may disagree over which production plan maximizes the firm's net market value. However, although shareholders will disagree on their implicit prices, they must agree on the equilibrium market values of all firms' production plans. Therefore, if a firm's production plan is spanned by other firms' production plans, there are observable market prices at which to value the firm's production proposals; all shareholders then agree on what maximizes the firm's net market value, and with competitivity this is the unanimously preferred objective.

Makowski (1983) provides an alternative set of assumptions which guarantee unanimity. His definition of competitivity when combined with a prohibition on short sales is sufficient to make an additional spanning assumption redundant. This may be a useful alternative route to take since it avoids the problem of firms being able to alter the set of marketed securities by exiting entirely from the market.

The final point to emerge from the literature in this area is that if firms are not competitive, then, in general, no objective will meet with unanimous approval by shareholders.

3.7 CONCLUDING REMARKS

This chapter has extended the discussion of the previous chapter by relaxing the assumption that the economy has a complete set of tradable primary securities. However, except for some slight latitude in section 3.5, it has not explicitly examined the effects of introducing information into the analysis.

The chapter has concentrated on finding conditions under which FPE can be attained despite the set of primary tradable securities being incomplete. To summarize the discussion, at a fundamental level the critical issue appears to be the constraints on trading created by informational incompleteness in the economy. With a certain degree of homogeneity of investor beliefs, an economy can attain FPE despite being informationally incomplete. With incompleteness due to institutional restrictions, the introduction of new derivative securities or of more frequent trading in long-lived securities may make a market effectively complete. But in this case, without the institutional restriction being explained in the first place it is not clear how, or why, or with what effect the institutional restriction is overcome.

Finally, although a fully satisfactory story has not been obtained, the chapter has considered the role of the firm in a stock market economy. This has shown that given certain assumptions, shareholders continue to prefer that the firm maximize its net market value.

All of the analysis to this point has assumed the absence of informational asymmetries between agents in the economy. It is arguable that in particular for a realistic theory of the firm, some informational asymmetry needs to be introduced into the model. This will be taken up towards the end of the book. However, we start our introduction to information in the following chapter by considering the effect of public information in market economies.

4

The Social Value
of Public Information

4.1 INTRODUCTION

Chapter 1 discussed the value of information in single-person decision problems. The main purpose of the present chapter is to discuss the value of information in a social context where several individuals interact with each other through trade in securities. By the end of this chapter the reader should have an understanding of the main ways in which information can influence the welfare of individuals and society as a whole.

In discussing the social value of information it is helpful to distinguish different types of information according to the time when the information is received and according to its distribution among economic agents. Figure 4.1 distinguishes four main types of information. The public/private

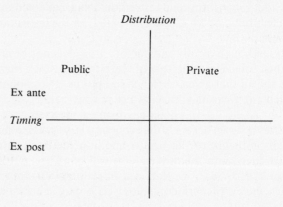

Figure 4.1 Types of information

distinction contrasts information that is freely observed by everyone in the economy with information that is observed by only a subset of individuals. The *ex ante/ex post* distinction focuses on the timing of the information relative to the time at which binding portfolio and investment decisions have to be made. *Ex ante* information is received before binding portfolio and investment decisions have to be made. *Ex post* information is received after binding portfolio and investment decisions have to be made.

The main purpose of this chapter is to investigate the social value of public information. Under certain conditions an improvement in public information can result in an outward shift in the Pareto efficient frontier of the economy. One major purpose of this chapter is to elucidate the precise conditions under which such outward shifts occur. A related purpose is to highlight the most important sources of social benefit from the provision of public information.

Section 4.2 provides an overview of the remaining sections and presents a set of conditions that are sufficient for public information to be of no social value. Section 4.3 focuses on the risk-sharing role of ex post information, and shows that such information can have social value if it permits an expansion in the set of enforceable risk-sharing arrangements. Section 4.4 focuses on the social value of public *ex ante* information in a context where there would be no risk-sharing role for information, that is, where the market, in the absence of information, is complete. Section 4.5 discusses the social value of public *ex ante* information in incomplete markets. Section 4.6 discusses the value of public *ex ante* information in a situation where some investors have access to private information production possibilities.

4.2   THE SOCIAL VALUE OF PUBLIC INFORMATION – AN OVERVIEW

Social Value Defined

Before discussing the social value of information it is important to define what it means to say that public information has social value. For present purposes we will say that a public information function has *social value* if its introduction results in an outward shift in the Pareto efficient frontier of the economy. We will say that the introduction of a public information function results in an *actual Pareto improvement* if the expected utility of all individuals is at least as great in the presence of the information as it was in its absence and if at least one individual has a higher expected utility in the presence of the information as in its absence.[1]

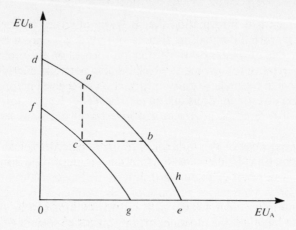

Figure 4.2   Pareto efficient frontier with and without public information

Note that it is quite possible for the introduction of a public information function to produce an outward shift in the Pareto efficient frontier without necessarily leading to an actual Pareto improvement. This possibility is illustrated in figure 4.2. In the figure *fcg* is the Pareto efficient frontier in the absence of information. The locus *dabe* is the Pareto efficient frontier in the presence of information. Since *dabe* lies to the 'north-east' of *fce* it is clear that this information has social value. Now suppose that the market mechanism reaches an equilibrium at point *c* in the absence of information. If the market mechanism in the presence of information reaches an equilibrium anywhere in the 'triangle' *acb* then we would say that the information produces an actual Pareto improvement. However, even if the economy in the presence of information is fully Pareto efficient, it is quite possible for the introduction of information to lead to some (but not all) individuals becoming worse off. For example, if the new equilibrium in the presence of information is at point *h* then individual B is actually worse off than in the absence of information. In cases such as these it may still be possible for society to realize an actual Pareto improvement if some way can be found to allow those individuals who gain from the outward shift in the Pareto efficient frontier to compensate those individuals who lose.

Conditions under which Public Information has no Social Value

The remainder of this chapter will consider the social value of public information in the setting of the two-period model developed in the previous two chapters. Within the context of such a model information whether received *ex ante* or *ex post* will have no social value if the following conditions are satisfied:

1   All individuals have time-additive utility functions, that is, the expected utility of the representative consumer can be expressed as follows:

$$U_i(C_{io}) + \sum_s V_i(C_{is}).\phi_{is}$$

where $U_i(C_{io})$ is individual i's utility of current consumption; $V_i(C_{is})$ is individual i's utility of consumption in state s^2; and ϕ_{is} is individual i's subjective probability of state s.

2   Individuals have homogeneous subjective state probabilities.
3   The securities market, in the absence of information, is complete.
4   Production decisions are given exogenously; that is, we have a pure trading model.
5   All individuals have homogeneous prior information and there are no private information production opportunities.

Condition 3 automatically rules out any value of *ex post* information since completeness implies that all contingencies are already freely tradable.

To prove our assertion that conditions 1 to 5 are also sufficient for *ex ante* information to have no social value it will be helpful to first prove the following proposition:

Proposition 1. In a two-period model in which conditions 1 to 5 are satisfied and in which the immediate consumption levels of all individuals are given exogenously, public information has no social value.

To establish proposition 1 consider any two states, s and r, which give rise to the same signal under the public information function. In the absence of information a Pareto optimal allocation must satisfy the following first-order conditions:

$$\frac{V_{is}.\phi_{is}}{V_{ir}.\phi_{ir}} = \frac{V_{js}.\phi_{js}}{V_{jr}.\phi_{jr}} \qquad \text{for all } i \text{ and } j \qquad (4.1)$$

The appendix to this chapter shows that these conditions still apply in the presence of information provided the prior probabilities in (4.1) are replaced by the appropriate revised probabilities, that is, $\phi_i(s/y)$ replaces ϕ_{is} where

$$\phi_i(s/y) = \phi_{is}/\phi_i(y) \qquad (4.2)$$

Now note that when the revised probabilities (4.2) are substituted into (4.1) the $\phi_i(y)$ terms cancel out leaving (4.1) unaffected. Hence any allocation that is Pareto optimal in the absence of information is also Pareto optimal in the presence of information. This establishes proposition 1.

We are now in a position to establish our earlier assertion.

Proposition 2. In a two-period model in which conditions 1 to 5 are satisfied, public *ex ante* information has no social value.

To prove proposition 2 first recall (from chapter 2) the first-order conditions for a Pareto optimal intertemporal allocation of state claims in the absence of information. In terms of the notation of this chapter we have:

$$U_i'/V_{is}.\phi_{is} = U_j'/V_{js}.\phi_{js} \qquad \text{for all } i \text{ and } j \text{ and all } s \qquad (4.3)$$

The appendix to this chapter shows that the following analogous conditions must hold following the receipt of an ex ante information signal y:

$$U_{iy}'/V_{isy}.\phi_i(s/y) = U_{jy}'/V_{jsy}.\phi_j(s/y) \qquad \text{for all } i \text{ and } j \text{ and all } s \qquad (4.4)$$

In (4.4), U_{iy}' represents the marginal utility of the ith individual's current consumption if signal y occurs, and V_{isy} represents the marginal utility of the ith individual's state s consumption if signal y occurs.

Using (4.2), we can rewrite (4.4) as follows:

$$U_{iy}'.\phi_i(y)/V_{isy}.\phi_{is} = U_{jy}'.\phi_j(y)/V_{jsy}.\phi_{js} \qquad (4.5)$$

Now if individuals have homogeneous beliefs the $\phi(y)$ terms will cancel in (4.5) and we can see that any allocation that satisfies (4.3) will also satisfy (4.5). Combining this observation with proposition 1 implies that any allocation that is Pareto efficient in the absence of information will also be Pareto efficient in the presence of information, that is, proposition 2 will hold.[3]

The intuition behind proposition 2 becomes clear once one recalls that the aggregate amount of time 0 consumption and state-contingent time 1 consumption is given exogenously. Within this context, therefore, information can only be used to alter the distribution of state-contingent claims between individuals, that is, to improve risk sharing. However, the assumption of market completeness guarantees that full Pareto efficient risk sharing will be achieved in the absence of information whilst the twin assumptions of homogeneous beliefs and time-additive utilities guarantees that there will be no demand to alter the risk-sharing arrangement following the release of any information. Hence information has no social value.

Proposition 2 implies that it is necessary to relax at least one of these conditions before it is possible to construct examples of economies where public information has social value. In fact the following sections will show that relaxing any one of these five conditions allows examples to be constructed of economies in which information has social value. In a sense, therefore, conditions 1–5 are both necessary and sufficient for information to have no social value.

If we leave aside the rather technical conditions 1 and 2 there would seem to be three important sources of potential benefit from the provision of public information:

1   An expansion of the set of risk-sharing arrangements where the market structure is incomplete.
2   An improvement in real production decisions.
3   The elimination or reduction of any social costs associated with asymmetric information.

These possibilities are considered in sections 4.3 to 4.6 as follows. Section 4.3 explains how *ex post* information can be used to expand the set of risk-sharing arrangements. Section 4.4 explains how *ex ante* information can be used to improve real production decisions and examines the efficiency of various market regimes in the presence of *ex ante* information. Section 4.5 explains how *ex ante* information can be used to complete an institutionally incomplete market. Section 4.6 reviews some of the early literature on asymmetric information and explains how the introduction of public information may result in social benefit to the extent that it induces a reduction in private information production.

4.3   THE CONTRACTUAL ROLE OF *EX POST* PUBLIC INFORMATION

In single-person decision problems, *ex post* information has no value. However, in a social context *ex post* information can have social value. To see why, consider an economy involving two individuals with state-contingent endowments as below:

	s_1	s_2	s_3
Individual 1	100	0	0
Individual 2	0	100	0

Assume that both individuals assign equal probabilities to the three states and both individuals are strictly risk-averse with identical utility functions.

Suppose first that the two individuals are both able to observe the state of the world *ex post*. Then they will be able to agree to a risk-sharing contract whereby they share the aggregate endowments equally in all states of the world. Now suppose that they can only observe their own endowments. For example, individual 1 observes 100 in state 1 and 0 in states 2 and 3. In this case the ideal risk-sharing contract will not be enforceable because, for example, individual 2 could claim that state 3 has occurred whenever state 2 occurs and individual 1 would be unable to challenge this claim. Hence an improvement in public *ex post* information can have social value to the extent that it permits an expansion in the set of enforceable risk-sharing contracts.

Four points should be noted about this *ex post* role of information. First, only information that is available to all parties to the contract can satisfy this role. Second, this role does not involve prediction. It simply involves *validation* of the actual state occurrence. Third, even though state prediction is not involved, the parties to a contract must be able to rely on the information being released *ex post*, otherwise they will not be able to base a contract upon it. Fourth, the observable effect of an improvement in the public *ex post* information function is an increase in the variety and complexity of state-contingent claims contracts.

Before ending this section we should pause to consider just how much *ex post* information is needed to complete the market. In other words just how fine does the *ex post* information partition need to be in order for full Pareto efficiency to be achieved? We can answer this question fairly easily by employing the analysis developed in chapter 3. Let us suppose that all individuals observe not only the information induced by their own state-contingent endowments but also the information induced by the state-contingent endowments of everybody else. Under this assumption the state-contingent endowments of all individuals will jointly induce a partition of the states of the world that is observed by all individuals. Two states will belong to the same element of this partition if and only if the endowment of every individual is the same in each state. We will refer to this partition as the '*minimum public partition*' (MPP).

Table 4.1 presents an example economy and its associated MPP. In the table, individual 1's endowment provides no information in relation to the realized state of the world. Individual 2's endowment distinguishes s_4 from the other states whilst individual 3's endowment distinguishes s_1 from the other states. By combining the information provided by all three endowments we are able to generate the MPP. We will refer to the elements of the

Table 4.1 Example of an economy and its minimum public partition

	s_1	s_2	s_3	s_4
Endowment of individual 1	100	100	100	100
Endowment of individual 2	100	100	100	200
Endowment of individual 3	200	300	300	300
Aggregate payoff	400	500	500	600
The MPP	$\{\{s_1\},$	$\{s_2,$	$s_3\},$	$\{s_4\}\}$

MPP as the 'events' of the MPP. Hence in our example there are three possible events of the MPP, $\{s_1\}$, $\{s_2, s_3\}$, and $\{s_4\}$.

Now notice that for this example what we have called the events of the MPP are in fact identical to the superstates we discussed in chapter 3. Hence we know that if the beliefs of investors, conditional on the events of the MPP, are homogeneous, the economy will achieve full Pareto efficiency on the basis of trade in supershares. More generally if beliefs contingent on the MPP are not homogeneous, *ex post* information finer than the MPP will be necessary if full Pareto efficient risk sharing is to be achieved. In particular the work of Amershi indicates that the public *ex post* information partition must be at least as fine as the partition induced by the minimal aggregate wealth sufficient statistic if full Pareto efficient risk sharing is to be achieved.

4.4 PUBLIC *EX ANTE* INFORMATION UNDER COMPLETE MARKETS

The previous section concentrated on the pure contractual role of information where improved *ex post* information is used to expand the set of tradable securities. This section focuses on the other pure case where information received *ex ante* has no effect on the set of tradable securities. Contractual effects are ruled out *a priori* by assuming that, in the absence of information, the market would be complete.

The first purpose of this section is to identify the conditions under which the introduction of information will have no effect on the Pareto efficient frontier and the conditions under which information can result in an outward shift of the Pareto efficient frontier. The second purpose is to examine the efficiency properties of alternative regimes of markets. Finally the section will identify sufficient conditions for the introduction of information in a market context to result in an actual Pareto improvement.

The Effect of Public Ex Ante *Information on the Pareto Efficient Frontier – the Effect of* Ex Ante *Information on Real Production Decisions*

The introduction of information into the central planner's problem discussed in chapter 2 can never result in a reduction in the optimum value of the planner's objective function (that is, it can never result in a reduction in social welfare). In the last resort the planner can always choose to ignore the information. In general, therefore, the Pareto efficient frontier will either shift outward or it will remain unaffected by the introduction of information. We say that an information function has social value if and only if its introduction results in an outward shift in the Pareto efficient frontier. If the frontier is not affected by the introduction of the information we say that the information has no social value. The purpose of this subsection is to identify situations under which a public information function does or does not have social value. We will focus on results for noiseless information functions. For a more general treatment the reader should consult Hakansson et al. (1982).

One situation in which information will have social value is in a production economy in which information comes available before binding production decisions have been made. Under such circumstances the introduction of information may allow the pattern of state-contingent production to be shifted in the direction of those states that are more likely to occur in the light of the information received. Suppose, for example, that the economy has the three alternative production plans below:

	s_1	s_2
Plan 1	150	0
Plan 2	100	100
Plan 3	0	150

Suppose also that, in the absence of information, all individuals assign equal probabilities to the two states. Then, in the absence of information, the socially optimum production plan will be plan 2. Now consider the implications of perfect *ex ante* information for this economy. In this case the optimum plan will be plan 1 if state 1 is going to occur and plan 3 if state 2 is going to occur. This decision rule will produce an aggregate payoff of 150 in both states compared to a payoff of only 100 in both states in the absence of information.

The Effect of Public Ex Ante
Information on the Pareto Efficient Frontier
when Production Decisions are given Exogenously

In section 4.2 we proved that information will have no social value when production decisions are given exogenously if individuals have homogeneous beliefs, time-additive utility functions and no private information and if the market structure (in the absence of information) is complete.

If beliefs are not homogeneous, in particular if signal beliefs differ, information may have social value. This possibility has been established by Hakansson et al. (1982) and its plausibility can be seen by comparing (4.3) and (4.5). This comparison shows that any allocation that satisfies (4.3) in the absence of information will inevitably violate (4.5) in the presence of information if signal beliefs differ. Hence information may have social value if signal beliefs differ.

So far, then, we have seen that *ex ante* information can have social value with endogenous production decisions and that it can have social value with exogenous production decisions if signal beliefs differ. There are, in fact, two further circumstances under which *ex ante* public information can have social value. To understand the first of these circumstances requires only a slight modification to the model we have been using so far. In particular we have so far assumed that an individual's utility function can be expressed in the additively separable form $U(.) + V(.)$ where $U(.)$ refers to the utility of current consumption and $V(.)$ refers to the utility of end-of-period consumption. In fact there is nothing inherent in the axioms of the expected utility theorem to imply that the two-period utility function can be written in this additively separable form. Hakansson et al. (1982) have shown that information can have social value in an exogenous production context if the utility functions of individuals are not additively separable even if they have homogeneous signal beliefs. The remaining circumstance under which *ex ante* public information can have social value is when individuals have asymmetric access to information. This circumstance is discussed briefly in section 4.6 and more fully in chapters 5 to 8.

The Economic Efficiency of Alternative Market Regimes in the
Presence of Ex Ante Information

The analysis of chapter 2 showed that, in the absence of information, competitive market equilibrium allocations are fully Pareto efficient provided there is a complete set of tradable securities. The question we consider in this subsection is whether the equilibria of market regimes will continue to be efficient in the presence of information. The analysis will show that the answer to this question depends on whether the market functions as if there is a complete set of tradable claims contingent on both the state of the world *and* the public *ex ante* information signal. In the interest of simplicity we will restrict our discussion to the pure trading case and confine mathematical details to the appendix.

To see that a market regime may fail to achieve Pareto efficiency in the presence of information consider the example economy below:

	s_1	s_2
Prior beliefs of both individuals	½	½
Endowment of individual 1	100	0
Endowment of individual 2	0	100

The example also assumes that both individuals are strictly risk-averse with identical utility functions.

In the absence of information the individuals can agree to share the aggregate payoff of 100 equally in both states of the world giving themselves a guaranteed payoff of 50. Now consider the effect of a perfect ex ante public information function that produces its signal before the individuals have had an opportunity to trade. If state 1 is signalled individual 1 will hold on to his endowment and individual 2 will receive nothing. If state 2 is signalled agent 1 will end up with nothing. Clearly, since both individuals are risk-averse, they will both be worse off in the presence of information. This effect occurs because of the revaluation of the endowments of the individuals induced by the information. For each individual this revaluation effect is favourable in one state and unfavourable in the other but, because of risk aversion, the overall effect is unfavourable for both individuals. Hirshleifer (1971) uses the term *distributive risk* to refer to this effect.

If the market regime in the presence of information is to achieve full Pareto efficiency it will be necessary to provide some mechanism whereby individuals can insure themselves against these endowment revaluation effects. Ohlson and Buckman (1981), following earlier work by Hirshleifer (1971) and Marshall (1974), discuss three alternative market regimes each of which is capable of achieving full Pareto efficiency. They refer to these regimes as the S, the A, and the I regimes.

Under the S (for standard) regime there is a single round of trade which takes place *before* any *ex ante* information is revealed. Trade takes place in the set of primary securities contingent on the realized signal. For example, suppose there are two states of the world, two primary securities and two possible information signals. Then in the S regime trade will take place in the following claims:

(i)   claims to units of security 1 if signal 1 occurs;
(ii)   claims to units of security 2 if signal 1 occurs;
(iii)   claims to units of security 1 if signal 2 occurs;
(iv)   claims to units of security 2 if signal 2 occurs.

In general if there are J primary securities and Y possible signals, trade will take place in $J \times Y$ claims.

Under the A regime (A after Arrow, the economist) trade takes place in two rounds. In the first round, which takes place *before* any information is released, individuals trade claims to generalized purchasing power contingent on the realized public information signal. Thus, for example, if there are just two possible signals, signal 1 claims are traded against signal 2 claims. In the second round of trading, which takes place after any information has been revealed, trade takes place in the original set of primary securities.

Both the S and the A regimes can be shown to achieve FPE. The appendix to this chapter provides a proof of the Pareto efficiency of the S and A regimes for the pure trading case (see Marshall, 1974, for the proof with production). The proof for the S regime follows a straightforward extension of the proof of the Pareto efficiency of complete markets outlined in chapter 2. The proof for the A regime requires the additional assumption that every consumer knows the second-round vector of security prices conditional on the realized signal. Given this assumption the economic efficiency of the A regime can be proved by showing that the A regime achieves the same equilibrium allocations as the S regime.

The third regime discussed by Ohlson and Buckman is the *iterated market regime* (the I regime for short). Under this regime trade takes place in two rounds. In both rounds only the primary securities themselves are traded; that is, there are no explicit signal-contingent trades. The first round of trade takes place before any information is released and the second round takes place after the release of information. Under the I regime individuals have no direct means of insuring themselves against revaluation effects but they do at least have an opportunity to trade in the primary securities before any information is released. It is instructive to compare the I regime with the A regime which, we already know, achieves full Pareto efficiency. Both regimes involve two rounds of trade, one before and one after the release of information. Both regimes involve trade in the set of primary securities in the second round. The only difference between the two regimes is that in the A regime trade takes place in a complete set of signal-contingent claims in the first round whilst in the I regime trade is confined to the set of primary securities. In the A regime the signal-contingent payoff matrix from the first round of trading will be as below:

	Claims to Signal 1 purchasing power	Claims to Signal 2 purchasing power	. . .	Claims to Signal Y purchasing power
Signal 1	1	0	. . .	0
Signal 2	0	1	. . .	0
$\vdots$	$\vdots$	$\vdots$	$\vdots$	$\vdots$
Signal Y . . .	0	0		1

This matrix shows the number of units of second-round purchasing power yielded by each security that is traded in the first round of trading. In the case of the A regime trade takes place directly in simple signal-contingent claims to second-round purchasing power and the matrix is a $Y \times Y$ identity matrix.

Under the I regime the first round of trade is restricted to the set of primary securities and claims to immediate consumption. If we assume that immediate consumption is the numeraire in the second round of trading the signal-contingent payoff matrix of the first round of the I regime can be expressed as below:

	Claims to current consumption	Claims to primary security 1	. . .	Claims to primary security J
Signal 1	1	P_{11}	. . .	P_{1J}
Signal 2	1	P_{21}	. . .	P_{2J}
$\vdots$	$\vdots$	$\vdots$	$\vdots$	$\vdots$
Signal Y	1	P_{Y1}	. . .	P_{YJ}

Here P_{yj} is the second-round price per unit of security j (relative to the price of one unit of current consumption) if signal y is revealed. The columns of this matrix, therefore, represent the signal-contingent purchasing power which a purchaser of one unit of a primary security' will receive in the second round of trading. The first round of the A regime permits trade in a complete set of signal-contingent claims whilst the I regime only permits trade in a set of $J + 1$ complex signal-contingent claims. By direct analogy with the analysis of chapter 2 we can see that the I regime will function as if there is a complete set of signal-contingent claims if and only if the rank of its signal-contingent payoff matrix is equal to Y. In fact, Ohlson and Buckman (1981) prove that this rank condition will always hold given our assumption that the market, in the absence of information, is complete. Hence, like the A and S regimes, the I regime also achieves full Pareto efficiency.

Finally we should mention one other regime considered by Ohlson and Buckman, namely, the NI regime (the *non-iterated* regime). This regime involves a single round of trade in the set of primary securities *after* the release of public information. The example given at the beginning of this subsection was a simple example of the NI regime. This regime hardly ever achieves full Pareto efficiency because it provides no insurance against revaluation effects.

Conditions for an Actual Pareto Improvement

Even though the introduction of information may result in an outward shift in the Pareto efficient frontier and even though the equilibrium allocations of the A, S and I regimes are Pareto efficient (assuming the rank condition holds in the case of the I regime) there is no guarantee that the introduction of information into any of these regimes will automatically result in everyone becoming better off. Consider, for example, figure 4.2 again.

Suppose c is the point on the inner frontier that will be achieved in equilibrium in the absence of information. If information is introduced into this economy the new pair of equilibrium expected utilities will lie somewhere on the frontier *dabe* but there is no guarantee that it will lie between point a and point b in the absence of a redistribution of initial endowments. Of course there will always exist a redistribution of initial endowments which will lead to a strict Pareto improvement following the release of information.

Several scholars have attempted to uncover conditions sufficient to guarantee that the introduction of information will lead to a strict Pareto improvement even in the absence of redistribution (see, for example, Jaffe, 1975; Hakansson et al., 1982; Kunkle, 1982). The basic result to emerge from this literature is that, if the initial endowments of individuals are their equilibrium endowments in the absence of information, then the introduction of *ex ante* information will result in a strict Pareto improvement (except, of course, in those special cases where information has no effect on the Pareto efficient frontier).

4.5 PUBLIC *EX ANTE* INFORMATION IN INSTITUTIONALLY INCOMPLETE MARKETS

Section 4.3 showed how *ex post* information can be exploited to expand the set of enforceable risk-sharing contracts. By using *ex post* information to introduce new tradable securities it may be possible to complete an otherwise incomplete market. Ohlson and Buckman (1981) have shown that a similar effect may be achieved by introducing *ex ante* information into an economy with an incomplete set of risk-sharing arrangements. The Ohlson and Buckman analysis is conducted in the context of a pure trading version of the two-period model. Before summarizing their main findings we need to review two further items of terminology.

Institutionally Constrained Pareto Efficiency

An allocation will be said to be *institutionally constrained Pareto efficient* if it is Pareto efficient subject to the restrictions imposed by the available resources and subject to the additional requirement that the end-of-period payoff to every individual must be a weighted sum of the payoffs on the set of tradable securities[4]. (This definition is a special case of the concept of constrained Pareto efficiency discussed in chapter 3.)

A Conditionally Complete Market

Let the matrix X be the state-contingent payoff matrix of the set of tradable securities, let η be a public *ex ante* information function, and let S_y be the set of states associated with signal y under information function η. Then X and η are said to constitute a *conditionally complete market* if for each signal y, the matrix formed by the columns of X associated with S_y is of full column rank. This definition is illustrated below:

	s_1	s_2	s_3	s_4
Payoff from security 1	1	1	1	1
Payoff from security 2	1	2	1	2
The partition induced by η	$S_{y_1} = \{s_1, s_2\}$		$S_{y_2} = \{s_3, s_4\}$	

In the absence of information the market structure is incomplete because there are four states and only two tradable securities. Under the information function η columns s_1 and s_2 are associated with signal y_1. The matrix formed by these two columns has a rank of 2. Similarly the matrix formed by columns s_3 and s_4 associated with signal y_2, is also of full rank. Hence this market structure is conditionally complete.

The main results established by Ohlson and Buckman are as follows:

1   The introduction of *ex ante* information enlarges the set of feasible allocations of state-contingent payoffs, hence the Pareto efficient frontier in the presence of information at least weekly dominates the Pareto efficient frontier in the absence of information.
2   The A and S regimes always achieve institutionally constrained Pareto efficiency and they achieve full Pareto efficiency if the market structure is conditionally complete.
3   The I regime will achieve institutionally constrained Pareto efficiency if a rank condition analogous to the one discussed in section 4.4 holds. Furthermore it will achieve full Pareto efficiency if the market is conditionally complete.
4   As in section 4.4, the NI regime will not normally achieve Pareto efficiency (either institutionally constrained or full).

For present purposes the most interesting of these findings is result 3. This establishes that it may be possible to complete an otherwise incomplete market by introducing *ex ante* information into an iterated market regime. This 'completion of markets' effect is similar to the effect achieved by the provision of *ex post* information but the mechanism of achieving this effect is different. In the case of *ex post* information, completion is achieved by introducing new risk-sharing contracts based on the new information. In the case studied in this section completion is achieved by introducing a further round of trading following the release of *ex ante* information whilst holding the number of tradable securities constant. This is identical to the effect of more frequent trading that we highlighted in section 3.5.

4.6   THE VALUE OF PUBLIC INFORMATION WHEN SOME INDIVIDUALS HAVE PRIVATE INFORMATION

Sections 4.3 to 4.5 explained two of the three main sources of social benefit from the provision of public information. The purpose of this section is to discuss the third possible source of social benefit.

This third source stems from the possibility that some individuals may have access to private information or private information production opportunities. The economics of information has focused on two main types of information asymmetry, namely, investor/investor asymmetry and outsider investor/insider manager asymmetry.

Investor/Investor Asymmetry

The investor/investor case of information asymmetry refers to the possibility that some investors may observe information that is not observed by other investors. This possibility was first rigorously examined by Hirshleifer (1971) and Fama and Laffer (1971). Further important insights were provided by Marshall (1974).

The main point to emerge from the analyses of Hirshleifer and Fama and Laffer is that circumstances can arise where there are considerable private benefits from having private access to information even though the social benefits of information are zero. To see this point consider the situation of an individual with sole access to perfect *ex ante* information in a pure trading model with homogeneous prior beliefs. Under the assumption that the trading activity of the investor will have no perceptible impact on market prices it is easy to see that the individual will benefit from private information even though, as demonstrated in section 4.4, such information is socially valueless. Since the investor has private foreknowledge of the future state of the world he can simply sell all his endowments to claims in the state that he knows is not going to occur and invest the proceeds in the state that he knows is going to occur. In this way he makes a private gain at the expense of other members of society by 'dumping' the claims which only he knows to be worthless on the less informed investors. In this context, therefore, the production of private information is a privately beneficial but socially valueless activity (and socially wasteful if it consumes real resources).

Marshall (1974) notes that this divergence between the private and social benefits of private information production may provide yet another rationale for the provision of public information. In particular, one possible way of reducing socially valueless private information production may be to produce information publicly. If public information production deters private information production there will be a net benefit to society to the extent that the costs of public information production fall short of the reduction in aggregate private information expenditure induced by the provision of public information.

The details of Marshall's (1974) argument can be criticized because it assumes that relatively uninformed investors will simply react passively to price signals even though they will be aware that they are likely to be 'scalped' by relatively well informed investors. In fact uninformed investors have at least two possible strategies available to protect themselves from trading with informed individuals:

1 They can refuse to trade with the more informed individual and/or insulate themselves from the trading activities of the more informed by adopting a passive 'buy and hold' strategy.
2 They may attempt to infer the information of the informed individuals from market prices.

In recent years a number of models have been developed that assume a greater degree of sophistication on the part of uninformed investors. In particular they assume that uninformed investors are able to infer some (and in some cases all) the information of informed investors from market prices. Further details on these more sophisticated models is given in chapter 5, but for present purposes the important point to emerge from these models is that Marshall's basic insight still holds so long as privately produced information is less than perfectly reflected in market prices.

Outsider Investor/Insider Manager Information Asymmetry

The case of outsider investor/insider manager information asymmetry is an issue that has cropped up from time to time in the literature on the economic theory of the firm under the rubric of 'separation of ownership from control'. The economics of information has focused on two main issues within this context. The first is the question of whether managers will have an appropriate incentive to truthfully reveal their private information to outside investors and the related question of whether any costs will be incurred in communicating this information. The two main types of models used to examine these issues are known as *signalling* and *screening* models. Both types of models are game-theoretic in nature and both involve two types of agents, namely, informed insiders and uninformed outsiders. The essence of a signalling or screening equilibrium is that the informed insiders reveal their information to uninformed outsiders by their own actions. For example, in some models the means by which the information available to an insider manager is publicly revealed is through the manager agreeing to a contract under which there is a substantial penalty if misrepresentation is established at a later date when the terms of the contract are fulfilled. It is interesting to note that *ex post* information is adequate to enforce this type of contract. In other models of signalling and screening such *ex post* validation is not possible. Chapter 7 supplies a review of the signalling and screening literature.

The second major issue which arises when managers have access to private information is the question of how to motivate managers to take decisions consistent with the outside shareholders' interests. A class of models known collectively as *agency theory* has recently helped to shed some light on this issue. In all agency models the manager has a number of decision variables under his control which are not directly observable by the outside shareholders. In some agency models the manager also has access to additional private information at the time he makes his decision choice. An agency problem arises where the manager's preference ranking over alternative levels of the decision variables differs from that of the shareholders. The literature often refers to decision variables such as the level of expenditure on perquisites or the manager's level of effort, but there are other, possibly more important, decision variables over which conflicts of interest can arise. For example, the manager and shareholders may disagree over what kinds of project risk are acceptable. In an agency context shareholders will demand information that helps them to infer which decision the manager chose, or that helps them to infer what information the manager had at the time he made his decision choice. For example, if the shareholders can observe both the manager's decisions and the manager's information they can achieve perfect control over his decisions. It is again worth noting that such information reported *ex post* would be just as effective in maintaining control as *ex ante* information. Chapter 8 provides a more detailed review of the agency theory literature.

4.7 CONCLUDING REMARKS

The previous sections have identified five potential sources of social benefits from the provision of public information:

1 Improved intertemporal allocation of claims when utility functions are not time-additive.
2 Improved intertemporal allocation of claims when prior beliefs are not homogeneous.
3 Improved real production decisions.
4 An expansion in the set of risk-sharing opportunities.
5 Reduction of the social costs associated with information asymmetries.

Whether or not any of these potential benefits are economically significant is ultimately an empirical question. Our prior beliefs, for what they are worth, are that the benefits from sources 1 and 2 are likely to be insignificant relative to the benefits from sources 3, 4 and 5.

The purpose of this appendix is to supply the technical details behind the analysis of sections 4.2 and 4.4. We begin by deriving the first-order conditions for full Pareto efficiency in the presence of information. We then demonstrate the Pareto efficiency of the S and A regimes. We focus entirely on the exogenous production case.

Notation

$Y=$ number of possible information signals and the set of information signals

$y=$ an element of Y, i.e. a particular signal

$S=$ the set of states

$S_y=$ the set of states that give rise to signal y

$\phi_{is}=$ prior probability of state s as assessed by consumer i

$\phi_i(y)=$ probability of signal y as assessed by consumer $i=\sum_{s\epsilon S_y}\phi_{is}$

$$\phi_i(s/y)=\begin{cases} \phi_{is}/\phi_i(y) & \text{if } s\epsilon S_y \\ 0 & \text{if } s\epsilon S_y \end{cases}$$

i.e. the revised probability of state s given y

$C_{i0y}=$ the immediate consumption of consumer i if signal y occurs

$C_{is}=$ the consumption of the ith consumer in state s

$M=$ the aggregate endowment of current consumption

$y_{js}=$ the aggregate payoff from firm j in state s

Given this notation the expected utility of the ith consumer can be expressed as follows:

$$EU_i = \sum_y [U_i(C_{i0y}) + \sum_{s\epsilon S_y} V_i(C_{is}).\phi_i(s/y)]\phi_i(y) \qquad (4A.1)$$

The expression inside the square bracket in (4A.1) is the expected utility of consumer i if signal y occurs. To get his overall expected utility we need to multiply by $\phi_i(y)$ and aggregate over all y.

First-Order Conditions for Pareto Efficiency

The conditions for full Pareto efficiency can be found along the lines of section 2.2 by considering the following central planner's problem:

$$\text{maximize } \sum_i k_i\Big\{ \sum_y [U_i(C_{i0y}) + \sum_{s\epsilon S_y} V_i(C_{is}).\phi_i(s/y)]\phi_i(y)\Big\} \qquad (4A2)$$

subject to $\sum_i C_{i0y} = M$ for all y (4A.3)

$\sum_i C_{is} = \sum_j y_{js}$ for all s (4A.4)

The first-order conditions for an optimum solution can be expressed as follows:

$$k_i \cdot U'_{iy} \cdot \phi_i(y) - \lambda_y = 0 \qquad \text{for all } y, \text{ all } i \qquad (4A.5)$$

$$k_i \cdot V_{isy} \cdot \phi_i(y) \cdot \phi_i(s/y) - \mu_s = 0 \qquad \text{for all } s, \text{ all } i \qquad (4A.6)$$

plus (4A.3) and (4A.4). (λ_y and μ_s are the Lagrange multipliers on (4A.3) and (4A.4) respectively.) U'_{iy} is the marginal utility of individual i's current consumption under signal y and V_{isy} is the marginal utility of individual i's state s consumption under signal y.

The reader can easily check that (4A.6) implies equation (4.1) employed in section 4.2 above. Also by dividing (4A.5) by (4A.6) it can be seen that equation (4.4) must hold.

The Pareto Efficiency of the S and A Regimes

In analysing the economic efficiency of the S and A regimes we can assume, without loss of generality, that a complete set of simple state claims is tradable in the absence of information.

The consumer's problem for the S regime can then be expressed as follows:

maximize $\sum_y [U_i(C_{i0y}) + \sum_{s \in S_y} V_i(C_{is}) \cdot \phi_i(s/y)] \cdot \phi_i(y)$ (4A.7)

subject to $\sum_y [p_{0y} \cdot C_{i0y} + \sum_{s \in S_y} p_{sy} \cdot C_{is}] = \bar{C}_{i0} \cdot \sum_y p_{0y} + \sum_y \sum_{s \in S_y} \sum_j \bar{x}_{ij} \cdot y_{sj} \cdot p_{sy}$

(4A.8)

Here p_{0y} is the price of a claim to immediate consumption contingent on
    signal y.
p_{sy} is the price of one unit of consumption in state s if signal y occurs;
    clearly p_{sy} will be zero if s is not an element of S_y.
$\bar{C}_{i0}$ is the ith consumer's initial endowment of current consumption.
$\bar{x}_{ij}$ is the ith consumer's proportional endowment of firm j.

The first-order conditions for an optimum can be expressed as (4A.8) plus the following:

$$U'_{iy} \cdot \phi_i(y) - \theta_i \cdot p_{0y} = 0 \qquad \text{for all } y \qquad (4A.9)$$

$$V_{isy}.\phi_i(y).\phi_i(s/y) - \theta_i.p_{sy} = 0 \qquad \text{for all } y \text{ and all } s\epsilon S_y \qquad (4A.10)$$

where θ_i is the Lagrange multiplier on (4A.8).

Comparing (4A.9) and (4A.10) with (4A.5) and (4A.6) it is readily apparent that all equilibria of the S regime are Pareto efficient. The converse proposition can be established along the lines of the proof suggested in chapter 2.

For the A regime the consumer's problem can be expressed as follows:

$$\text{maximize } \sum_y \left[U_i(C_{i0y}) + \sum_{s\epsilon S_y} V_i(C_{is}).\phi_i(s/y) \right].\phi_i(y) \qquad (4A.11)$$

$$\text{subject to } \sum_y C_{iy}.P_y = 0 \qquad (4A.12)$$

$$\text{and } C_{i0y} + \sum_{s\epsilon S_y} C_{is}.P_{sy} = \bar{C}_{i0} + \sum_{s\epsilon S_y} \sum_j \bar{x}_{ij}.y_{sj}.P_{sy} + C_{iy} \qquad \text{for all } y$$
$$(4A.13)$$

Here (4A.12) is the consumer's first-round budget constraint.

    P_y is the price per unit of signal y contingent purchasing power carried forward to the second round of trading.

    C_{iy} is the number of units of signal y purchasing power carried forward to the second round of trading.

    (4A.13) is a set of Y equations, one for each possible signal. This represents the signal-contingent budget constraint of the consumer in the second round of trading.

    P_{sy} is the price of state s consumption relative to immediate consumption if signal y occurs.

The analysis assumes that P_{sy} is known before first-round trading takes place and that P_{sy} is equal to what it would have been under the S regime, namely, p_{sy}/p_{0y}. In addition it is assumed that P_y is the same as its S regime counterpart, p_{0y}.

First-order conditions are (4A.12) and (4A.13) plus the following:

$$U'_{iy}.\phi_i(y) - \gamma_{iy} = 0 \qquad \text{for all } y \qquad (4A.14)$$

$$V_{isy}.\phi_i(y).\phi_i(s/y) - \gamma_{iy}.P_{sy} = 0 \qquad \text{for all } y \text{ and all } s\epsilon S_y \qquad (4A.15)$$

$$-\beta_i.P_y + \gamma_{iy} = 0 \qquad \text{for all } y \qquad (4A.16)$$

where β_i is the Lagrange multiplier on (4A.12), and the γ_{iy} are the Lagrange multipliers on (4A.13). By setting β_i equal to θ_i and recalling that (by assumption) $P_{sy} = p_{sy}/p_{0y}$, and $P_y = p_{0y}$, it is easy to see that these conditions are equivalent to the corresponding conditions for the S regime, namely, (4A.9) and (4A.10). Hence, since the S regime is Pareto efficient, the A regime must also be Pareto efficient.

5

Rational Expectations Equilibrium

Previous chapters have considered the efficiency properties of equilibrium under alternative regimes of production and exchange in stock market economies. Two informational issues have been analysed. Chapter 1 dealt with the value of information in the single-person case, while chapter 4 introduced information into a variety of capital market settings. But in this second case, attention was largely restricted to the value of information made available to all individuals in the economy – the 'value of public information' problem. Until now, little consideration has been given to the impact of heterogeneous information on capital markets. Yet it is a fundamental characteristic of modern stock markets that different agents receive different information signals.

The main purpose of this chapter is to provide an introduction to a fairly recent body of literature concerned with the definition and analysis of equilibrium in an economy in which different economic agents come to the capital market with different information. The term *rational expectations equilibrium* (REE) has been used to describe this problem. The one characteristic that distinguishes this branch of equilibrium economics from previous developments is that economic agents are now assumed to treat the market prices of securities as additional sources of information.

In the context of a capital market this is a natural assumption to adopt. When investors purchase the equity securities of companies, the eventual payoffs from those securities are not known with certainty at the time of purchase. In the terminology adopted in this book, the eventual payoffs depend upon the state of the world. Now if prices are established as the outcome of a process equilibrating aggregate demands and supplies, and if economic agents enter the market with different non-price information, then security prices themselves will convey information. To take a simple example, if private research by a number of stockbroking firms uncovers evidence that leads them to increase their subjective probabilities that the future demand for oil will fall, the prices of equity shares in oil companies will be bid down. It would then be short-sighted of an individual investor who knew nothing first-hand of this information, to simply act parametrically with respect to the price change. A natural response would be to attempt to infer some information from the price change and to treat price as an additional information signal. The problem of characterizing equilibrium in an economy in which agents learn from prices as well as from their own non-price information has generated an enormous literature in recent years. This chapter will concentrate on characterizing an REE with particular emphasis on the implications for information in the economy. More technical aspects concerned with the existence of an REE are not addressed here.

The chapter begins in section 5.1 with an exposition of the concept of an REE and of the main differences between an REE and alternative concepts of equilibrium in the presence of heterogeneous information. Section 5.2 illustrates these concepts using a numerical example. Some of the main results on REE that have appeared in the literature are analysed in the following two sections. These results are illustrated by examples of situations where individuals may learn all agents' non-price information by simply observing prices (section 5.3), and where individuals may learn some but not all information from prices (section 5.4). Where appropriate, references are made to the original literature and an attempt is made to link the results illustrated by the simple examples with the more general results appearing in their original sources. A preliminary analysis of the relationship between the concepts of a rational expectations equilibrium and of full Pareto efficiency is given in section 5.5. Section 5.6 offers some concluding remarks.

5.1 THE CHARACTERIZATION OF
A RATIONAL EXPECTATIONS EQUILIBRIUM

In all previous competitive equilibrium models in this book, agents behaved parametrically with respect to price. This meant that in the decision problem facing any individual, security prices entered only through the individual's budget constraint. When agents use security prices as an additional signal, security prices enter their objective function directly. This is because beliefs, or expectations, over states of the world are conditioned not only on the non-price information available to individual agents but also on the signals generated by prices.

Equilibrium in a Walrasian economy in which different agents receive different non-price information signals before trade takes place but in which agents do take prices as given, can be characterized as follows. Let η_i denote the information function of the ith agent in the economy. We will refer to the vector of information functions $(\eta_1, \eta_2, \ldots, \eta_I)$, as the *information structure* of the economy. Given a specific set of information signals $(y_1, y_2, \ldots, y_I)$, where y_i is the signal received by individual i from η_i, each individual will revise his beliefs over states of the world. Demands for the available securities[1] will then be formed and equilibrium security prices equating total demand and supply for each security will be established for the particular set of information signals $(y_1, y_2, \ldots, y_I)$. Similarly, for any other set of information signals, $(y'_1, y'_2, \ldots, y'_I)$, an equilibrium set of security prices would be established in the same way. An overall Walrasian equilibrium for this differential information economy with information structure $(\eta_1, \eta_2, \ldots, \eta_I)$ would be a price function, or in probability terminology, a price random variable, comprising a mapping from each possible set of information signals from information structure $(\eta_1, \eta_2, \ldots, \eta_I)$ to the corresponding equilibrium set of security prices.

In an Arrow–Debreu economy all agents share the same information from the start of trading and no further information is introduced. The equilibrium price function therefore collapses to a single set of equilibrium security prices which can be considered as corresponding to a public null information signal. Equilibrium in the Walrasian economy with differential information involves an extension of the Arrow–Debreu equilibrium. An equilibrium set of security prices is now defined for each of the possible sets of information signals from the information structure, and the overall equilibrium is a function from sets of information signals to sets of equilibrium security prices.

Given this extension of the Arrow–Debreu economy to the case of differential information with no learning from prices, the extension to an REE is conceptually, if not analytically, straightforward. A heuristic justification for this learning-from-prices phenomenon has been argued by many authors by analogy with the previous equilibrium concept. To follow the argument, imagine a Walrasian capital market economy in which agents act parametrically with respect to price. Assume that this economy essentially repeats itself over a number of trading periods. In this economy, if different investors have different information, relatively uninformed investors should eventually be able to learn something of the relationship between share prices and the information available to informed investors. For example, uninformed investors who took prices as given would eventually learn that high share prices for companies tended to be followed by favourable economic conditions for the companies concerned, and similarly for low prices and unfavourable conditions. Given enough replications of the economy, the uninformed investor would eventually be able to construct a model linking share prices to states of the world. The sophisticated investor would then use share price as an additional signal about the true state of the world.

This behaviour inevitably leads to a departure from the Walrasian equilibrium previously considered. If agents revise their beliefs on the basis of price as well as non-price information, then their investment demands will differ from demands based solely on the latter source of information. In turn, the previous equilibrium prices from the Walrasian economy will no longer be market clearing. The concept of equilibrium now required for the differential information structure $(\eta_1, \eta_2, \ldots, \eta_I)$ can be developed as follows. A set of equilibrium security prices is required for each non-price information signal $(y_1, y_2, \ldots, y_I)$, such that when investors form demands, given beliefs or expectations conditional on both the non-price information received and the information revealed by prices, security markets clear at those very same prices. It is in this respect – that conjectures about prices are self-fulfilling – that expectations are said to be rational. The overall REE is then, as before, a price function from each set of information signals from the information structure $(\eta_1, \eta_2, \ldots, \eta_I)$ to a set of (self-fulfilling) equilibrium security prices.

5.2 ILLUSTRATION OF A RATIONAL EXPECTATIONS EQUILIBRIUM

In this section, some of the concepts discussed in the previous section are illustrated with the aid of a numerical example.

Consider a simple economy comprising two firms, X and Y. State-contingent cash payoffs in the (single) future period are given exogenously as below:

		s_1	s_2	s_3	s_4	s_5
Firms	X	1	1	2	1	3
	Y	2	2	2	1	1
	$X+Y$	3	3	4	2	4

Obviously, this description is in no sense intended to be realistic, but the example lends itself to a simple understanding which can then be generalized in a straightforward manner.

Assume two individuals, A and B, in the economy with identical utility functions over future wealth levels x, of the form, $u(x) = \ln x$. Our intention in introducing this assumption is solely to simplify the numerical calculations to follow. However, as we have seen in chapters 2 and 3, this assumption in addition means that in the absence of heterogeneous beliefs, the allocation that achieves FPE results in each individual consuming the same proportion of market wealth in each state of the world. Notwithstanding this special result, the discussion of all numerical examples throughout this chapter will proceed as if we were considering individuals with different functional forms for their utility functions. In fact, as we shall see below when we specify the types of contracts that individuals can enter into, this simplification becomes superfluous to the analysis.

We will assume that subjective beliefs over states of the world are as below:

	s_1	s_2	s_3	s_4	s_5
ϕ_A	1/3	1/6	1/6	1/6	1/6
ϕ_B	1/4	1/8	1/8	1/4	1/4

Individual A is assumed to be endowed with all ownership interest in firm 1 while individual B is similarly endowed with all ownership interest in firm 2.

The general decision problem facing any individual is to contract on the basis of commonly observable contingencies in order to maximize the expected utility of future payoff subject to a budget constraint.

This still leaves the problem of specifying the precise set of enforceable contingencies on which individuals can strike contracts. In fact, the formal analysis of the remainder of this chapter would go through whatever the precise specification adopted, although the characterization of the corresponding REE would alter. But it seems appropriate here, in considering equilibrium in economies with heterogeneous information, to abstract entirely from institutional restrictions on trade in order to focus exclusively on informational issues. Accordingly, individuals are assumed to observe, in the future period, the cash flows of the individual firms in the economy. As a result, the contingencies revealed by cash flows form a minimal set of mutually observable contingencies on which contracts can be struck now, with terms being fulfilled when the actual contingency is revealed in the future. Similarly, when information is introduced into the analysis so that individuals are endowed with private information functions, individuals are assumed to be able to trade on the basis of commonly observable contingencies where this includes contingencies revealed by their private information functions. This treatment is in the spirit of Radner (see, for example, Radner, 1982, p. 948). It is distinct from what we have called a stock market economy in which individuals are restricted to trade in ownership shares of the entire vector of a firm's state-contingent cash flows.

Given the foregoing, individuals in this economy will be unable to distinguish only between states s_1 and s_2. This means that trade is constrained to the basic securities below:

	s_1	s_2	s_3	s_4	s_5
H_1	1	1	0	0	0
H_2	0	0	1	0	0
H_3	0	0	0	1	0
H_4	0	0	0	0	1

So, for example, H_1 represents a claim to a payoff of 1 if either s_1 or s_2 occurs. An alternative description would be that H_1 represents a claim to a payoff of 1 contingent on the cash flow payoff from firm X being 1 and the cash flow payoff from firm Y being 2. The partition of contingencies, or states or the world, defined by cash flows is therefore

$$\Gamma(X, Y) = \{\{s_1, s_2\}, \{s_3\}, \{s_4\}, \{s_5\}\}$$

The partition of event-conditional belief homogeneity, which can be calculated according to the procedure outlined in chapter 3, is

$$\Gamma(\psi_A, \psi_B) = \{\{s_1, s_2, s_3\}, \{s_4, s_5\}\}$$

Given the argument in chapter 3 it follows that this economy achieves FPE through trade in the basic securities, $\{H_j\}$. This is despite the fact that, with only four linearly independent securities, the market is incomplete. The reader can also note that given the set of tradable securities assumed here, any numerical examples that involve homogeneous utility functions do not in fact lead to any further simplification of the conditions required for FPE. If we assume that individuals can contract on the basis of commonly observable contingencies as revealed by distinct firm cash flows, then sharing of market risk can already be achieved and so any relaxation of this requirement is redundant.

Endowments of firms translate into endowments of basic securities as below:

	A	B
H_1	1	2
H_2	2	2
H_3	1	1
H_4	3	1

The Arrow–Debreu Equilibrium

The framework for analysis is developed by considering initially the Arrow–Debreu equilibrium in which individuals receive no further information prior to trade. The Arrow–Debreu equilibrium for this economy can be solved for in the same manner as for the market equilibrium in example 2.3 of chapter 2. However, it might be useful to be reminded of that development here. The equilibrium is solved for in two stages:

1 each individual's decision problem is solved for basic security demands as functions of the (as yet unknown) equilibrium prices; and
2 aggregate demands are equated with total supply and the system is solved for equilibrium prices.

Letting Hs, appropriately subscripted, denote the demands by individuals for basic security, equilibrium prices can be solved for as follows. Basic security H_1 is taken to be numeraire. Individual A's decision problem written out in full is:

$$\underset{\{H_{Aj}\}}{\text{maximize}} \quad u(H_A) = \frac{1}{2}\ln H_{A1} + \frac{1}{6}(\ln H_{A2} + \ln H_{A3} + \ln H_{A4})$$

subject to $H_{A1} + p_2.H_{A2} + p_3.H_{A3} + p_4.H_{A4} = 1 + 2p_2 + p_3 + 3p_4$

Forming the Lagrangean function and differentiating partially with respect to the arguments of A's objection function gives the four equations:

$$H_{A1} = \frac{1}{2\theta}; \ H_{A2}p_2 = \frac{1}{6\theta}; \ H_{A3}p_3 = \frac{1}{6\theta}; \ H_{A4}p_4 = \frac{1}{6\theta}$$

where θ is the multiplier on A's budget constraint. Substitution into the budget constraint yields

$$1/\theta = W_A$$

where $W_A \ (= 1 + 2p_2 + p_3 + 3p_{4\text{p}})$ is A's initial wealth. A's basic security demands as functions of equilibrium prices are therefore

$$H_{A1} = W_A/2; \ H_{A2} = W_A/6p_2; \ H_{A3} = W_A/6p_3; \ H_{A4} = W_A/6p_4$$

A similar procedure gives individual B's demands as

$$H_{B1} = 3W_B/8; \quad H_{B2} = W_B/8p_2; \quad H_{B3} = W_B/4p_3; \quad H_{B4} = W_B/4p_4$$

where $W_B \ (=2+2p_2+p_3+p_4)$ is B's initial wealth.

Moving on to stage 2, total demands are now equated with total supplies and the system is solved for the equilibrium basic security prices. Equating demands and supplies gives

$$
\begin{aligned}
(10+14p_2+7p_3+15p_4)/8 &= 3 \\
(10+14p_2+7p_3+15p_4)/24p_2 &= 4 \\
(8+10p_2+5p_3+9p_4)/12p_3 &= 2 \\
(8+10p_2+5p_3+9p_4)/12p_4 &= 4
\end{aligned}
$$

These four equations comprise a set of three linearly independent equations in three unknowns which can be solved to give (three) relative prices,

$$(p_1, p_2, p_3, p_4) = (1, 1/4, 21/29, 21/58)$$

Interpreting the (numeraire) price of basic security H_1 as corresponding to prices of $1/2$ attached to cash flows in each of states s_1 and s_2, allows the equilibrium market values of firms X and Y to be computed as the inner products

$$V(X) = (1, 1, 2, 1, 3).(1/2, 1/2, 1/4, 21/29, 21/58) = 96/29$$
$$V(Y) = (2, 2, 2, 1, 1).(1/2, 1/2, 1/4, 21/29, 21/58) = 104/29$$

Each individual's final allocation can also be derived. For example, for individual A,

$$(H_{A1}, H_{A2}, H_{A3}, H_{A4}) = (48/29, 64/29, 16/21, 32/21).$$

This portfolio can be considered in terms of ownership of basic securities issued through an intermediary holding the market portfolio. Alternatively, the portfolio can be interpreted, for example, as individual A receiving a $19/58$ ownership interest in firm Y in addition to A's complete ownership of firm X, if and only if either state s_1 or s_2 is revealed to have occurred. The expected utilities of A and B can also be calculated by substituting the equilibrium allocations back into the objective functions.

The Differential Information Walrasian Equilibrium

Differential information can now be introduced into this simple economy. Specifically, assume that individual A becomes the informed investor and receives the following information function before trade takes place:

$$\eta_A$$

$$\{s_1, s_2, s_3\} \mapsto y_{A1}$$
$$\{s_4, s_5\} \mapsto y_{A2}$$

In other words, individual A knows that when the signal arrives he will know either that the event $\{s_1, s_2, s_3\}$ has occurred or that the event $\{s_4, s_5\}$ has occurred. Individual B on the other hand, is assumed to receive no private information and is therefore the uninformed individual. This is a case of asymmetric information, individual A receiving a finer information function than individual B. However, asymmetric information is a special case of the more general differential information description and the analysis to follow does not rely on the special case.

Initially, the assumption that agents act parametrically with respect to price is maintained. This places the example in a Walrasian economy with differential information.

The competitive equilibrium can now be computed for each signal received by individual A. Thus if y_{A1} is the signal received then A will revise prior beliefs of $(1/3, 1/6, 1/6, 1/6, 1/6)$ for states $(s_1, s_2, s_3, s_4, s_5)$ to conditional beliefs of $(1/2, 1/4, 1/4, 0, 0)$. Individual A will then solve the following decision problem:

$$\underset{\{H_{Aj}\}}{\text{maximize}} \; u(H_A) = \frac{3}{4}\,\ln H_{A1} + \frac{1}{4}\,\ln H_{A2}$$

$$\text{subject to } H_{A1} + p_2 H_{A2} = 1 + 2p_2 + p_3 + 3p_4$$

Solving in the same way as before gives A's demands as[3]

$$H_{A1} = 3W_A/4; \; H_{A2} = W_A/4p_2$$

Individual B's decision problem is unchanged so that B's demands are exactly as they were for the previous economy. Again, total demands and supplies can be equated and solved for basic security prices for signal y_{A1}. This gives relative prices as

$$(p_1, p_2, p_3, p_4) = (1, 1/4, 5/13, 5/26)$$

In a similar way, if y_{A2} is the signal received then A's conditional beliefs become $(0, 0, 0, 1/2, 1/2)$ and A faces the following decision problem:

$$\underset{\{H_{Aj}\}}{\text{maximize}} \; u(H_A) = \frac{1}{2}\ln H_3 + \frac{1}{2}\ln H_{A4}$$

$$\text{subject to } p_3 H_{A3} + p_4 H_{A4} = 1 + 2p_2 + p_3 + 3p_4$$

A's demands now become

$$H_{A3} = W_A/2p_3; \; H_{A4} = W_A/2p_4$$

B's demands are again as before. Solving for the equilibrium basic security prices now gives for signal y_{A2}

$$(p_1, p_2, p_3, p_4) = (1, 1/4, 11/3, 11/6)$$

The overall competitive equilibrium appropriate to the information structure

$$\eta_A \qquad\qquad\qquad \eta_B$$
$$\{s_1, s_2, s_3\} \mapsto y_{A1} \qquad\qquad \{S\} \mapsto y_B$$
$$\{s_4, s_5\} \mapsto y_{A2}$$

is therefore that below:

(y_A, y_B)	$\tilde{p}$
(y_{A1}, y_B)	$(1, 1/4, 5/13, 3/26)$
(y_{A2}, y_B)	$(1, 1/4, 11/13, 11/6)$

It can be seen that the concept of an equilibrium price is that of a price function, or in more familiar terms, a price random variable, mapping from possible information signals to equilibrium price vectors.

The Rational Expectations Equilibrium

What we now wish to develop is an REE appropriate to this differential non-price information economy. By this is meant that for each non-price information signal received, when beliefs are conditioned on both non-price information and the information revealed by the price vector, markets clear at that very same price vector. To begin with, the solution itself is simply stated. The reader can verify, by solving the individual decision problems, that the solution does represent an REE. The precise solution procedure is explained more fully in the following section.

Assume that individual A on receiving the non-price signal y_{A1} and observing the price vector (1, 1/4, 0, 0) revises prior beliefs of (1/3, 1/6, 1/6, 1/6, 1/6) to conditional beliefs (1/2, 1/4, 1/4, 0, 0). Similarly, assume that individual B on observing the null information signal y_B and the price vector (1, 1/4, 0, 0) revises prior beliefs of (1/4, 1/8, 1/8, 1/4, 1/4) to conditional beliefs (1/2, 1/4, 1/4, 0, 0). Then by going through the individuals' decision calculus the market clearing price vector is indeed found to be (1, 1/4, 0, 0).

If individual A receives the signal y_{A2} and observes the price vector (0, 0, 1, 1/2) – where basic security H_3 is now numeraire – then assume that beliefs are revised to (0, 0, 0, 1/2, 1/2). Individual B again receives the null non-price information signal y_B but on observing the price vector (0, 0, 1, 1/2) revises beliefs to (0, 0, 0, 1/2, 1/2). Again, the market clearing price vector can be solved for and found to be (0, 0, 1, 1/2).

This gives the REE appropriate to the information structure (η_A, η_B) as below:

(y_A, y_B)	$\tilde{p}$
(y_{A1}, y_B)	(1, 1/4, 0, 0)
(y_{A2}, y_B)	(0, 0, 1, 1/2)

In this REE, individuals effectively conjecture a model of how non-price information signals are mapped into prices. Then when this information is used to condition beliefs, these prices become self-fulfilling. The description 'effectively' is used above because individuals in fact conjecture a partition over states of the world generated by the observed price vector. Thus, when the price vector (1, 1/4, 0, 0) was observed by individual B, the conjecture was that either s_1, s_2 or s_3 had occurred, and similarly for the price vector (0, 0, 1, 1/2) and states s_4 and s_5. But this was precisely the partition generated over states by the information signals (y_A, y_B).

Finally, it can be noted that individuals agree on which equilibrium price vector is associated with each event, or set of states of the world. For example, they agree that the price vector (1, 1/4, 0, 0) is associated with the event $\{s_1, s_2, s_3\}$. However, they need not agree on the probability distribution of the equilibrium price random variable. For example, referring back to the prior probabilities, individual A believes that (1, 1/4, 0, 0) will be the equilibrium price vector with probability 2/3, whereas B attaches a probability of 1/2 to this event.

5.3 FULLY REVEALING RATIONAL EXPECTATIONS EQUILIBRIUM

This section illustrates some of the results that have appeared in the literature. The first set of results concerns the existence of a fully revealing rational expectations equilibrium (FRREE). That is, when will the REE price function reveal to each agent the non-price information of all agents collectively. In fact the immediately previous example from section 5.2 constituted an FRREE. However, rather than repeat that example, further examples are developed here in an attempt to illustrate what is required for an REE to be fully revealing and in the process to show how an FRREE is computed.

The examples assume an economic setting similar to that of the previous section. That is, individuals are assumed to trade in cash flows of firms contingent on common information. In so doing, individuals augment their non-price information with the information revealed by the price signal. An equilibrium is a price random variable for which beliefs are self-fulfilling or rational.

The example below assumes two firms with state-contingent cash payoffs over eight states of the world as follows:

	s_1	s_2	s_3	s_4	s_5	s_6	s_7	s_8
X	1	1	2	1	2	2	3	3
Y	1	1	1	3	2	3	2	2
	2	2	3	4	4	5	5	5

The economy again has two individuals, A and B, with subjective beliefs over states given as below:

	s_1	s_2	s_3	s_4	s_5	s_6	s_7	s_8
ϕ_A	0.1	0.2	0.15	0.04	0.06	0.05	0.1	0.3
ϕ_B	0.12	0.24	0.18	0.06	0.1	0.1	0.05	0.15

The assumption that individuals can contract on the basis of the commonly observed contingencies as revealed by distinct firm cash flows, means that A and B are unable to distinguish only between states s_1 and s_2 and between states s_7 and s_8. It can be seen that for the identification of Amershi's minimal aggregate wealth sufficient partition (see chapter 3), the condition on market wealth levels requires the partition of tradable contingent events $\Gamma(X+Y)=\{\{s_1, s_2\}, \{s_3\}, \{s_4, s_5\}, \{s_6, s_7, s_8\}\}$. It can also be calculated that the condition on individual beliefs of event-contingent homogeneity defines the partition $\Gamma(\psi_A, \psi_B) = \{\{s_1, s_2, s_3\}, \{s_4\}, \{s_5\}, \{s_6\}, \{s_7, s_8\}\}$.[4] From this it can be seen that the partition of states required for the achievement of FPE is, for this example, precisely that partition identified by the vectors of firm cash flows

$$\Gamma(X, Y) = \{\{s_1, s_2\}, \{s_3\}, \{s_4\}, \{s_5\}, \{s_6\}, \{s_7, s_8\}\}$$

The corresponding set of tradable securities is therefore as below:

	s_1	s_2	s_3	s_4	s_5	s_6	s_7	s_8
H_1	1	1	0	0	0	0	0	0
H_2	0	0	1	0	0	0	0	0
H_3	0	0	0	1	0	0	0	0
H_4	0	0	0	0	1	0	0	0
H_5	0	0	0	0	0	1	0	0
H_6	0	0	0	0	0	0	1	1

The assumption that individual A is endowed with 100 per cent ownership of firm X and B with 100 per cent ownership of firm Y is maintained. This implies the ownership of tradable securities as below:

	A	B
H_1	1	1
H_2	2	1
H_3	1	3
H_4	2	2
H_5	2	3
H_6	3	2

The information functions with which A and B are assumed to be costlessly endowed are given as

η_A

$\{s_1, s_2, s_3, s_4, s_5\} \mapsto y_{A1}$
$\{s_6, s_7, s_8\} \mapsto y_{A2}$

η_B

$\{s_1, s_2, s_3\} \mapsto y_{B1}$
$\{s_4, s_5, s_6, s_7, s_8\} \mapsto y_{B2}$

Neither individual is assumed to be better informed than the other here, so that this represents the more general case of differential information. The question now is, will the REE corresponding to this information structure and the economy as outlined, be fully revealing? That is, will the equilibrium price random variable reveal to each agent the non-price information of A and B collectively?

The collective non-price information of A and B can be seen to be

$$\Gamma(\eta_A, \eta_B) = \{\{s_1, s_2, s_3\}, \{s_4, s_5\}, \{s_6, s_7, s_8\}\}$$

Consistent with the general differential information assumption, this is a finer information partition than is available to either A or B individually.

However, for this example, we can say that the REE will reveal to each individual their collective information partition – the REE will be fully revealing. The reason is that the minimal aggregate wealth sufficient (MAWS) partition over states of the world defined by the set of tradable contingent events,

$$\Gamma(X, Y) = \{\{s_1, s_2\}, \{s_3\}, \{s_4\}, \{s_5\}, \{s_6\}, \{s_7, s_8\}\}$$

is at least as fine as the partition defined by the information functions of A and B collectively,

$$\Gamma(\eta_A, \eta_B) = \{\{s_1, s_2, s_3\}, \{s_4, s_5\}, \{s_6, s_7, s_8\}$$

Given this result, the REE is found by employing the 'trick' of calculating the equilibrium price random variable in which both individuals receive the information structure (η_A, η_B), but no learning from prices occurs. This equilibrium price random variable is then precisely the FRREE price random variable for the economy in which individual A receives only the non-price information function η_A, individual B receives only the non-price information function η_B, but both individuals condition their beliefs also on the price information signal. This was the procedure adopted in solving for the rational expectations equilibrium in the previous section.

A rough justification for this procedure can be given. Recall from chapter 2 condition (2.11b):

$$U_{i1s}\phi_{is} = p_s\theta_i \qquad \text{for all } s \qquad (2.11b)$$

This condition holds when the economy attains FPE. Now if any individual, i, has received information that an event cannot occur then by (2.11b) the prices of the corresponding tradable securities must be zero if FPE obtains. Since different sets of information signals will result in different tradable securities having zero prices, the REE price random variable will distinguish between the sets of signals received.

To give a precise characterization for the above example, assume initially that the signals y_{A1} and y_{B1} are received by A and B respectively. By adopting the artificial construct that A and B both know that the event $\{s_1, s_2, s_3\}$ has been revealed, then using the solution technique employed previously, the equilibrium price vector is calculated as (1, 1/3, 0, 0, 0, 0). Thus individual A on receiving the signal y_{A1} and observing the price vector (1, 1/3, 0, 0, 0, 0) revises beliefs of (0.1, 0.2, 0.15, 0.04, 0.06, 0.05, 0.1, 0.3) to conditional beliefs (2/9, 4/9, 1/3, 0, 0, 0, 0, 0). Similarly individual B on receiving y_{B1} and observing the same price vector revises prior beliefs of (0.12, 0.24, 0.18, 0.06, 0.1, 0.1, 0.05, 0.15) to the conditional set of beliefs (2/9, 4/9, 1/3, 0, 0, 0, 0, 0). Computing individual security demands, equating total demands with supplies, and solving for the equilibrium price vector gives (1, 1/3, 0, 0, 0, 0) as must be the case.

The pair of signals (y_{A1}, y_{B2}) can be considered in an identical fashion. The equilibrium price vector here will reveal the event $\{s_4, s_5\}$. By appropriate calculations the equilibrium can be characterized as follows. Individual A receives y_{A1} and observes the price vector (0, 0, 1, 13/34, 0, 0) – letting security H_3 be numeraire – and revises beliefs to (0, 0, 0, 2/5, 3/5, 0, 0, 0). Individual B receives y_{B1} and observes the same price vector and revises beliefs to (0, 0, 0, 3/8, 5/8, 0, 0, 0). Again the conjecture of which events are associated with which price vector is self-fulfilling.

Finally, for the pair of signals (y_{A2}, y_{B2}) and the price vector (0, 0, 0, 0, 1, 17/9) – letting security H_5 be numeraire – individual A forms conditional beliefs (0, 0, 0, 0, 0, 1/9, 2/9, 2/3), individual B forms conditional beliefs (0, 0, 0, 0, 0, 1/3, 1/6, 1/2) and the equilibrium price vector is again self-fulfilling. The fully revealing REE for the non-price information structure (η_A, η_B) is therefore as below.

(y_A, y_B)	$\tilde{p}$
(y_{A1}, y_{B1})	(1, 1/3, 0, 0, 0, 0)
(y_{A1}, y_{B2})	(0, 0, 1, 13/34, 0, 0)
(y_{A1}, y_{B2})	(0, 0, 0, 0, 1, 17/9)

For this example, both individuals learn more information by conditioning their beliefs on price as well as non-price information. It is also still the case that while the model linking security prices to environmental events is agreed, individuals do not agree on the probability distribution of price vectors.

Results of the type illustrated by these examples are well known in the literature. Grossman (1976, 1978, 1981) analyses the ability of equilibrium prices to aggregate all the information in the economy. For example, Grossman (1976) takes the special mean–variance case of investors with exponential utility functions dividing their initial wealth between a risk-free asset and a single risky asset with a normally distributed future cash payoff. The non-price information signal observed by trader i is simply the future payoff per unit on the risky asset perturbed by some noise unique to trader i. The model is chosen for tractability and in order to allow a closed form expression for the risky asset's equilibrium price as a function of all traders' information signals to be derived.

The basic result of Grossman is that the equilibrium price perfectly aggregates the diverse information of investors. In technical jargon, the REE price function is a sufficient statistic for the information signals received by all traders taken together. Intuitively what this means is that given the REE price random variable, the information signals received by traders reveal no further information. More technically, we would say that the conditional distribution (given the REE price random variable) of traders' information signals is independent of the future payoff of the risky asset. Therefore, given the equilibrium price, being told the value of something that is independent of the future payoff obviously gives no information about that future payoff.

When the number of possible states is finite, the REE price function will be a sufficient statistic for the combined information of traders if the partition induced by the REE price function is at least as fine as the partition induced by the combined information of traders. This idea can be explained within the context of the previous numerical example. There also, the REE price function was a sufficient statistic for the information signals of the two traders A and B. The partition induced by the equilibrium price function was seen to be

$$\Gamma(\bar{p}) = \{\{s_1, s_2, s_3\}, \{s_4, s_5\}, \{s_6, s_7, s_8\}\}$$

This can in turn be seen to be sufficient for the partition defined by the combined information structure of individuals A and B, $\Gamma(\eta_A, \eta_B)$, in the sense that $\Gamma(\bar{p})$ is at least as fine as $\Gamma(\eta_A, \eta_B)$. Of course, the underlying condition which generated this result was that the partition given by commonly tradable events $\Gamma(X, Y)$ was at least as fine as $\Gamma(\eta_A, \eta_B)$.

More general results have been obtained by Radner (1979, 1982), who is specifically concerned with the existence of an REE that is fully revealing. Radner does not restrict his analysis to discrete state spaces but does assume that the number of alternative information signals available to traders is finite. Radner proves that for his model, the existence of a fully revealing REE is *generic*. This can be explained by assuming that the parameters of the economy under consideration (for example, the prior probabilities of the individuals in the economy and the economy's information structure) are chosen randomly from the set of all possible values of these parameters.

In this case, it is only by accident that the combination of values of the parameters chosen will result in non-existence. If the selection of parameters is done randomly enough then there is a zero probability that such an accident will occur. The existence of an FRREE is then said to hold generically. Two points facilitate comparisons between Radner's results and the simpler though more restrictive result illustrated by the previous numerical example of an REE. First, Radner's analysis introduces the concept of a *forecast function*. In the terminology of this chapter this is the conjecture that traders make about how events are mapped into price vectors. Second, the crucial condition which ensures the existence of an REE that is fully revealing is that the dimension of the price space exceeds the dimension of the space of private information. Again, this requirement can be interpreted in terms of the previous example. There, the REE was fully revealing, and the condition that ensured this was that the partition $\Gamma(X, Y)$ was at least as fine as $\Gamma(\eta_A, \eta_B)$. In other words, the dimensionality of tradable events was at least as great as the dimensionality of private information. This meant that there was potentially sufficient variation in the equilibrium price vector to reveal to all traders the information possessed by all traders taken together.

5.4 PARTIALLY REVEALING RATIONAL EXPECTATIONS EQUILIBRIUM

Having given a simple example of an FRREE, this section illustrates the case where the REE fails to be fully revealing. This will clarify the condition on partitions of observable events and information structures required for full revelation. The same setting as in the previous section is assumed. Thus, there are two firms with uncertain future payoffs defined over eight states of the world. Individuals A and B have utility functions and endowments as before. For this example, A and B are assumed to agree that states are equally likely to occur – introducing heterogeneity into the example would not alter the main result. The future payoffs to firms X and Y are now as below:

	s_1	s_2	s_3	s_4	s_5	s_6	s_7	s_8
X	2	2	2	2	2	2	3	3
Y	1	1	1	1	3	3	3	3
	3	3	3	3	5	5	6	6

The tradable partition of events is again taken to be defined by distinct state-contingent payoff vectors. Thus the partition of enforceable contingencies is

$$\Gamma(X, Y) = \{\{s_1, s_2, s_3, s_4\}, \{s_5, s_6\}, \{s_7, s_8\}\}$$

Given the assumption of homogeneous beliefs, this partition also corresponds to the partition of superstates (see chapter 3) which ensures full Pareto efficiency of this exchange economy.

The tradable partition, $\Gamma(X, Y)$, defines the set of tradable supershares given below:

	s_1	s_2	s_3	s_4	s_5	s_6	s_7	s_8
Z_1	1	1	1	1	0	0	0	0
Z_2	0	0	0	0	1	1	0	0
Z_3	0	0	0	0	0	0	1	1

Original endowments in firms X and Y correspond to endowments of supershares as follows:

	A	B
Z_1	8	4
Z_2	4	6
Z_3	6	6

It remains to specify the individuals' private information functions. Here it is assumed that individual A is the informed individual, A and B being costlessly endowed with the following information functions:

$$\begin{array}{ll} \eta_A & \eta_B \\ \{s_1, s_2, s_5, s_6\} \mapsto y_{A1} & \{S\} \mapsto y_B \\ \{s_3, s_4, s_7, s_8\} \mapsto y_{A2} & \end{array}$$

The partition defined by the information functions of A and B together is

$$\Gamma(\eta_A, \eta_B) = \{\{s_1, s_2, s_5, s_6\}, \{s_3, s_4, s_7, s_8\}\}$$

Comparing this with the partition

$$\Gamma(X, Y) = \{\{s_1, s_2, s_3, s_4\}, \{s_5, s_6\}, \{s_7, s_8\}\}$$

we see immediately that these partitions cannot be ranked in terms of fineness. This means that the REE price random variable cannot be fully revealing but will only be partially revealing. For example, the set of supershares is incapable of distinguishing the event $\{s_1, s_2\}$ from the event

$\{s_3, s_4\}$, so that when individual A receives the signal y_{A1}, the equilibrium price vector will reveal that the event $\{s_1, s_2, s_3, s_4, s_5, s_6\}$ has occurred. But individual B will not be able to learn from observing price that the event $\{s_3, s_4\}$ has not occurred.

However, it is still possible to calculate the partially revealing REE. For example, for signals (y_{A1}, y_B) we assume that individual A learns that the event $\{s_1, s_2, s_5, s_6\}$ has occurred, but that individual B learns only that the event $\{s_1, s_2, s_3, s_4, s_5, s_6\}$ has occurred. Beliefs contingent on these events are then taken as fixed and the appropriate equilibrium price vector is calculated. A similar analysis applies to signals (y_{A2}, y_B). This allows the REE to be characterized as follows.

When individual A receives the non-price signal y_{A1} and observes the price vector $p = (1, 8/9, 0)$, beliefs are revised to $(1/4, 1/4, 0, 0, 1/4, 1/4, 0, 0)$. Individual B receives the null non-price signal y_B and observes $p = (1, 8/9, 0)$. B then revises beliefs to $(1/6, 1/6, 1/6, 1/6, 1/6, 1/6, 0, 0)$. Calculation of individual supershare demands establishes the self-fulfilling equilibrium price vector as $p = (1, 8/9, 0)$. Similarly, when individual A receives the signal y_{A2} and observes $p = (1, 0, 16/21)$ beliefs are revised to $(0, 0, 1/4, 1/4, 0, 0, 1/4, 1/4)$. Individual B on receiving y_B and observing $p = (1, 0, 16/21)$ revises beliefs to $(1/6, 1/6, 1/6, 1/6, 0, 0, 1/6, 1/6)$. The self-fulfilling price vector $p = (1, 0, 16/21)$ then clears markets. The partially revealing REE price random variable is therefore as below:

(y_A, y_B)	$\bar{p}$
(y_{A1}, y_B)	(1, 8/9, 0)
(y_{A2}, y_B)	(1, 0, 16/21)

Following on from Radner (1979, 1982), a number of papers (Allen, 1981; Jordan and Radner, 1982; Jordan, 1982) have examined more closely the conditions required for an REE to be fully revealing. The crucial condition again concerns the dimensionality of the space of private information relative to the dimensionality of the price space. Some insight into this highly technical and complex literature can be gained by considering this requirement in the context of the previous example. There the REE was only partially revealing. This was because the partition $\Gamma(X, Y)$ was not finer than $\Gamma(\eta_A, \eta_B)$. In other words, the dimensionality of tradable events was not greater than the dimensionality of private information. This meant that the equilibrium price vector could reveal some but not all of the information possessed by all traders taken together.

Noisy Rational Expectations Equilibrium

To end this section, we explicitly model a situation that has become popular in the literature for explaining the existence of costly information acquisition activities. This form of REE has been called a *noisy* REE. In fact, it is essentially a partially revealing REE, but the technique by which it has been generated has become so popular that a simple illustration is provided here in a discrete state space.

Take initially an identical setting to our previous examples and assume a two-firm economy with total future payoffs as follows:

	s_1	s_2	s_3	s_4	s_5	s_6
X	2	2	2	2	1	1
Y	1	1	1	2	1	2

To illustrate the existence of an FRREE with respect to this economy, take the pair of subjective beliefs below:

	s_1	s_2	s_3	s_4	s_5	s_6
ϕ_A	1/12	1/12	1/12	1/3	1/12	1/3
ϕ_B	1/8	1/8	1/8	1/4	1/8	1/4

and assume the following costless information functions:

$$\eta_A \qquad\qquad\qquad \eta_B$$
$$\{s_1, s_2, s_3, s_4\} \mapsto y_{A1} \qquad\qquad \{S\} \mapsto y_B$$
$$\{s_5, s_6\} \mapsto y_{A2}$$

Assuming that individuals A and B can contract to trade contingent on the events distinguished by total future payoffs, then since the MAWS partition

$$\Gamma(X, Y) = \{\{s_1, s_2, s_3\}, \{s_4\}, \{s_5\}, \{s_6\}\}$$

is at least as fine as

$$\Gamma(\eta_A, \eta_B) = \{\{s_1, s_2, s_3, s_4\}, \{s_5, s_6\}\}$$

the REE is fully revealing.

Now one method which has been used in the literature to ensure that the REE is not fully revealing has been to introduce noise into the economy. For the simple example above this is achieved as follows. Assume that instead of total future payoffs from firms X and Y being commonly observable, only the future payoff per ownership share is commonly observable. In addition, suppose that the supply of shares in firm X is uncertain. Specifically, assume that while individual B is endowed with the single ownership share in firm Y, individual A is endowed with either one or two shares in firm X. Of course, share ownership is still assumed infinitely divisible. Individual A is assumed to be endowed with the same information function as immediately above. In addition individual A learns of his share endownment in firm X and hence knows the supply of securities of firm X. This also ensures measurability of endowments, by which we mean that individuals are assumed to know the information partition revealed by distinct cash flows of their own endowment. Individual B remains uncertain as to A's endowment. Thus, the future unit payoffs per share from the two firms can be denoted according to whether individual A is of type I, endowed with the only share in firm X, or of type II, endowed with two shares in firm X, as below:

	A_I						A_{II}					
	s_1	s_2	s_3	s_4	s_5	s_6	s_1	s_2	s_3	s_4	s_5	s_6
X	2	2	2	2	1	1	1	1	1	1	1/2	1/2
Y	1	1	1	2	1	1	1	1	1	2	1	2
	s_1'	s_2'	s_3'	s_4'	s_5'	s_6'	s_7'	s_8'	s_9'	s_{10}'	s_{11}'	s_{12}'

As can be seen, the unit payoffs from firm X for type A_{II}, are simply one half of those for type A_I, while the payoffs from firm Y are simply repeated. This extra dimension of uncertainty over security supplies can be considered as simply extending the state space. This extended state space of twelve states of the world is denoted by the prime notation.

Beliefs over the original states s_1 to s_6 are assumed to be as before. In addition, both individuals agree that individual A is equally likely to be type A_I as type A_{II}. The partition of contingent events distinguished by the unit payoffs from X and Y that determines the set of tradable securities is now

$$\Gamma(X, Y) = \{\{s_1', s_2', s_3'\}, \{s_4'\}, \{s_5', s_7', s_8', s_9'\}, \{s_6', s_{10}'\}, \{s_{11}'\}, \{s_{12}'\}\}$$

This partition is still MAWS and so trade on the basis of this partition would achieve FPE. The information functions of A and B are

$$\eta_A$$
$$\{s_1', s_2', s_3', s_4'\} \mapsto y_{A1}$$
$$\{s_5', s_6'\} \mapsto y_{A2}$$
$$\{s_7', s_8', s_9', s_{10}'\} \mapsto y_{A3}$$
$$\{s_{11}', s_{12}'\} \mapsto y_{A4}$$

$$\eta_B$$
$$\{S\} \mapsto y_B$$

Clearly, the partition defined by the information functions of both traders together is

$$\Gamma(\eta_A, \eta_B) = \{\{s_1', s_2', s_3', s_4'\}, \{s_5', s_6'\}, \{s_7', s_8', s_9', s_{10}'\}, \{s_{11}', s_{12}'\}\}$$

It can be seen immediately that $\Gamma(X, Y)$ is not finer than $\Gamma(\eta_A, \eta_B)$. This means that the corresponding REE will not be fully revealing. For example, take the case where individual A receives signal y_{A2}. This means that individual A is endowed with the single ownership share in firm X from which the payoff is 1 for certain. However, individual B will only be able to infer from the REE price vector that the event $\{s_5, s_6, s_7, s_8, s_9, s_{10}\}$ has occurred. In other words, uninformed individual B will be unable to tell whether a particular price vector has occurred because supply is low or because a relatively unfavourable event for firm X has occurred. The random supply introduces noise into the REE and produces a partially revealing REE. It can also be noted from this example that the REE price random variable can be fully revealing for some information signals but not for others.

The idea of a noisy REE appears to be originally due to Lucas (1972) and to have been introduced to the literature on information flows between traders by Green (1973). But the model has been used in numerous subsequent studies including Grossman and Stiglitz (1976, 1980), Hellwig (1980), Diamond and Verrecchia (1981) and Verrecchia (1982). One particularly interesting strand of this literature has addressed the problem of how costly information is revealed by prices. Grossman and Stiglitz (1980) consider the problem of costly information acquisition in a model in which there are two assets, one a riskless asset and the other a risky asset. Traders can acquire a single piece of information which gives the risky asset's return perturbed by some random error. Traders are informed or uninformed depending on whether or not they spend an exogenously specified sum to acquire this item of information. Uninformed traders learn about the information only through observing the price of the risky asset. However, the price does not perfectly reveal the information that informed traders have acquired because of noise in the form of a random supply of the risky asset. On average when informed traders receive favourable news about the return on the risky asset, its price will be bid up. But its price could also be high because of a supply shortage. Observing this price therefore reveals the informed traders' information to the uninformed but it does this imperfectly.

An overall equilibrium is an REE in which the expected utility from becoming an informed trader is the same as from remaining an uninformed trader. This equality of expected utility will occur as the number of informed traders increases, for two reasons. First, as the number of informed traders increases, their effect on the price of the risky asset via aggregate demand increases. This allows uninformed traders to get a more accurate estimate of informed traders' information. The scope for exploiting differences in information is therefore reduced. The second reason is that as more traders become informed, and so less uninformed, there are less gains to be made by each informed trader by trading with the smaller uninformed groups.

Verrecchia (1982) can be considered as extending the model of Grossman and Stiglitz to the case where traders must decide not only on whether or not to become informed but also on the amount or quality of information they wish to acquire. In the Grossman and Stiglitz paper there are two initially unknown factors that affect the determination of the price of the risky asset. By becoming informed, a trader learns the value of one of these factors and each informed trader receives the same piece of information. In the Verrecchia model informed traders learn the return on the risky asset perturbed by a random error (as in the Grossman and Stiglitz model), but with the random error being unique to each trader and independent of the noise in other traders' information signals. Moreover, traders can reduce the random error in their information signal by expending more resources.[5] Verrecchia establishes the existence of an REE in which price partially aggregates the information signals of all traders taken together and in which traders' conjectures about how information is revealed through price are fulfilled by their own information acquisition activities.

Both Grossman and Stiglitz and Verrecchia provide comparative static analyses of an REE with costly information. In both papers, the price system is found to be more informative as the cost of acquiring information decreases and as the risk tolerance of traders increases. Grossman and Stiglitz find that in their model, reducing the noise in the aggregate supply of the risky security results in an offsetting smaller proportion of traders becoming informed with the result that the informativeness of the price system is unchanged. By contrast, Verrecchia finds in his model that the reduction in noise more than offsets the corresponding reduction in the amount of information traders acquire with the result that the price system becomes more informative.

5.5 RATIONAL EXPECTATIONS EQUILIBRIUM AND FULL PARETO EFFICIENCY

Amershi (1981) has proved that if an economy achieves FPE given any set of signals from the private information functions of the individuals in the economy, then the economy must reach an FRREE with respect to those information functions. To see the intuition behind this, consider initially a market setting in which the REE is only partially revealing. As a concrete case, return to the first example of the previous section illustrating a partially revealing REE. The set of enforceable contingencies there was

$$\Gamma(X, Y) = \{\{s_1, s_2, s_3, s_4\}, \{s_5, s_6\}, \{s_7, s_8\}\}$$

while the collective information structure was defined by individual A's information partition

$$\Gamma(\eta_A) = \{\{s_1, s_2, s_5, s_6\}, \{s_3, s_4, s_7, s_8\}\}$$

since individual B received a null private information signal. In the absence of any private information, the MAWS partition corresponded to the partition of distinct total market payoffs:

$$\Gamma(X + Y) = \{\{s_1, s_2, s_3, s_4\}, \{s_5, s_6\}, \{s_7, s_8\}\}$$

since individuals A and B were assumed to have homogeneous beliefs *a priori*.

Now assume individual A receives the signal y_{A1} revealing that the event $\{s_1, s_2, s_5, s_6\}$ has occurred. What is crucial here is the revised beliefs of individuals A and B. Individual A's beliefs, conditional on the signal y_{A1} will be given by (1/4, 1/4, 0, 0, 1/4, 1/4, 0, 0), but individual B's beliefs conditional on a null private information signal and on the information revealed by prices will be given by (1/6, 1/6, 1/6, 1/6, 1/6, 1/6 0, 0), since B is unable to tell from observing prices that the event $\{s_3, s_4\}$ has not occurred. Given the signal y_{A1}, the set of enforceable contingencies is necessarily still sufficient to accommodate variations in total market payoffs. But, the condition for FPE given the signal y_{A1} that the set of tradable contingencies be sufficient to accommodate side-bets on the state of the world – defined by the requirement of event-contingent homogeneity of beliefs – now defines the partition[6]

$$\{\{s_1, s_2, s_5, s_6\}, \{s_3, s_4\}, \{s_7, s_8\}\}$$

Combined with the condition on total market payoffs, the MAWS partition is now

$$\{\{s_1, s_2\}, \{s_3, s_4\}, \{s_5, s_6\}, \{s_7, s_8\}\}$$

and so FPE cannot obtain.

For FPE to be achieved given the set of private information signals $\{y_{A1}, y_B\}$, the set of tradable contingencies must accommodate the separate events $\{s_1, s_2\}$ and $\{s_3, s_4\}$. Similarly, in the general case, for FPE to obtain given a set of private information signals, the partition of tradable events must be at least as fine as the partition defined by the information signals of all individuals taken together. This must be the case if the condition for FPE of event-contingent belief homogeneity (calculated now on the basis of the revised beliefs given the private information signals and the information revealed by prices) is to be met. This necessarily means that the equilibrium will be fully revealing.

5.6   CONCLUDING REMARKS

This chapter has attempted to illustrate a relatively recently developed idea in economic theory. This is that in a world of uncertainty and differential information, individuals use the price system itself as a source of information. Prices in such a world not only clear markets, as in their traditional Walrasian role, but they also serve to transmit information. This learning-from-prices phenomenon requires a new equilibrium concept. If individuals infer information from prices and revise their beliefs and demands for securities accordingly, then those very same prices must be market clearing for the system to be in equilibrium. More precisely, a rational expectations equilibrium requires that the conjectures made by individuals about how events are mapped into security prices be self-fulfilling.

The chapter has also analysed the extent to which prices reveal information in an REE. In a fully revealing REE the price system reveals the collective information of all individuals taken together. In a partially revealing REE the price system reveals some but not all of this information. In a particular economic setting the chapter has illustrated the conditions required for either of these results to hold. Finally the chapter has briefly examined the relationship between an FRREE and FPE.

An issue which has not been examined explicitly is that of whether an REE will be fully or partially revealing in a stock market economy (although the illustration of a noisy REE is one step in this direction). Also the discussion of the relationship between an FRREE and FPE is incomplete. For example, the chapter has not considered whether an economy can achieve an FRREE while not achieving FPE.

Some of the results of this chapter will be used in the following chapter to explain the concept of informationally efficient capital markets.

6

Informational Efficiency

In section 2.2 we drew attention to the two senses in which the word efficiency is used in the finance literature. On the one hand concepts of allocative or Pareto efficiency are used in assessing the welfare properties of equilibrium market resource allocations. On the other hand concepts of informational efficiency are used in discussions concerned with the relationship between market prices and information.

This chapter is concerned with the concept of *informational efficiency* (IE). Roughly speaking, in this text we equate the degree of IE of an economy with the extent to which prices reflect information. Earlier literature has used alternative terms to refer to the same idea. Fama (1970, 1976b) uses the terms 'efficient capital markets' and 'market efficiency' where we use the term IE. Beaver (1981a, 1981b) also refers to 'market efficiency'. More recently Jensen and Smith (1985a) refer to 'efficient market theory' in connection with the idea that prices reflect information. Finally Merton (1985) has introduced the 'rational market hypothesis' to refer to the relationship between market prices and information.

It is important to distinguish between the concepts of allocative efficiency and IE. At the current stage of theoretical research into these concepts, the precise relationship between the two is not clear. Adding the qualifier 'informational' to efficiency therefore identifies more precisely the set of issues with which the concept is concerned.

Most of the published literature on IE is concerned with empirical tests of the hypothesis of IE. As has been noted on a number of occasions, these empirical papers have often preceded the formal development of any adequate theoretical statement of the concept of IE. This chapter will make no attempt to survey the vast and rapidly expanding empirical literature. Rather its main purpose is to explore the precise meaning of IE by reference to published definitions of the concept.

The chapter begins in section 6.1 by making a preliminary attempt at explaining IE by introducing the concept of 'ideal' markets. This provides a kind of benchmark against which the behaviour of prices in actual economies can be compared. Section 6.2 reviews the pioneering attempts by Fama to provide an operational definition of IE. These attempts were directed mainly at providing a theoretical foundation for empirical work on IE. A fundamental problem in testing for IE is discussed with reference to the recent work on the volatility of the stock market in section 6.3. Section 6.4 presents Beaver's 'state of the art' definition of IE. This provides a useful vehicle for introducing the traditionally accepted taxonomy of IE. Beaver's definition is related to the concept of an FRREE discussed in the previous chapter and we consider the question of whether market prices will reveal the information of different individuals in the economy at a point in time. Section 6.5 goes on to consider whether the market is efficient with respect to new information that is disclosed through time. To examine this issue we allow for trade both prior to and subsequent to the information release. As we will see, the issue of efficiency turns on the types of trading contract that individuals can enter into. Section 6.6 attempts an overall appraisal of IE, and section 6.7 offers some concluding remarks.

6.1 IDEAL MARKETS

In general terms there seems to be fairly widespread agreement in the literature as to the meaning of the term IE. Dyckman and Morse (1986) provide a typical definition:

> A securities market is generally defined as [informationally] efficient if (1) the prices of the securities traded in the market act as though they fully reflect all available information and (2) these prices react instantaneously, and in an unbiased fashion to new information.

Similar definitions can be found in Fama (1970), Keane (1983), Begg (1982), Minford and Peel (1983) and Sheffrin (1983).

Difficulties arise with such definitions with regard to the precise meaning of the terms 'fully reflect', 'available information' and 'unbiased'. One possible first approach towards these difficulties is to relate the actual behaviour of prices to the way that prices would behave under ideal conditions.

Consider the following set of conditions used to describe ideal markets:

1 Perfect competition: all economic agents behave as though they have no market power over prices.

2 Frictionless markets: there are no transactions costs or restrictions on trade, either institutional or informational, and all assets are perfectly divisible.
3 Homogeneous beliefs and information: all individuals have homogeneous prior beliefs and receive the same information function.
4 Individual rationality: all individuals are rational expected utility maximizers.

We can use the behaviour of prices in ideal markets as the basis for a definition of the IE of less than ideal markets. We can say that a market is informationally efficient if market prices are identical to those prices that would rule in ideal markets in which the information under consideration is received by all individuals.

An important advantage of this definition is that the analysis of the behaviour of prices in ideal markets is relatively straightforward. In particular by combining the assumption of ideal markets with elementary models of expected returns formation it is often possible to generate testable implications relating to the stochastic behaviour of share prices in relation to new information.

An early contribution in this spirit is Samuelson (1965, 1973). Samuelson (1973) combines an assumption equivalent to one of ideal markets with the assumption that the price of a security at any point in time is equal to the market's expectation of all future dividends discounted at a constant rate[1] to give

$$P_{jt} = \sum_{T=1}^{\infty} E_t [\tilde{x}_{jt+T}/(1+r_j)^T]$$

where r_j is the discount rate appropriate to security j; P_{jt} is the equilibrium price of security j at time $t+T$; $\tilde{x}_{jt+T}$ is the uncertain dividend paid on security j at time $t+T$; and E_t is the expectation conditional on information available at time t.

Given these assumptions Samuelson is able to derive the *martingale property* of stock prices which states that at any point in time the equilibrium price of security j is set such that the expected one-period return on the stock is equal to the discount rate r_j. That is, the expected return on security j conditional on the information available at time t is equal to the unconditional expected return r_j. An alternative way of explaining this result is that if stock prices have the martingale property, the current price is a sufficient statistic for the next period expected price in the sense that the latter is equal to the former compounded at a rate that is independent of the realization of the information available.

Prior to Samuelson's theoretical contribution, several statisticians had already noted that stock prices tend to fluctuate randomly in the sense that stock returns exhibit a very low degree of serial correlation (see, for example, Working, 1934; Kendall, 1953; Osborne, 1959, 1962). The importance of Samuelson's contribution was the demonstration that such apparently erratic price behaviour is to be expected in ideal markets. If prices reflect all currently available information and change to their new equilibrium values immediately and only on the receipt of new information then price changes will be uncorrelated.

6.2 FAMA'S DEFINITIONS OF INFORMATIONAL EFFICIENCY

Fama (1970, 1976a) has made two important attempts to provide a statement of the concept of IE in a form suitable for empirical testing. Because of the emphasis on empirical testing Fama implicitly assumes all individuals have the same information functions and, at least conditional on the information under consideration, they share the same beliefs. This allows Fama to use the terms 'the *market*', 'the information available to the *market*', and 'the expectation of the *market*' or 'the *market*'s assessed probability distribution', without any ambiguity.

The Fair Game Model

Fama's 1970 formulation of IE is based on two key assumptions. These are first that the conditions of market equilibrium can be expressed in terms of expected returns and second that all currently available information is used by the market in forming equilibrium expected returns and thus current equilibrium prices.

Fama represents the idea that the conditions of market equilibrium can be expressed in terms of expected returns as follows:

$$E(\tilde{p}_{jt+1}/\Phi_t) = [1 + E(\tilde{r}_{jt+1}/\Phi_t)] p_{jt} \qquad (6.1)$$

where Φ_t is the information available at time t; E is the expected value operator; $\tilde{p}_{jt+1}$ is the uncertain price of security j at time point $t+1$; and $\tilde{r}_{jt+1} = (\tilde{p}_{jt+1} - p_{jt})/p_{jt}$ is the one-period return on security j.

According to Fama the assumptions that the conditions of market equilibrium can be expressed in terms of expected returns and that currently available information is used in setting current prices have one major empirical implication. They rule out the possibility of trading systems based on currently available information to generate abnormal returns, where abnormal returns are defined as

$$z_{jt+1} = r_{jt+1} - E(\bar{r}_{jt+1}/\Phi_t) \tag{6.2}$$

The inability to generate abnormal returns on the basis of available information is known as the fair game property and it can be stated as follows:

$$E(\bar{z}_{jt+1}/\Phi_t) = 0 \tag{6.3}$$

In words, (6.3) says that the sequence of abnormal returns, z_{jt+1}, follows a fair game with respect to currently available information, Φ_t.

Commenting on Fama's 1970 article, Leroy (1976) argued that Fama's formulation was tautological and, therefore, empirically vacuous. Leroy pointed out that given the definition of $\bar{r}_{jt+1}$, any set of values satisfying (6.1) and (6.2) must necessarily satisfy (6.3). Hence the fair game property as stated by Fama appears to be tautological.

Fama's Response

Fama disputed Leroy's accusation of tautology but acknowledged that his 1970 formulation possessed a degree of ambiguity. In an attempt to rectify any perceived ambiguity, Fama (1976a) advances an alternative formulation of IE which subsequently has become widely accepted.

The new formulation assumes that all events of interest take place at discrete points in time: t, $t+1$, and so on. Fama defines the following terms:

Φ_t is the information available at time t;

Φ_t^m is the information actually used by the market at time t;

$f(P_{t+1}/\Phi_t)$ is the true joint probability density function of the vector of security prices, P_{t+1}, at time $t+1$ implied by Φ_t;

$f_m(P_{t+1}/\Phi_t^m)$ is the joint probability density function of the vector of security prices at time $t+1$ as assessed by the market at time t.

Fama defines the market as informationally efficient if the following two conditions are satisfied:

$$f_m(P_{t+1}/\Phi_t^m) = f(P_{t+1}/\Phi_t) \qquad \text{and} \qquad \Phi_t^m = \Phi_t$$

In words, these two conditions state that the market is informationally efficient if it behaves as if the actual probability distribution used in setting current prices at time t is the true conditional distribution implied by all the information available to the market at time t. Fama suggests that for the purposes of empirical testing, the actual link between the vector of current security prices and the market assessed density function $f_m(.)$ will be given by the chosen model of market equilibrium.

6.3 TESTING FOR INFORMATIONAL EFFICIENCY

By combining Fama's concept of IE with a theory of equilibrium price determination it is possible to generate testable implications for the stochastic behaviour of share prices. For example, by combining the assumption of IE with the assumption that expected returns are constant one can derive the implication that actual returns are intertemporally uncorrelated.[2]

From the viewpoint of the empiricist the ability to generate testable implications from relatively simple models must be regarded as a major advantage of the methodology suggested by Fama. Indeed for almost twenty years from 1959 to 1978 numerous tests of IE were carried out along these lines with the overwhelming majority resulting in the conclusion that the stock market is informationally efficient at least with respect to information that is publicly available.

Difficulties arise with the interpretation of such tests, however, when they report evidence of price behaviour that is inconsistent with the joint assumptions of IE and the particular equilibrium model of price determination underlying the test. The problem is that any test of IE is inevitably a joint test of IE and the assumed equilibrium model of price determination. Hence whenever negative evidence against the joint hypothesis is found, it is difficult, if not impossible, to determine whether the evidence is indeed evidence against IE or alternatively evidence against the particular model of price determination used to generate the null hypothesis. This jointness problem is particularly well illustrated by the controversy surrounding the recent volatility tests of IE.

Volatility Tests of Market Efficiency

To the observer of financial markets in general, and of stock markets in particular, one of their most fascinating features is the frequency and rapidity with which large changes in prices occur. At times, the fluctuations are so large that they call into question the collective rationality of the market.

Starting with Shiller (1981a, 1981b) and Leroy and Porter (1981) a number of studies have attempted to assess whether observed levels of share price volatility are a sign of collective irrationality on the part of stock markets or whether they are consistent with the kind of fluctuations one would expect to arise naturally from the response of rational investors to new information. From a policy viewpoint this work is very important because strong evidence in favour of the view that the stock market is too volatile might easily lead to a demand for increased government intervention in the allocation of real investment.

The simplest and best known of the many volatility tests is the one presented by Shiller (1981a). In devising the test, Shiller first assumes that investors exhibit rational expectations with respect to future dividends. This means that investors are assumed to use all available information in forming their expectations. Second he assumes that at any point in time the aggregate value of all outstanding shares is equal to the present value of expected future real dividends discounted at a constant real rate of return. We can express this assumption as

$$P_t = \sum_{k=1}^{\infty} E_t(D_{t+k})/(1+r)^k \qquad (6.4)$$

where P_t is the real aggregate value of all outstanding shares at time t; D_{t+k} is the aggregate real dividend at time $t+k$; E_t is the expectation conditional on information available at time t; and r is the required rate of return.

Shiller's theoretical hypothesis is derived from these first two assumptions by defining a term P_t^* as follows:

$$P_t^* = \sum_{k=1}^{\infty} D_{t+k}/(1+r)^k \qquad (6.5)$$

Here D_{t+k} is the actual dividend paid at time $t+k$. Shiller refers to P_t^* as the 'ex post rational' or 'perfect foresight' price. It represents the present value at time t of the actual future dividend stream. As the expectations operator is linear it can be taken to the left of the summation sign in (6.4), which when combined with (6.5) gives

$$P_t = E_t(P_t^*)$$

This states that the market price of shares at time t according to the chosen equilibrium model is equal to the expected ex post rational price, where this expectation is conditioned on the information available at time t. Denoting by e_t the market's error in forecasting P_t^* gives

$$P_t^* = P_t + e_t$$

As e_t is a rational forecast error, according to the assumptions of the model it must be uncorrelated with any information used in conditioning expectations at time t; in particular, it must be uncorrelated with P_t. Hence, since the variance of e_t can never be negative, the following variance bound must hold given Shiller's first two assumptions:

$$\text{var}(P_t^*) \geq \text{var}(P_t) \tag{6.6}$$

The variance of the actual price should be lower (that is, it should be less volatile) than the variance of the ex post rational price. Shiller proceeds to test (6.6) by invoking a third assumption. This states that aggregate real dividends follow a finite-variance stationary stochastic process with a deterministic exponential trend rate of growth. Without this or some similar assumption, the variance relation in (6.6) cannot be tested since only one observation on P_t^* and P_t can be made. But given Shiller's third assumption, the sample variances of the detrended time series for P_t^* and P_t can be used to test the variance bound.

Shiller (1981a) provides two tests of (6.6). Both tests use annual data. The first test is based on the Standard and Poor's Composite Stock Price Index for the years 1871 to 1979. Shiller estimates the standard deviation of P_t^* as 8.968 and the standard deviation of P_t as 50.12, giving a gross violation of (6.6). The second test is based on a modified Dow Jones Industrial Average Index for the period 1928 to 1979. Shiller estimates the standard deviation of P_t^* as 26.8 and the standard deviation of P_t as 355.9, again giving a gross violation of (6.6).

This finding and the related findings reported by Leroy and Porter (1981) have been interpreted by some academics as strong evidence against IE. For example, Ackley (1983) expresses the view that 'Robert Shiller's recent paper appears to demolish the possibility that movements of US stock prices can be explained by the rational expectations of shareholders'. However, before this conclusion can be drawn, one should consider the possibility that there may be other explanations for Shiller's findings. In fact, following the publication of the early volatility tests several papers have either criticised or devised alternative explanations of the volatility tests which taken together call into question the informational inefficiency interpretation.

First, both Flavin (1983) and Kleidon (1986) have shown that Shiller's estimates of $\text{var}(P_t^*)$ and var (P_t) suffer from a degree of small sample bias. However, both of these authors admit that the small sample bias is not sufficient to explain the gross violations of the variance bound detected by Shiller (1981a).

Second, one can question the assumption of a constant real discount rate. In particular Leroy and LaCivita (1981) have shown that the volatility of share prices relative to the volatility of dividends can increase without bound as the degree of risk aversion of individuals in the economy increases. This explanation of excessive volatility has been tested by Grossman and Shiller (1981). Grossman and Shiller show that pathologically high levels of risk aversion are needed to explain the gross violations of the variance bound detected by Shiller (1981a). Here we see an indication of the joint hypothesis problem. If we adopt equation (6.4) as our equilibrium model of share price determination we report gross violations of the variance bound. If we adopt a model along the lines of Leroy and LaCivita the gross violations are eliminated, though in this case for reasonable levels of risk aversion smaller violations of the variance bound are still reported.

Third, one might attempt to explain excess volatility as the result of the market reacting to changes in the perceived likelihood of some major event of low probability (such as a nuclear war) which never actually occurred within the sample period. However, as noted by Shiller (1981a), 'such an explanation is "academic" in that it relies fundamentally on unobservables and cannot be evaluated statistically'.

Finally, and crucially, several authors have focused on the implications of relaxing the third assumption of Shiller's model, that detrended dividends follow a stationary stochastic process. Shiller (1984) has acknowledged this line of criticism as the most important in calling into question the early claims of excessive volatility. Papers by Flavin (1983), Kleidon (1985), and Marsh and Merton (1986) show that the early findings of excessive volatility can be explained away by replacing this stationarity assumption with an assumption that allows detrended dividends to follow a non-stationary stochastic process. Moreover, and particularly damaging for the early tests, Marsh and Merton (1986) have shown that the variance bound (6.6) actually reverses itself if dividends follow the kind of stochastic process proposed in their paper. However, a recent paper by Mankiw et al. (1985) has reported results for a new form of volatility test which is not dependent on the stationarity assumption. These new tests still report evidence of excessive volatility although the evidence is not as strong as that reported by Shiller (1981a).

The development of the volatility tests and the discussions that they have provoked illustrate well the difficulties of testing for IE. However, it remains true that the evidence on volatility taken as a whole is to date the most damaging to proponents of the IE of stock markets.

6.4 BEAVER'S CONTRIBUTION

A major conceptual problem with Fama's revised definition of IE is that it makes use of the ill-defined term, 'the market'. According to Fama it is the market that assesses the joint probability density function of future prices, and the market that sets current prices. A related problem with Fama's second definition is that it refers to the 'true' density function of security prices implied by the 'information available'.

From a theoretical point of view, all of this is unsatisfactory. In a world in which individuals have heterogeneous beliefs and differential information, the relationship between the beliefs of individuals and the beliefs of the market are not well defined; nor are the concepts of the 'true' density function of security prices or the 'information available'. Partly in an attempt to overcome these difficulties Beaver (1981a,b) has advanced an alternative definition of IE which has been described by one author as 'the state of the art' (Latham, 1986).

Beaver's definition is both illuminating and instructive:

a distinction will be made between information system efficiency (called η-efficiency) and signal efficiency (called y-efficiency) as follows:

y-efficiency

A securities market is efficient with respect to a signal y_t if and only if the configuration of security prices $\{P_{jt}\}$ is the same as it would be in an otherwise identical economy (i.e. with an identical configuration of preferences and endowments) except that every individual receives y_t as well as y_{it} [individual i's private signal].

η-efficiency

A securities market is efficient with respect to η_t if and only if y-efficiency holds for every signal (y_t) from η_t.

One useful feature of this definition is that it allows us to consider IE with respect to alternative information functions. The generally accepted taxonomy of IE is contained in Fama (1970). Fama distinguishes between three information structures that might be reflected in market prices. Since each successive structure simply adds more information to the previous structure, each can be considered as inducing a successively finer partition over the set of states of the world.

First, the capital market is said to be *weak form efficient* if equilibrium security prices reflect the information available in previous share prices. An immediate consequence of weak form efficiency is that investors will be unable to earn abnormal returns from exploiting any patterns in share prices whether from charting price movements or from an investment strategy employing some mechanical formula based on past prices. Second, the capital market is said to be *semi-strong form efficient* if equilibrium security prices reflect all information that is publicly available where this obviously includes the past history of share prices. Semi-strong form efficiency precludes earning abnormal returns from so-called fundamental analysis (that is, from the study of published accounting reports and other publicly available information such as take-over bid announcements, dividend announcements, money supply announcements, and so on). Finally, the market is said to be *strong form efficient* when equilibrium share prices reflect not only publicly available information but also information to which an investor might have monopolistic access. This threefold distinction provides a convenient device for classifying empirical tests of IE. However, from a theoretical point of view, these distinctions provide only a crude partitioning of the information sets of potential interest. By defining IE with respect to a specific information function, Beaver's definition allows the researcher to be more precise as to the specific information function of interest.

Perhaps the most important advantage of Beaver's definition from a theoretical point of view is that it employs the Marschak–Radner information economics framework of information systems and signals that has been employed throughout this text. This feature is particularly important because it allows Beaver's definition to be represented in terms of the concepts introduced in the previous chapter. In particular, Amershi (1981) has argued that Beaver's concept of IE is equivalent to the concept of an FRREE. According to Amershi, Beaver's definition of signal efficiency is concerned with the ability of traders to make inferences from the price vector observed at a single market date. The fact that the price vector would not change even if the particular information signal was received by all traders is equivalent to the property of an FRREE that prices fully reveal the information signal. The conjecture by traders of how information signals are mapped into distinct price vectors – in Radner's terminology, the forecast function – is self-fulfilling, and traders learn the information signal simply by observing prices. Since prices already fully reveal the information signal, no change in beliefs would occur if the signal were to be received directly by all traders.

We can best illustrate this idea by returning to the example in section 5.3. There we considered an economy with eight states of the world in which the private information functions received by our two individuals, A and B were as follows:

$$\eta_A \qquad\qquad\qquad \eta_B$$

$$\{s_1, s_2, s_3, s_4, s_5\} \mapsto y_{A1} \qquad\qquad \{s_1, s_2, s_3\} \mapsto y_{B1}$$

$$\{s_6, s_7, s_8\} \mapsto y_{A2} \qquad\qquad \{s_4, s_5, s_6, s_7, s_8\} \mapsto y_{B2}$$

The collective non-price information of A and B therefore defined the partition

$$\Gamma(\eta_A, \ \eta_B) = \{\{s_1, \ s_2, \ s_3\}, \ \{s_4, \ s_5\}, \ \{s_6, \ s_7, \ s_8\}\}$$

We then found that the REE price vector for this information structure was as below:

$(y_A, \ y_B)$	$\tilde{p}$
$(y_{A1}, \ y_{B1})$	(1, 1/3, 0, 0, 0, 0)
$(y_{A1}, \ y_{B2})$	(0, 0, 1, 13/34, 0, 0)
$(y_{A1}, \ y_{B2})$	(0, 0, 0, 0, 1, 17/9)

The question we can now ask is, with respect to which information signals and/or functions is this securities market efficient?

First, we can note that the information functions of individuals A and B cannot be ranked in terms of fineness. However, we can say that this securities market is efficient with respect to the information signals of both individuals A and B and therefore also with respect to their information functions.

As an illustration, let us consider first the signal y_{B1}. When individual B receives y_{B1}, individual A receives y_{A1} and so learns directly only that the event $\{s_1, s_2, s_3, s_4, s_5\}$ has occurred. But, conditioning beliefs on the equilibrium price vector (1, 1/3, 0, 0, 0, 0) as well as the signal y_{A1}, A learns that the event $\{s_1, s_2, s_3\}$ has occurred. The price vector fully reveals the signal y_{B1} and if y_{B1} was made available directly to individual A – 'in addition' to y_{A1} – the equilibrium price vector would not change.

A more interesting example occurs when individual A receives y_{A1} and individual B receives y_{B2}. The same argument as given above shows that the market is efficient with respect to these two signals. If either signal was made available to the other trader, the equilibrium price vector would be unchanged. But in this case, the information revealed by prices is finer than either of the signals y_{A1} and y_{B2}. In this case the market is efficient with respect to the signal that the event $\{s_4, s_5\}$ has occurred. Even if this signal was received by each trader in addition to their private signals, no change in prices would result.

The finest set of signals with respect to which the market is efficient in this example is

$$\{s_1, \ s_2, \ s_3\} \mapsto y_1$$
$$\{s_4, \ s_5\} \mapsto y_2$$
$$\{s_6, \ s_7, \ s_8\} \mapsto y_3$$

Clearly, the market must be efficient to any coarser set of signals and similarly to any information function coarser than $\{y_1, y_2, y_3\}$.

We can develop this idea further by returning to the first example of a partially revealing REE in section 5.4. The private information functions received by the two individuals there were

$$
\begin{array}{cc}
\eta_A & \eta_B \\
\{s_1, s_2, s_5, s_6\} \mapsto y_{A1} & \{S\} \mapsto y_B \\
\{s_3, s_4, s_7, s_8\} \mapsto y_{A2} &
\end{array}
$$

When A receives signal y_{A1} and B receives y_B the REE price vector (1, 8/9, 0) reveals only that the event $\{s_1, s_2, s_3, s_4, s_5, s_6\}$ has occurred. The price vector does not fully reveal that the event $\{s_1, s_2, s_5, s_6\}$ has occurred and the market is inefficient with respect to signal y_{A1}. If y_{A1} was revealed to individual B as well as to A, individual B would revise beliefs to (1/4, 1/4, 0, 0, 1/4, 1/4, 0, 0). It can be calculated that the REE price vector would become (1, 6/5, 0). Similarly, when A receives signal y_{A2} and B receives y_{B1}, the REE price vector (1, 0, 16/21) reveals only that the event $\{s_1, s_2, s_3, s_4, s_7, s_8\}$ has occurred. If individual B also received y_{A2} the REE price vector would change to (1, 0, 1).

In both of these cases, to use Beaver's terminology, the configuration of security prices changes when individual A's information signals are publicly revealed. Therefore, the market cannot be efficient with respect to A's information signals. However, we can say that if any of the traders were to receive the private information partition $\{\{s_1, s_2, s_3, s_4\}, \{s_5, s_6\}, \{s_7, s_8\}\}$, or a coarser partition, then the market would be efficient with respect to any of these signals and with respect to the corresponding information function.

6.5 DYNAMIC INFORMATIONAL EFFICIENCY AND NEW INFORMATION

The previous section implicitly considered IE at a single market date. We asked whether traders could infer an information signal from an REE price vector. If they could, then making all traders receive the signal would not result in any change in the equilibrium price vector. An equally interesting question of IE and one that it is probably useful to consider separately, concerns efficiency with respect to information to be released in the future.

This issue has been addressed in two papers in the academic literature. Milgrom and Stokey (1982) contrast the 'static rational expectations model' of the previous section with a 'dynamic rational expectations model'. In the dynamic model there are markets both before and after traders receive information. In an earlier paper, Rubinstein (1975) defines the necessary and sufficient conditions for 'new information' to be reflected in prices albeit for a rather specialized economy. However, both papers derive essentially identical conditions for IE.

Rubinstein's Model

To begin with Rubinstein's development, we shall again adopt a numerical example to illustrate the results of his paper. The example is slightly more complex than previous examples because of its explicit two-date nature, but the increased complexity is purely in terms of the expansion of the problem; the solution technique remains exactly as in previous examples.

To convey the essentials of Rubinstein's model we will consider a two-date economy where uncertainty unfolds as shown by figure 6.1. In this figure uncertainty in one period's time is represented by the two possible events (or states) e_1 and e_2 that can occur at $t = 1$. Similarly, uncertainty in two periods' time is represented by the two possible events, s_1 and s_2, that can occur at $t = 2$. Denoting the set of states at $t = 1$ and $t = 2$ by $E = \{e_1, e_2\}$ and $S = \{s_1, s_2\}$ respectively, the model really comprises an economy with four states of the world given by the Cartesian product

$$E \times S = \{(e_1, s_1), (e_1, s_2), (e_2, s_1), (e_2, s_2)\}$$

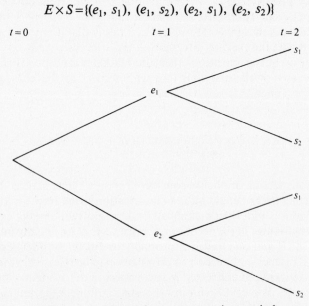

Figure 6.1 Uncertainty over two time periods

Rubinstein assumes that, in this economy, traders meet at $t=0$ to trade in claims contingent on the events that can occur at $t=1$, and separately in claims contingent on the events that can occur at $t=2$. These are provisional portfolio choices which we shall denote as E_i and S_i for $i=1, 2$. When one period has elapsed, it is publicly revealed which of e_1 and e_2 has occurred, the spot market in $t=1$ claims reopens, and traders make final $t=1$ choices and final $t=2$ state-contingent portfolio choices. We shall denote these final choices as $\bar{E}_i$ and $\bar{S}_i$ for $i=1, 2$. The question Rubinstein poses is, under what condition will trader's final choices coincide with their provisional choices? Where no portfolio revision takes place, Rubinstein interprets this as the absence of any desire to speculate on the information revealed by the state that has occurred at $t=1$. The absence of speculation, or trade, can only occur if the revision of beliefs caused by the information revealed at $t=1$ is precisely offset by the change in relative prices of $t=2$ state-contingent claims. In effect, for this to happen, all traders must agree on the interpretation of the information revealed at $t=1$. In this case, prices change, no trade occurs, and the market is efficient with respect to the new information revealed at $t=1$.

It is important to note at this stage that Rubinstein has implicitly imposed an extra degree of market incompleteness in this economy, and one that is not otherwise justified by the information available to traders. In particular, at $t=0$ traders are assumed to be unable to exchange claims contingent on the states (e_1, s_1), (e_1, s_2), (e_2, s_1) and (e_2, s_2) that can occur at $t=2$. Instead, their provisional choices of $t=2$ claims must be constant within each of the two pairs of states $\{(e_1, s_1), (e_2, s_1)\}$ and $\{(e_1, s_2), (e_2, s_2)\}$. Because of this imposed restriction, for no trade or speculation to occur at $t=2$, a special condition on beliefs must be satisfied. We shall illustrate this by considering two alternative sets of beliefs in turn.

We will again assume a competitive two-person economy. Initial resource endowments are distributed such that if at $t=1$, e_1 occurs, trader A receives 2 units of a consumption commodity while trader B receives nothing. If e_2 occurs, the traders' endowments are reversed. Similarly, if at $t=2$, s_1 occurs, trader A again receives 2 units of the commodity, trader B receives nothing, and vice versa if s_2 occurs. Setting out these details in their most complete form gives the table of endowments below:

		(e_1, s_1)	(e_1, s_2)	(e_2, s_1)	(e_2, s_2)
$t=1$	A	2	2	0	0
	B	0	0	2	2
$t=2$	A	2	0	2	0
	B	0	2	0	2

The information revealed by these endowments is assumed to be available to both traders. Therefore, in the absence of further restrictions we see that at $t=2$ the history of endowments will reveal perfectly which of the four states has occurred. However, we will follow Rubinstein's artificial restriction of trade at $t=2$, to s_1- and s_2-contingent claims.

The first set of beliefs, which illustrates Rubinstein's non-speculation condition is as below:

	(e_1, s_1)	(e_1, s_2)	(e_2, s_1)	(e_2, s_2)
ϕ_A	1/8	7/24	3/8	5/24
ϕ_B	1/16	7/16	3/16	5/16

Assuming logarithmic utility functions and, for simplicity taking a zero discount factor for $t=1$ and $t=2$ consumption, we can set out trader A's individual portfolio problem at $t=0$ as

$$\text{maximize } \frac{5}{12} \ln E_1 + \frac{7}{12} \ln E_2 + \frac{1}{2} \ln S_1 + \frac{1}{2} \ln S_2$$

$$\text{subject to } E_1 + p_2 E_2 + q_1 S_1 + q_2 S_2 = 2 + 2q_1$$

where $(5/12, 7/12, 1/2, 1/2)$ are A's subjective probabilities of (e_1, e_2, s_1, s_2) as can be calculated from the set of beliefs assumed above, and p_2, q_1 and q_2 are the prices of e_2-, s_1- and s_2-contingent claims respectively, e_1-contingent claims being taken as numeraire.

Trader B's problem can be similarly formulated and the solution procedure proceeds exactly as in the examples of previous chapters (the only difference here being that the state probabilities as posed in this two-period problem will sum to 2).

The reader should check that the relative prices $(p_2, q_1, q_2) = (47/41, 31/41, 57/41)$ clear markets and that the provisional portfolio choices are as below:

	E_1	E_2	S_1	S_2
A	30/41	42/47	36/31	12/19
B	52/41	52/47	26/31	26/19

Now assume that at $t=1$ state e_1 occurs. Traders will revise beliefs about states s_1 and s_2 and markets will reopen in sure contracts in $t=1$, e_1 claims and in uncertain $t=2$, s_1- and s_2-contingent claims. Trader A's problem will now be as follows:

$$\text{maximize } \ln \bar{E}_1 + \frac{3}{10} \ln \bar{S}_1 + \frac{7}{10} \ln \bar{S}_2$$

$$\text{subject to } \bar{E}_1 + \bar{q}_1 \bar{S}_1 + \bar{q}_2 \bar{S}_2 = \frac{52}{41} + \frac{26}{31} \bar{q}_1 + \frac{26}{19} \bar{q}_2$$

where $\bar{q}_1$ and $\bar{q}_2$ are the new prices of s_1- and s_2-contingent claims relative to the numeraire time 1 consumption commodity. The reader can check that the competitive equilibrium price vector is $(\bar{q}_1, \bar{q}_2) = (31/164, 133/164)$ and final consumption choices are as below:

	$\bar{E}_1$	$\bar{S}_1$	$\bar{S}_2$
A	30/41	36/31	12/19
B	52/41	26/31	26/19

Obviously, prices have changed. But they have changed so as to counteract precisely the change in beliefs of the two traders. For example, trader A believed *a priori* that s_1 and s_2 were equally likely to occur, but conditional on e_1, A believes *a posteriori* that s_2 is 7/3 times more likely to occur than s_1. But prices of s_1- and s_2-contingent claims have changed from (32/41, 57/41) to (31/164, 133/164) and the price of s_2-contingent claims are now 7/3 times more expensive than s_1-contingent claims. A similar analysis applies to trader B. As a result, the final set of consumption choices are identical to the provisional set. No trade or speculation takes place.

The reader can check as an exercise that if at $t = 1$, state e_2 occurs then (taking e_2 consumption as numeraire) the competitive equilibrium price vector becomes $(\bar{q}_1, \bar{q}_2) = (93/138, 95/138)$ and final consumption choices again coincide with provisional choices.

The condition on beliefs that guarantees these results is that traders should agree on the conditional beliefs $\phi(e_i/s_j)$, $i, j = 1, 2$. For the array of beliefs assumed above, these are as below:

	$\phi(e_1/s_1)$	$\phi(e_1/s_2)$	$\phi(e_2/s_1)$	$\phi(e_2/s_2)$
A	1/4	7/12	3/4	5/12
B	1/4	7/12	3/4	5/12

and can be seen to satisfy the condition.

An interpretation of this condition in the light of the results of previous chapters runs as follows. The result that beliefs over e conditional on s (where e and s are generic notation for the states that occur at $t = 1$ and $t = 2$ respectively) are homogeneous across investors is equivalent to the result that beliefs over (e, s) conditional on s are homogeneous. This latter result defines the following partition over states of the world for our simple example:

$$\Gamma(\phi((e, s)/s)) = \{\{(e_1, s_1), (e_2, s_1)\}, \{(e_1, s_2), (e_2, s_2)\}\}$$

What this effectively means is that even if trades could be struck independently, for example, on the states (e_1, s_1) and (e_2, s_1) this would not allow a more efficient allocation of resources and would not alter the trades that take place; it is sufficient for trade to be made contingent on the entire event, s_1 (or, to be more exact, the event $\{(e_1, s_1), (e_2, s_1)\}$). Referring back to the decision tree depicted in figure 6.1, in the absence of any arbitrary informational restrictions, the natural assumption would be that at $t = 2$, traders would not only know which of s_1 and s_2 has occurred but would also remember which of e_1 and e_2 had occurred at $t = 1$. This property of information available through time, depicted by a decision tree structure as shown, where at each point in time new information is learned in addition to what is already known, is referred to as an increasing *filtration*. Rubinstein imposes an artificial informational incompleteness whereby trades for time 2 can be made conditional only on s_1 or s_2 and not, in addition, on the information as to whether e_1 or e_2 has occurred at $t = 1$. But, given the condition of non-speculative beliefs, this is a redundant incompleteness and there is no need for portfolio revisions in any spot markets beyond $t = 0$. The market is efficient with respect to the new information.

To illustrate the situation where within Rubinstein's model beliefs are speculative, portfolio revision occurs, and the market is inefficient with respect to the information revealed at $t = 1$, we can consider a second set of beliefs as below:

	(e_1, s_1)	(e_1, s_2)	(e_2, s_1)	(e_2, s_2)
ϕ_A	1/8	3/8	7/24	5/24
ϕ_B	1/16	3/16	7/16	5/16

Assuming traders with the same characteristics as before (including resource endowments) and following the same solution procedure, prices $(p_2, q_1, q_2) = (57/31, 41/31, 47/31)$ clear markets, and provisional portfolio choices are as below:

	E_1	E_2	S_1	S_2
A	36/31	12/19	30/41	42/47
B	26/31	26/19	52/41	52/47

If we now assume that at $t = 1$, e_1 occurs, beliefs will be revised (the reader can check that beliefs will in fact be homogeneous, although this is not a general result). The new competitive equilibrium price vector is $(\bar{q}_1, \bar{q}_2) = (1/4, 3/4)$. Final consumption choices are such that trader A consumes $30084/29653$ times more than trader B at $t = 1$ and $t = 2$ (regardless of which of s_1 and s_2 occurs).[3]

So for this set of beliefs, when e_1 is revealed at $t = 1$, speculation – or trade – does occur. Provisional portfolio choices are revised. A similar result can be shown to hold if e_2 is revealed to have occurred at $t = 1$. The reason that speculation occurs in this example is that beliefs over (e, s) conditional on s are not homogeneous. The informational incompleteness that trade is restricted to contracts contingent on s_1 and s_2 at $t = 2$ is a real restriction. When $t = 1$ comes around and the event e is revealed, traders will wish to revise their portfolios. Within the type of model Rubinstein assumes, there is no reason why the market should not be efficient for some events, say e, at $t = 1$ and inefficient with respect to other events, say e'. But, a more general and important issue is that the informational incompleteness is exogenously imposed. Without it, Rubinstein's market would necessarily be efficient with respect to new information that was publicly revealed to all traders. The more general question of whether the market would be efficient with respect to any private information that is revealed at any point in time concerning future states would involve a proper consideration of the conditions of the previous section.

The Milgrom–Stokey Model

Milgrom and Stokey (henceforth M–S) examine a pure exchange economy in which an initial round of trading occurs in commodities contingent upon the state of the world. The state of the world comprises two components so that the generic state of the world is denoted $w = (\theta, x)$ – in the M–S notation – where only $\theta \epsilon \Theta$ is payoff-relevant. After the initial round of trading, information in the form of a signal $x \epsilon X$ is revealed and markets reopen. M–S ask the question whether prices in the subsequent trading round will reveal the information disclosed. M–S show that the subsequent price vector will fully reveal the information if traders' prior beliefs are *concordant*.

Concordant beliefs satisfy the condition

$$\phi_1(x/\theta) = \ldots \ldots \ldots = \phi_n(x/\theta) \qquad \text{for all } x$$

where n is the number of traders. M–S give the useful interpretation of this condition that regarding x as information about θ, concordant beliefs mean that traders agree about how this information should be interpreted.

It should be apparent that the property of concordant beliefs is essentially identical to the Rubinstein property of non-speculative beliefs. Relabelling the M–S notation of (θ, x) in terms of Rubinstein's notation of (s, e), the analysis of the previous subsection applies equally to the M–S result.

6.6 AN APPRAISAL OF INFORMATIONAL EFFICIENCY

The answer to the question of whether prices will reflect information in a more general setting in which no institutional restrictions on trade are imposed, can be examined by imposing the M–S trading sequence on the type of example used to illustrate an REE in chapter 5. So, repeating the example of section 5.2, let the cash payoffs to firms X and Y and the beliefs of individuals A and B be as below:

	s_1	s_2	s_3	s_4	s_5
X	1	1	2	1	3
Y	2	2	2	1	1
ϕ_A	1/3	1/6	1/6	1/6	1/6
ϕ_B	1/4	1/8	1/8	1/4	1/4

Maintaining the original assumptions over endowments and trading in basic securities, then if we allow for a prior round of trading before the receipt of any information, we know from our previous solution to the Arrow–Debreu equilibrium that given the set of basic tradable securities below

	s_1	s_2	s_3	s_4	s_5
H_1	1	1	0	0	0
H_2	0	0	1	0	0
H_3	0	0	0	1	0
H_4	0	0	0	0	1

the equilibrium price vector is

$$(p_1, p_2, p_3, p_4) = (1, 1/4, 21/29, 21/58)$$

with basic security allocations

$$H_A = (48/29, 64/29, 16/21, 32/21)$$

$$H_B = (39/29, 52/29, 26/21, 52/21)$$

Now assume that information is released and that traders then engage in a second round of trading. Consider information that is costlessly available. Let us first examine the hypothesis of weak form efficiency. Remember that this refers to the information available in previous share prices. In our example, disclosure of the equilibrum price vector $(p_1, p_2, p_3, p_4) = (1, 1/4, 21/29, 21/58)$ will result in no revision of beliefs, prices, or equilibrium trades. In the setting assumed, the capital market is necessarily weak form efficient since individuals already take into account all available information in forming their demands, and the history of past prices is already available information. So let us move on to consider costless public information. Assume that the publicly available information is

$$\{s_1, s_2, s_3\} \mapsto y_1$$
$$\{s_4, s_5\} \mapsto y_2$$

Consider first the case where the signal y_1 is publicly revealed. From the REE of section 5.2, we know that when the signal y_1 is publicly revealed the equilibrium price vector becomes $(1, 1/4, 0, 0)$, and when signal y_2 is revealed it becomes $(0, 0, 1, 1/2)$. Clearly, for tradable securities that are now revealed by the public information to be worthless, price falls to zero. But for other basic tradable securities, relative prices remain unchanged, and similarly, equilibrium allocations will remain unchanged. But, in general, the equilibrium price vector necessarily changes and as it is this that is used to value complex securities, the equilibrium market values of firms will necessarily change as public information is received, although the market is informationally efficient.

Finally considering strong form efficiency we can say that this economy will reveal the information structure

$$\{s_1, s_2\} \mapsto y_1$$
$$\{s_3\} \mapsto y_2$$
$$\{s_4\} \mapsto y_3$$
$$\{s_5\} \mapsto y_4$$

or any coarser partition where this function is constructed from the information functions of all individuals taken together. Thus, in this example, even if an individual had monopolistic access to the above information function it would be of no value since the information would be revealed by prices to all individuals.

To end this section we can return to the issue of costly information acquisition referred to in section 5.4. A paradox that has been posed in the literature is that a capital market cannot be efficient with respect to information that is costly to acquire. For if it was, then there would be no incentive for any individual to acquire the information because of its cost; but if no individual acquires the information, then it cannot be reflected in prices. More formally, Grossman and Stiglitz (1980) prove that in their model when the noise in aggregate supply disappears, an REE with costly information does not exist. It is perhaps useful to consider the issue of costly information within the context of a partially revealing (or noisy) REE. If prices cannot fully reveal an item of information then that piece of information is potentially valuable. This will create a demand for the information and as a result it will command a price – information can be costly to acquire. This is one way of interpreting the results of Grossman and Stiglitz and others.

6.7   CONCLUDING REMARKS

This chapter has attempted to shed some light on a complex area in finance – the relationship between market prices and information. Although all finance academics would claim an intuitive understanding of the term informational efficiency, a rigorous and operational definition of IE has proved elusive. This has not prevented numerous empirical tests of IE being carried out that have generally come out in support of the view that capital markets are efficient with respect to publicly available information. However, at least one recent area of research – tests of the volatility of share prices – casts some doubt on this conclusion. A review of this area of research has served to highlight the problems of testing for IE.

The chapter has reviewed Beaver's attempt to provide a rigorous definition of IE and has interpreted the generally accepted taxonomy of IE in terms of this definition. Beaver's definition can be linked with the literature on REE and it provides a useful way of analysing IE, as we have attempted to show in sections 6.4 to 6.6. The importance of distinguishing the concepts of IE and allocative efficiency is probably best illustrated by considering an economy that fails to be fully informational efficient (fails to achieve an FRREE). Some finance academics would they say that the market is 'inefficient'. We have seen that a partially revealing REE fails to achieve IE, and this is one means of explaining the existence of costly information. But costs of information are no less real than costs of production; no market failure is implied. The only danger here is that the concept of IE becomes empirically vacuous as the presence of unmeasured costs of information are adduced to explain any departure from IE.

7

Signalling and Screening

The previous two chapters have analysed various aspects of the competitive market equilibrium that results when traders have differential information. All of the analysis was conducted within a model of pure exchange. The analysis of this chapter can be regarded in some respects as a special case of the general differential information model in that it considers the issues arising from information asymmetry between what might be called insiders and outsiders to a market-mediated agreement. In addition, the present chapter includes a first attempt at analysing the behaviour of firms in the real-world situation in which information asymmetries exist. There are in fact a number of situations which arise naturally in the context of capital markets, in which two groups of agents interact and in which one group, which can be considered as comprising outsiders (typically investors of some form), is initially imperfectly informed about the quality of products purveyed by the other, inside group (typically the firm or its management). The insiders, on the other hand, have either perfect information about product quality or at least superior information to outsiders.[1] In other words, there is at the outset an information asymmetry between the insiders and the outsiders.

In the absence of further information, this information asymmetry can cause markets to break down or even disappear altogether. Borrowing from Akerlof (1970), who originally analysed the phenomenon in a general product market setting, the reasoning is as follows. Imagine a market in which informed sellers offer products of different quality to buyers who, while being aware that the quality differences exist, are unable to tell the quality of particular products. Given that buyers are unable to distinguish between products of different quality, the price offered for those products must reflect their average quality. If sellers of the product have a reservation price below which they are unwilling to market their product then, initially, sellers of the highest quality products may withdraw their products from the market. This will reduce the average quality of products marketed and so the price offered by buyers will fall. Sellers of the next highest quality products may now withdraw their product from the market. So the process can continue until only the poorest quality products are marketed or the market disappears altogether.

However, a second major phenomenon that characterizes markets of this type is the concern of this chapter. Given that sellers are better informed than buyers there will be an incentive on the part of sellers to alter the initial information asymmetry and inform the buyers about the quality of their product. This incentive will obviously be greatest for those purveyors of the highest quality products. But, if they succeed, then the incentive to distinguish the next highest quality products from inferior products will filter down the quality range. In the terminology that has been adopted in the literature, sellers will have an incentive to *signal* their quality. An alternative way of viewing this phenomenon is to say that buyers will have an incentive to sort or *screen* sellers of different quality products. Although not exactly equivalent, as will be more fully explained later, signalling and screening devices are alternative ways of viewing the same phenomenon.

All the models of signalling and screening involve the so-called *self-selection principle*. Essentially this means that sellers choose courses of action that vary systematically with the quality of their product. Buyers, observing these actions learn something about the product quality of each individual seller. Sellers reveal their information through their own selections.

For this self-selection procedure to work it must be non-optimal for lower quality sellers to imitate the actions of higher quality sellers. Consider a single-period model in which sellers of quality-differentiated goods come to the market to confront uninformed buyers. Assume that penalties against misrepresentation are unenforceable at law – at least without significant costs. Alternatively, and perhaps more realistically, assume there is residual uncertainty in quality so that poor quality can result from an expectation of low quality or, with reduced probability, from an expectation of high quality. In this setting, a verbal assertion from high quality sellers could be matched at no cost by low quality sellers – in the case where there is residual uncertainty in product quality no claim could be subsequently disproved. Buyers would remain uninformed. Clearly, for a signalling device to be effective, the costs of signalling must vary inversely with the degree of quality. More precisely, the marginal cost of the signalling activity must be lower for sellers of higher quality products. This simply represents a more rigorous version of the catchphrase, 'money speaks louder than words'.

To give a simple model of how signalling might allow higher quality insiders to distinguish themselves consider the following example. Assume there are five entrepreneurs who each wish to sell an idea for a new project. Each project's payoff is normally distributed and the expected payoffs from the five projects are £100, £200, £300, £400 and £500 respectively (homogeneous beliefs are assumed here). Given the assumption of normal distributions, all of the projects can give rise to the same actual cash payoffs, so that observing the eventual cash payoff is not sufficient to identify what the expected payoff from each project was. This means that contingent contracts cannot be struck on the basis of the cash payoff. Assuming risk neutrality on behalf of all agents and for simplicity assuming a zero discount rate, if the projects remain undistinguished, all projects will be sold off for the average present value of £300. Now suppose that for a fixed, exogenous fee of £100 the true present value can be signalled to the market.[2] The entrepreneur with the £500 present value project will pay £100 in order to recoup £400 rather than receive £300. This lowers the average present value of undistinguished projects to £250. The entrepreneur with the £400 present value project will then prefer to pay £100 in order to receive £300 rather than £250. This leaves the new average present value of remaining undistinguished projects as £200. The entrepreneur with the £300 present value project now sees no advantage in paying the 'certification' fee and the three lower quality projects are pooled at an average value of £200. The signalling equilibrium results in the two higher quality projects being distinguished and the three lower quality projects remaining pooled. This example is rather simple but some of the basic ideas underlie the models to be reviewed below.

The aim of this chapter is to describe some applications of signalling and screening which have appeared in the capital market literature. The chapter begins in section 7.1 with a brief review of some of the main areas in finance to which the theory of screening and signalling has been applied. Section 7.2 discusses a distinction that has been made in the literature between a *dissipative* and a *non-dissipative* signalling equilibrium. The following three sections then describe in more depth the three areas of finance in which signalling or screening models have been most successfully applied. These areas are capital structure (section 7.3), dividend policy (section 7.4), and credit rationing (section 7.5). The final section offers some concluding remarks.

7.1 SIGNALLING AND SCREENING IN CAPITAL MARKETS

It might be useful in order to get a better appreciation of signalling and screening to give some examples of the areas in finance to which the models have been applied. At the same time this will serve to identify the relevant relationships that drive the major result in each case. Some of these examples will be elaborated upon later in the chapter.

One of the first areas in finance to which the theory of signalling was applied was that of the firm's capital structure decision. As explained in chapter 2, according to the Modigliani–Miller theorem, capital structure is irrelevant to the value of the firm. Firm value is determined by underlying cash flows from assets, and how those assets are financed, or equivalently how those cash flows are parcelled out among the various claims on them, is immaterial. The firm's optimal capital structure is indeterminate. However, if firms themselves have superior (inside) information about some aspect of the firm then the choice of capital structure can serve to signal this information to the outside capital market. Leland and Pyle (1977) analyse the case where entrepreneurs are seeking to finance a project (or firm) on which they have inside information about the expected return. The means by which this can be signalled to uninformed investors is through the retained insider position in the project. The cost of signalling consists of the increased risk from holding a less than fully diversified portfolio which arises from the extra insider investment in the project. But this increased risk costs less where the expected return is higher and so financial structure, in the sense of the equity retained by original owners, can signal quality and result in an optimal level of inside equity.[3] Ross (1977) considers the more typical choice between debt and equity finance as a signal of quality. In his model, managers are considered to have superior information to investors about the return on the firm. This information is signalled to the market by managers issuing debt and designing themselves a remuneration package that involves a heavy penalty should the firm be unable to meet its debt obligations. The level of gearing is a viable signal since the expected costs of bankruptcy for a given level of debt will be greater for firms with lower expected returns.

It has long been recognized in finance that the dividend decisions of firms might signal information to the stock market. Lintner (1956) found, *inter alia*, that firms pursue target dividend policies and only alter these target policies as long-term considerations justify. If the market recognizes that firms do behave in this way then changes in dividend policy might signal information to investors. Such effects have been documented in empirical research on the share price reaction to changed dividend policies. In the theoretical literature Bhattacharya (1979) assumes that outside investors have imperfect information about firms' profitability. Proposed dividends function as a signal of expected cash flows. The costs of signalling comprise the higher taxation of dividends relative to capital gains and the assumed transactions costs of meeting any shortfall of the cash flow from the proposed dividend. In Bhattacharya (1980) dividends again signal firm profitability to uninformed outside investors. The required signalling cost function is established through insiders precommitting themselves to an ex post adjustment of the selling price of their shareholding as a function of the discrepancy between the dividend and the actual earnings of the firm. In both articles the marginal cost of the dividend signal is lower for higher profitability firms. Miller and Rock (1985) analyse the situation where the firm's managers know more than outside investors about the true state of the firm's current earnings. The net distribution of funds by the firm signals its unannounced earnings to outsiders. The cost of higher net distributions is the consequent reduction in investment. This opportunity cost of a higher net dividend decreases with increases in the firm's current earnings. John and Kalay (1985) consider a case where dividend reductions can signal good news. In their model, there is an information asymmetry about the type of a firm's investment opportunities. Because recourse to outside finance is costly, by pre-committing the firm to dividend restrictions, shareholders can signal their true investment opportunities. If the lower quality firm attempts to imitate the precommitment of the higher quality firm then it is forced to overinvest, which produces the costs of false signalling.

One area of finance to which a model of screening has been applied is the theory of credit rationing. In this case, borrowers are selling debt claims to banks (the buyers). When the borrower first approaches a bank for a loan, the bank will be unable to tell whether the borrower is a good credit risk or not. One means of screening good borrowers from bad borrowers is through the terms of the loan agreement offered. For example, the interest rate that borrowers are willing to pay on the loan may serve to sort out potential borrowers. Those willing to pay higher interest rates on borrowed funds are, on average, likely to be the worse risks. In other words if borrowers have projects with identical expected returns, those having projects with more speculative returns will be willing to borrow at higher rates. This is because there is an increased probability of a higher payoff to the borrower whereas the increased probability of a lower payoff has no effect on the worst event that can happen to the borrower which is that he defaults on the bank loan.

7.2 NON-DISSIPATIVE *v.* DISSIPATIVE SIGNALS

One distinction that has been drawn in the literature between different signalling models is whether the resulting equilibrium signal is dissipative or not. This distinction turns on whether the information to which the seller initially has superior access can be verified by the buyer at a subsequent date when the contract is fulfilled.

In the case of non-dissipative signals, or what Spence (1976) has called contingent contracts, the range of quality signals available to the seller is created by the buyer's subsequent ability to observe the seller's quality directly. So, if sellers know their quality or type, they declare this publicly. Contingent upon their claim subsequently being substantiated, they are then paid accordingly but with a penalty if actual quality is subsequently found to be different from that reported. With suitable penalties there will be a negative correlation of signalling costs with quality and sellers will report truthfully. In effect, the signal in non-dissipative models serves to bring forward the timing of communication of sellers' (insiders') information. The resulting signalling equilibrium is indistinguishable from an equilibrium in which both buyers and sellers share information to begin with.

In the case of sellers knowing their quality or type with certainty no signalling costs are actually incurred. Alternatively, in the more general case where sellers know something about their quality but there remains some residual uncertainty, some risk will be absorbed by the sellers. But this result is still equivalent to a symmetric information equilibrium under uncertainty. Pareto efficiency still requires some risk sharing and so the return to sellers will be random. Most models interpret this as penalties in the contract being incurred and thus giving rise to actual signalling costs. These costs can be considered as being equivalent to the uncertain payoffs in a symmetric information equilibrium under uncertainty.

In the case of dissipative signals, or what Spence calls exogenously costly signals, buyers cannot subsequently validate the quality claims of sellers. A signalling cost structure based on commonly observable contingencies cannot be created. In these models, there are activities that involve an exogenous or third-party cost, varying with quality, which sellers engage in directly and independently of buyer behaviour. The resulting equilibrium is termed dissipative because these costs are actually incurred by sellers and so there is a welfare loss in comparison to the (unattainable) symmetric information equilibrium.

We can gain some further insight into the difference between these two signalling models by using the framework developed in previous chapters. Suppose that a group of individuals each have the ownership rights to a project. Given any project there is uncertainty over the cash flow outcome and for risk-sharing purposes the owners wish to issue securities against these cash flows. However, for (outsider) potential security holders there is an extra layer of uncertainty in that *a priori* they are uncertain whether any project is a good (type 1) project or a bad (type 2) project. The information asymmetry is created by assuming that the (insider) owners do know their project type prior to securities being sold. Assume there are an equal number of good and bad projects and that everyone knows this. In the absence of further information, securities will be priced to reflect the average quality of projects. This will create an incentive on the part of owners of good projects to signal their quality to security holders.

Suppose that the cash flow structures are as below:

	s_1	s_2	s_3	s_4
$X(1)$	5	5	4	4
$X(2)$	2	3	2	3

Here, the cash flow from the project, X, depends first on whether it is a type 1 or type 2 project and second upon the state of the world that occurs in the future. Essentially, from the viewpoint of buyers of securities there is an extended state space of the form

$$S' = S \times T = \{(s, t): s \in \{s_1, s_2, s_3, s_4\} = S, \ t \in \{1, 2\} = T\}.$$

This can be laid out as below:

s_1'	s_2'	s_3'	s_4'	s_5'	s_6'	s_7'	s_8'
$\{s_1, 1\}$	$\{s_2, 1\}$	$\{s_3, 1\}$	$\{s_4, 1\}$	$\{s_1, 2\}$	$\{s_2, 2\}$	$\{s_3, 2\}$	$\{s_4, 2\}$

| X | 5 | 5 | 4 | 4 | 2 | 3 | 2 | 3 |

Now, *a priori*, the outsiders who buy the securities have the null information function with respect to this extended state space. But the insiders who sell the securities have the information partition $\{\{s_1', s_2', s_3', s_4'\}, \{s_5', s_6', s_7', s_8'\}\}$. The question is whether the information known by insiders can be communicated costlessly to outsiders. In the above example it should be apparent that it can. In fact the question resembles the question posed in chapter 5 as to whether an REE will be fully revealing. A non-dissipative signalling equilibrium can be achieved for this example because the partition of states generated by commonly observable cash flows

$$\Gamma(X) = \{\{s_1', s_2'\}, \{s_3', s_4'\}, \{s_5', s_7'\}, \{s_6', s_8'\}\}$$

is at least as fine as the partition of states generated by the private information of insiders. Equivalently, cash flows are a sufficient statistic for project type. By contracting on the basis of subsequently observed contingencies insiders can signal their project type to outsiders.

An even simpler version of the non-dissipative signalling equilibrium is where there is no uncertainty over the cash payoff given the project type, but where, *a priori*, only insiders are informed about project type. In this case the extended state space corresponds exactly to the range of project types. To see this, consider an example where there are three possible project types with future payoffs as follows:

$$
\begin{array}{ll}
X(1) & a \\
X(2) & b \\
X(3) & c
\end{array}
$$

This is equivalent to the extended state space

$$
\begin{array}{cccc}
 & s_1 & s_2 & s_3 \\
X & a & b & c
\end{array}
$$

with an assumption that insiders are perfectly informed *a priori* as to which state has occurred. In this case the future cash payoff fully reveals the state of the world or, equivalently, the project type; trade can take place contingent on the project type.

To illustrate the alternative case of the dissipative signal, consider the following cash flow structure:

	s_1	s_2	s_3	s_4
$X(1)$	2	3	3	3
$X(2)$	2	2	2	3

This has the corresponding extended state space

	s_1'	s_2'	s_3'	s_4'	s_5'	s_6'	s_7'	s_8'
	$\{s_1, 1\}$	$\{s_2, 1\}$	$\{s_3, 1\}$	$\{s_4, 1\}$	$\{s_1, 2\}$	$\{s_2, 2\}$	$\{s_3, 2\}$	$\{s_4, 2\}$
X	2	3	3	3	2	2	2	3

Again, assume that *a priori* outsiders have the null information function over this extended state space. Insiders, on the other hand, are endowed with the information partition

$$[\{\{s_1', s_2', s_3', s_4'\}, \{s_5', s_6', s_7', s_8'\}\}]$$

and receive a signal before trade takes place as to whether their project is type 1 or type 2. Now in this case a non-dissipative signalling equilibrium is unattainable. The reason is that the owner of a type 2 project could mimic any verbal claims of a type 1 owner and the claim could never be disproved. This is because observation of the cash flow is insufficient to distinguish between the two project types. In the technical terminology we have employed so far, the partition generated by commonly observable cash flows $\Gamma(X) = \{\{s_1', s_5', s_6', s_7'\}, \{s_2', s_3', s_4', s_8'\}\}$ is not finer than the partition of states generated by the insiders' private information – cash flows are not a sufficient statistic for project type.

In this setting, a signalling equilibrium that reveals project type to outsiders may still be possible if there is some activity whose cost is negatively correlated with project quality. In this case project type is revealed by self-selection since it does not pay owners of lower quality projects to mimic the signalling activities of owners of higher quality projects. A more detailed version of this type of model with an explicit treatment of the signalling costs is given in section 7.3 below.

Note that in the second illustration above, signalling costs are incurred and so there is a deadweight cost by comparison with a setting in which both insiders and outsiders are costlessly informed of project types *a priori*. Hence the term dissipative. However the comparison is rather misleading from a welfare point of view. It is only because of the inability to substantiate project quality ex post from observing cash flows that there is the demand for the signalling activity from insiders and thus the cost of the signalling activity. Similarly, in the non-dissipative case, no costs are incurred because the existing public information structure perfectly reveals the private information of insiders and so there cannot be any additional cost to signalling. In a general equilibrium setting private information costs only arise when all costless public sources of information fail to fully reveal that private information. In this respect, non-dissipative signalling models are to some extent an artificial construct. Viewed in terms of information problems alone,[4] since cash flows are a sufficient statistic for quality type, insiders' qualities will be revealed to outsiders whether they like it or not regardless of any deliberate attempt at signalling.

7.3 SIGNALLING AND CAPITAL STRUCTURE

One of the earliest applications of signalling in finance appears in a paper by Ross (1977). Ross presents a model in which the management of a firm knows more about the firm's future returns than do outside investors. A two-period economy is assumed with assets being priced in the market on a risk-neutral basis. The information that is common to all participants is that managers are rewarded by a known incentive or remuneration schedule and that firms have random future returns, X, assumed to have a uniform distribution between 0 and t. The information asymmetry is introduced by assuming that only managers have the inside information on the precise value of t and hence on the true value of the firm. Outsiders know only the range of possible t values, $t \in [c, d]$. The means by which managers signal their inside information to outsiders is through their choice of capital structure for the firm.

Because the general structure of the signalling equilibrium used in the Ross paper is one that is common to other papers in the area and because the mathematics is relatively tractable the model is developed below. The precise equilibrium concept is that of an equilibrium function relating the inferred market value (or t value) of the firm to the inside management's choice of capital structure from which the market inference is made. This equilibrium function must satisfy two conditions. First, management chooses the firm's capital structure in order to maximize expected utility (given according to the known remuneration schedule) in the knowledge of how outside investors use this as a signal of the true value of the firm. Second, the equilibrium function is self-fulfilling or informationally consistent in that for any choice of capital structure the inference that investors make about the true value of the firm on the basis of the observed choice of capital structure is correct.

The incentive schedule for management, which is known by all market participants, takes the form

$$M = (1 + r)\gamma_0 V_0 + \gamma_1 E \left\{ \begin{array}{ll} X & \text{if } X \geq F \\ X - L & \text{if } X \leq F \end{array} \right\}$$

where r is the riskless interest rate; γ_0, γ_1 are positive constants; V_0 is the initial market value of the firm; F is the nominal value of debt issued in the first period; L is a bankruptcy penalty; and E is the expectations operator with respect to the random return X.

This management remuneration schedule can be interpreted as follows: (a) at time 0 the manager gets paid a wage that is proportional to the current value of the firm, V_0; and (b) at time 1 the manager receives a compensation that depends on the terminal value of the firm, X.

The essence of the signalling mechanism is that investors use the nominal value of debt as a signal of the firm's type, t, a greater nominal value of debt indicating a larger t value. Moreover, this will be a credible signal because for a given value of t higher gearing increases the probability that the bankruptcy penalty will be incurred, resulting in a smaller compensation to management.

Given the face value of debt issued by the firm, the market's perception of firm type can be denoted $t(F)$. The corresponding market valuation of the firm given risk neutrality and the uniform return distribution is then

$$V_0 = \frac{t(F)/2}{(1+r)}$$

Given this market valuation, managers maximize their reward which can now be expressed as

$$M = \gamma_0 t(F)/2 + \gamma_1(t/2 - LF/t) \tag{7.1}$$

For any $t(F)$ schedule, the solution to this optimization problem results in an optimal value of F which depends upon t. Specifically, differentiating M with respect to F and assuming an internal maximum gives

$$\gamma_0 t'(F)/2 = \gamma_1 L/t \tag{7.2}$$

which defines F implicitly as a function of t, $F^* = F^*(t)$. This is the first condition required for a signalling equilibrium: the inside management chooses the level of the signal (here the face value of debt) in the light of the feedback effect this has on the outside market's perception of the firm's value in order to maximize a given objective function.

The requirement for an equilibrium $t(F)$ schedule is that the firm's true type be correctly identified, that is,

$$t[F^*(t)] = t \tag{7.3}$$

Equation (7.3) is the second condition required for a signalling equilibrium. This is that the equilibrium function mapping management's choice of the face value of debt into firm type be self-fulfilling or informationally consistent; that is, the inference that the market makes about firm type on the basis of the management's (utility-maximizing) choice of debt is correct. Conditions (7.2) and (7.3) must be satisfied simultaneously at the signalling equilibrium. Differentiating (7.3) with respect to t gives

$$t'(F^*) = \frac{1}{dF^*/dt}$$

Combining this with (7.2) then gives

$$dF^*/dt = \gamma_0 t/2\gamma_1 L \tag{7.4}$$

Equation (7.4) is the differential equation relating management's choice of the face value of debt and the market's inferred firm type when the two conditions (7.2) and (7.3) for a signalling equilibrium are satisfied. The equilibrium function is the solution to (7.4) which the reader can confirm is given by the general solution

$$F^*(t) = \frac{\gamma_0 t^2}{4\gamma_1 L} + b$$

where b is a constant of integration. Since the least attractive firm with type $t = c$ has no incentive to signal, it will set $F^*(c) = 0$, which implies $b = -\dfrac{\gamma_0 c^2}{4\gamma_1 L}$, giving the specific solution

$$F^*(t) = \frac{(t^2 - c^2)\gamma_0}{4\gamma_1 L} \tag{7.5}$$

To put some numbers into this model, let us assume that $\gamma_0 = \gamma_1 = 0.01$, and $[c, d] = [£1m, £10m]$. With these assumed values the management of a £10m value firm has every incentive to set the value of L at a level that will just permit full discrimination without increasing bankruptcy penalties unnecessarily. If it chooses a value of $L = £4.5m$ and so issues debt with nominal value of £5.5m then the management of a type £1m firm will be just indifferent between receiving a remuneration of

$$0.01(£1m) = £10,000$$

from choosing $F = 0$ and a remuneration of

$$(1/2)(0.01)(10) + 0.01(0.5 - 4.5) = £10,000$$

from falsely signalling a type £10m firm. (The bankruptcy penalty is incurred with certainty in this example.)

Condition (7.5) ensures that no other managers have incentives to give false signals. So, a manager of an £8m value firm sets $F = £3.5m$, the firm is correctly identified by the market and the manager's remuneration is, from (7.1), £60,312.5. The signal works because the market knows that given the managerial incentive schedule, an issue of £3.5m nominal value debt implies an £8m firm. At the same time, if the manager issued more debt, the increase in the expected bankruptcy penalty would outweigh the benefit of the higher market value attached to the firm, whereas, if less debt was issued, the loss from the reduced market value would outweigh the reduced bankruptcy penalty. In the Ross model, the management's remuneration schedule amounts to a contingent contract and so the resulting signalling equilibrium is non-dissipative.

A second application of signalling to the theory of capital structure was developed at the same time as the Ross paper in a paper by Leland and Pyle (1977). They consider a setting in which an entrepreneur has to decide on the optimum form of finance for a risky investment project. What makes the problem interesting is that initially only the entrepreneur knows the expected payoff from the project. Potential investors know only that project payoffs are normally distributed about the *a priori* unknown mean. The assumption of a normal distribution ensures that cash flows cannot be a sufficient statistic for project type since the cash flow support is independent of project type.[5] The resulting signalling equilibrium is therefore dissipative – entrepreneurs are willing to incur some cost to signal their project type. The model of Leland and Pyle can be considered as a more general and complete version of the simple numerical example that we used to motivate the idea of a dissipative signalling equilibrium in section 7.2.

The means by which entrepreneurs can signal the quality of their project to potential investors is via the fraction of equity they retain in the project. The cost of this activity is the forgone diversification opportunities from holding a larger equity proportion in their own firms by comparison with a setting in which project quality is common information. Investors will view the retained equity position as a signal of the true expected payoff from the project. The signalling equilibrium used in the Leland and Pyle paper is in essence the same as that used in the Ross paper. The concept is again that of an equilibrium function here mapping the entrepreneur's retained equity position into expected project payoffs such that two conditions are satisfied. First, entrepreneurs choose their retained equity position in order to maximize expected utility in the knowledge that investors will use this as a signal of the true expected project payoff. Second, the equilibrium function is self-fulfilling or informationally consistent in that for any project undertaken, the inference that investors make about the true expected project payoff on the basis of the observed retained equity position is correct.

The mathematics of the Leland and Pyle paper perhaps obscures rather than illuminates the underlying concept of a signalling equilibrium. But the solution technique is essentially the same as in the Ross paper. The Leland and Pyle signalling equilibrium involves solving the entrepreneur's problem of choosing the retained equity position to maximize expected utility in the light of the feedback effect that this has on the valuation of the project. The equilibrium condition that project type be correctly identified is then invoked. This results in a differential equation describing the effect that the choice of retained equity has on the inferred expected project payoff when the two conditions required for a signalling equilibrium are satisfied. The equilibrium function is the solution to this differential equation.

In both the Ross and Leland and Pyle papers the signalling equilibrium differs in significant respects from the corresponding models with no information asymmetries. In both cases, the value of the firm depends upon its capital structure; the Modigliani–Miller capital structure irrelevance proposition no longer holds.

7.4 SIGNALLING AND DIVIDENDS

It is well known that in perfect markets with symmetric information the firm's dividend policy has no effect on its market value. Given the firm's investment decision, financing an increased dividend by issuing new equity capital (or decreasing the dividend and repurchasing equity) merely involves a transfer of ownership; the underlying cash flows to security holders, which determine the value of the firm, remain unchanged. This irrelevance of dividend policy in theory is in conflict with the importance attached to dividend policies in practice. One way of explaining the relevance of dividends in practice has been to examine dividend policy under conditions of asymmetric information.

As an example of a non-dissipative signalling equilibrium, Bhattacharya (1980) uses a structure that is very similar to Ross's to provide an explanation of how firms signal their profitability to the market via their dividend policy. In the model it is assumed that there is a cross-section of firms each holding assets with differing future payoffs, X_t, at times $t = 1, 2$. Insider managers know their own firm's profitability. The market, on the other hand, is unable to distinguish firms *a priori*, knowing only the distribution of firm profitabilities. However, it is assumed that firm profitability can be observed by the market at date $t = 2$. Managers are assumed to act in the best interests of current shareholders who plan to sell out to new shareholders at $t = 1$.

The signalling mechanism is the dividend to which the firm initially commits itself. The market uses the dividend to identify firm profitability, and so to value shares sold at $t = 1$. At the same time, initial shareholders agree to an ex post adjustment to this liquidation value as a function of the discrepancy between the declared dividend and the first-period earnings.

Given a suitable specification of the adjustment function and the market's valuation as a function of the dividend, management selects a dividend that balances the benefits of a higher liquidation valuation against the costs of a subsequent adjustment penalty. Given this behaviour by management, at the signalling equilibrium firm profitability is correctly inferred from the dividend signal, allowing perfect discrimination between firm types.

Miller and Rock (1985) present a dissipative dividend signalling equilibrium model. In their model, directors are assumed to know more than outside investors about the true state of the firm's current earnings. The intuition behind the dividend signalling equilibrium and the costs it imposes relative to the symmetric information case is as follows. Other things being equal, higher (net) dividends (excess of dividends over new security issues) indicate higher current earnings for the firm. However, if the market reacts naïvely to dividend announcements there will be an incentive to sacrifice investment in order to pay out excessive dividends. If the market reacts naïvely to the dividend, shareholders can sell their shares before the market learns the truth about the firm's investment policy. But this would not be informationally consistent since the inference that the market makes about the firm is subsequently proved incorrect; new shareholders lose out. A signalling equilibrium requires the market to infer the current earnings from the dividend signal in the full knowledge of the incentive of insiders to increase the dividend at the expense of investment. Similarly, insiders select an appropriate dividend payout in the knowledge of the market's assessment. The equilibrium is achieved when the assessment that the market makes is correct.

To illustrate the signalling equilibrium of Miller and Rock, assume that the current earnings of the firm, X, are known only to the firm's directors. Directors have to decide on a net dividend distribution, D, and an amount to invest, I. The investment will result in future earnings, $\bar{X}_2 = F(I) + \bar{\epsilon}$ where $I = X - D$ is the firm's investment and $\bar{\epsilon}$ is a random disturbance with zero mean. The firm is assumed to be dissolved on the distribution of future earnings, $\bar{X}_2$.

Thus the true value of the firm assessed on the information of directors is

$$V^{\mathrm{d}}(X, D) = D + \frac{F(X-D)}{1+i}$$

where i is an appropriate risk-adjusted discount rate for the firm's earnings. But for market outsiders who observe only D, the value of the firm is given by

$$V^{\mathrm{m}}(D) = D + \frac{F[X(D)-D]}{1+i}$$

The objective function that directors are assumed to maximize consists of a weighted average of these two valuation functions:

$$\max_{D} W = kV^m + (1-k)V^d$$

with weights k and $(1-k)$ given by the fraction of shareholders who plan to sell and hold shares respectively. This objective function is posited on the grounds that it resolves any conflict of interest between short- and long-term shareholders; the benefit to one group of a change in dividend is exactly offset by the cost to the other group in the objective function.

We have that directors maximize the objective function

$$\max_{D} W = kV^m(D) + (1-k)V^d(X, D)$$

which can be rewritten as

$$= k\left\{D + \frac{F[X(D)-D]}{1+i}\right\} + (1-k)\left\{D + \frac{F(X-D)}{1+i}\right\}$$

The first-order condition for a maximum is

$$k\left\{1 + \frac{F'(X(D)-D)(X'(D)-1)}{1+i}\right\} + (1-k)\left\{1 - \frac{F'(X-D)}{1+i}\right\} = 0 \tag{7.6}$$

Equation (7.6) gives the first condition required for a signalling equilibrium; the directors choose the level of dividend, knowing the effect that this has on the market's perception of the firm's current earnings, in order to maximize a known objective function. The second condition for the signalling equilibrium of information consistency is that the inference that the market makes about the firm's current earnings on the basis of its dividend be correct. This ensures that the market's valuation of the firm agrees with the directors' valuation. We can write the condition simply as

$$X = X(D) \tag{7.7}$$

where D satisfies the first-order condition (7.6). Substituting (7.7) into (7.6) gives

$$1 + \frac{kF'(X(D)-D)X'(D)}{1+i} - \frac{F'(X(D)-D)}{1+i} = 0$$

or rearranging in terms of the signalling function, $X(D)$,

$$X'(D) = \frac{F'(X(D)-D)-(1+i)}{kF'(X(D)-D)} \qquad (7.8)$$

Equation (7.8) is the differential equation giving the effect of the directors' optimizing choice of dividend on the current earnings inferred by the market. The solution to this differential equation gives the general solution to the signalling equilibrium. A specific solution which Pareto dominates all others is obtained by assuming that the firm with lowest current earnings has no incentive to deviate from the dividend–investment choice it would make in the absence of any information asymmetry.

To illustrate these results for a specific case, Miller and Rock provide the following example. Assume the production function takes the following form:

$$F(I) = a \ln(I+b); \; a, \; b > 0$$

In the symmetric information case, the optimal investment policy requires setting the marginal return on investment equal to the market-required rate of return, or

$$\frac{a}{(I+b)} = 1 + i$$

giving

$$I^* = \frac{a}{(1+i)} - b$$

The solution to the signalling equilibrium is obtained by substituting for the production function in (7.8), giving

$$X'(D) = \frac{a - b(1+i)}{ak} - \frac{(1+i)(X-D)}{ak} \qquad (7.9)$$

with endpoint condition $\underline{X}(D^*(\underline{X})) = \underline{X}$, where $I^* = \underline{X} - D^* = a/(1+i) - b$ and $\underline{X}$ denotes the lowest possible current earnings.

It can be confirmed that the solution to (7.9) can be written as

$$X(D) - D = I^* - \frac{ak}{1+i}\{1 - \exp[-(1+i)(D-D^*)/ak]\} \qquad (7.10)$$

Since the second term on the right hand side is positive, the signalling equilibrium requires directors to underinvest relative to the symmetric information optimum level in order to signal the firm's earnings to the market via dividends.

To take a numerical example, let us specify

$$a = 1.725 \ (\pounds m)$$
$$b = 1.0 \ (\pounds m)$$
$$i = 15\%$$
$$k = 0.2$$
$$X = 0.4 \ (\pounds m)$$

The directors in the firm with the lowest level of current earnings will declare net dividends of $-\pounds 0.1m$ (they will issue new securities to the value of $\pounds 0.1m$), allowing them to achieve the optimal level of investment of $\pounds 0.5m$. For the firm with current earnings of $\pounds 0.5m$ the optimal level of investment in a symmetric information equilibrium would again be $\pounds 0.5m$ with a zero net dividend. However, the reader can check that by (7.10), this firm will distribute a dividend of (approximately) $\pounds 183,330$. Given this dividend, the market will correctly value the firm as having current earnings of $\pounds 0.5m$ and as a result only investing $\pounds 316,670$. Similarly, knowing the market's reaction, the dividend that is distributed and the consequent investment policy maximizes the directors' objective function. The reader can also check that a firm with current earnings of $\pounds 1m$ would distribute $\pounds 784,260$ and invest $\pounds 215,740$, while the equivalent figures for a firm with earnings of $\pounds 1.5m$ would be $\pounds 1,297,150$ and $\pounds 202,850$. A sketch of the equilibrium function is shown as figure 7.1.

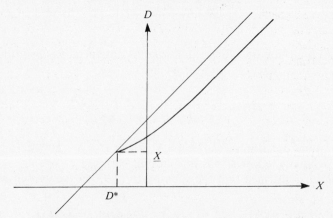

Figure 7.1 Dividend signalling equilibrium function

Similar to the case of capital structure, introducing information asymmetries into the dividend problem of the firm destroys the dividend irrelevance proposition of Miller and Modigliani (1961) in the sense that if dividends signal information to outside investors the market value of the firm will depend upon the firm's chosen dividend. However as a number of authors have pointed out, it is still the cash flows of the firm that determine firm value. Dividends are used only to convey the information about cash flow, and not for any intrinsic value of their own. Indeed Miller (1983) has reversed the line of causation between dividends and firm value in suggesting that in a rational signalling equilibrium it is firm value that determines the firm's dividend policy and not the other way round.

7.5 SCREENING AND CREDIT RATIONING

We suggested earlier that signalling and screening are alternative ways of describing the same phenomenon. This equivalence may be sufficiently accurate for the analysis of this chapter where we are concerned with the intuition behind asymmetric information equilibrium models. In particular we have implicitly assumed the existence of a unique equilibrium. However, it is useful to be aware of the different approaches that have been used in the literature in constructing signalling and screening models. This difference in approach can be important when considering the existence and uniqueness of the resulting equilibrium.

The distinction that Stiglitz and Weiss (1983) draw between signalling and screening models concerns the order in which market participants move. In the signalling models, informed agents move first and uninformed agents react to the signalling activity of the informed. In screening models, by comparison, the uninformed move first, offering a menu of contracts to the informed, designed to screen their qualities; the uninformed self-select themselves by their choice of contract. The principal result of the Stiglitz–Weiss paper is to show that the set of equilibria to the screening models is a subset of the set of equilibria to the signalling models. This explains why theoretical papers on signalling often find the equilibrium to be non-unique while in screening models non-existence of an equilibrium is typically the problem.

Stiglitz and Weiss (1981) apply a model of screening to the problem of credit rationing in which borrowers with different probabilities of repayment apply for loans from banks who are initially unable to distinguish different credit risks. The means by which banks screen prospective borrowers is through the terms of the loan contract offered.

Basic terms such as the interest rate charged or the amount of security required can change the distribution of borrowing types who apply for loans. For example, higher interest rates can shift this distribution towards worse risks who view their probability of total default to be higher. Similarly, increased security requirements can shift the distribution towards wealthier, less risk-averse individuals.

Stiglitz and Weiss consider a model where single-project firms apply for equal amounts of bank finance. All projects have the same expected return but some are riskier than others. Banks are unable to distinguish between projects of different risk *a priori*. When firms borrow from banks they effectively have a call option on their project. If the project succeeds and its value exceeds the repayment on the loan, the bank will be paid and the project effectively repossessed. Alternatively, if the project fails then the firm, with limited liability, simply reneges on the loan, losing any security that has been pledged. This means that for given terms of the loan contract, borrowing will be more attractive to riskier firms. These firms gain more from the increased probability of the project succeeding, but are unconcerned about the increased probability of failure since the worst that can happen is that they lose the security on the loan. The result of this is that, as the bank raises its interest rate on loans, the effect of attracting greater risk applicants may outweigh the increased return from projects that succeed.

A simple setting in which the interest rate serves to distinguish different borrowers is where there are only two types of firm. 'Safe' firms are assumed willing to borrow only at interest rates below r_1, while 'risky' firms are assumed willing to borrow up to an interest rate $r_2 > r_1$. Given this borrowing behaviour the return, ϱ, to the bank can be depicted as in figure 7.2. Here, the optimal interest rate is given by r_1. In the more general case of a discrete number of different risk types, the saw-tooth depiction of figure 7.2 will become less accentuated but there will be a unique optimal interest rate which the bank should charge, since higher interest charges screen out the safer applicants.

Stiglitz and Weiss present a diagrammatic analysis of a screening equilibrium in which credit rationing occurs. With credit rationing, at the interest rate that maximizes the return to banks there is an excess demand for finance. But the interest rate will not rise to equilibrate demand and supply because this lowers the return to banks. The credit rationing equilibrium is shown in figure 7.3. Here, the relation between the expected return to the bank and the interest rate charged on loans is shown as a continuous curve in the upper right hand quadrant. This is the equivalent to figure 7.2 when there is a large number of firm types. Once again it shows that the expected return to the bank does not increase monotonically

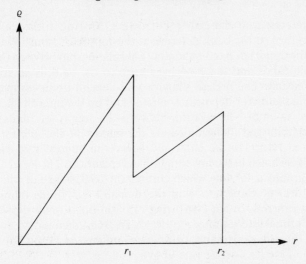

Figure 7.2 Returns to the bank for various interest rates

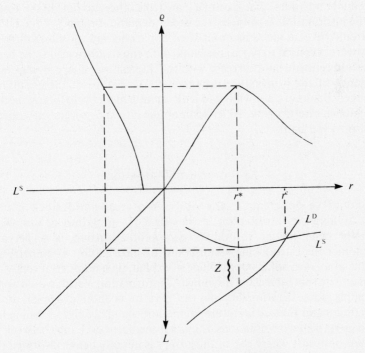

Figure 7.3 Credit rationing equilibrium

with the interest rate charged to borrowers. Moving anticlockwise, the expected return to the bank determines the supply of funds by the bank shown in the upper left hand quadrant. The relationship between the supply of loanable funds and the expected return to the bank is assumed here to be increasing. The precise shape would depend upon competition in the banking sector for depositors' money and on the interest elasticity of depositors' savings. The relation between the supply of funds and the interest rate charged (determined via the impact of the interest rate on the expected return to the bank and hence the interest rate offered to depositors) is shown in the lower right hand quadrant. The lower left hand quadrant graphs a 45° line which ensures the consistency of the supplies of funds drawn. Superimposing the demand for funds (shown as a decreasing function of the borrowing rate) on this supply shows that at the bank optimal interest rate, r^*, there is an excess demand, Z, for funds. Although this excess demand would be eliminated at r^e, no bank would wish to increase its interest rate above r^*.

With the assumed information asymmetry, the screening equilibrium results in credit being rationed in the sense that among a set of identical potential borrowers some receive a loan while others do not. In the absence of the information asymmetry the excess demand for loans at the interest r^* would be eliminated as unsatisfied borrowers bid up the interest rate they were prepared to pay to the bank; with equal information, the bank's expected return would increase with the interest rate charged. But in the presence of the information asymmetry, the nature of the equilibrium changes. Banks are not willing to lend out at a higher rate than r^* because the higher rate attracts riskier loan applicants and lowers the expected return to the bank.

7.6 CONCLUDING REMARKS

It should be apparent to any observer of real-world stock markets that asymmetric information in the sense of one group of individuals initially being better informed than another group is a pervasive phenomenon. Introducing assumptions of information asymmetry into financial models holds out the hope of explaining a number of real-world phenomena that, at least in a symmetric information world, would appear to imply some irrationality on the part of economic agents. In the economics and finance literature, models of signalling and screening have been used to analyse situations of market-mediated exchange between two groups of agents where one of the groups is initially better informed than the other group.

In this chapter the primary aim has been to illustrate examples of models of screening and signalling in capital markets. Applied to the capital structure and dividend debates, inside management is assumed to be better informed than outside investors about some aspect of the firm. If this is the case, the firm's choice of capital structure or dividend can signal this information to the uninformed investors. This chapter has shown how a signalling equilibrium is developed. One important result is that in a world of asymmetric information, capital structure and dividend policies become relevant to the valuation of the firm. However, it is important to remember that firm value is determined simultaneously with the level of the signalling activity in these models. No line of causation from the signalling activity to the value of the firm is implied. In this sense, the signalling activity is not something that managers can manipulate independently to signal what they would like outside investors to believe about the firm. In the signalling equilibrium investors anticipate a level of signalling activity for any value of the unobservable variable (for example, cash flow) that determines firm value. Managers automatically choose the signal appropriate for the inside information they possess. The costs of signalling ensure that the appropriate signals are made.

The chapter has also illustrated a simple situation of asymmetric information in the market for loans. Because banks are initially assumed to have no information on the relative riskiness of particular loan applicants, the interest rate charged on loans can serve to screen out higher risks with the result that credit is rationed at the screening equilibrium.

The next chapter goes on to consider further aspects of information asymmetries. This will provide additional insights into the implications of information asymmetries for the role of the firm and for contractual arrangements in general.

8

Agency Theory

8.1 INTRODUCTION

This chapter continues the theme of the previous chapter but from a different perspective. Both this chapter and chapter 7 are concerned with issues that arise when insider managers have an information advantage over the outside investors of the firm. Chapter 7 considered ways in which insiders could be induced to disclose their information via some form of signalling or screening strategy. This chapter is concerned with questions relating to the control of the behaviour of the relatively well informed by the relatively less informed. This subject area has come to be known in the economic literature as *agency theory*. Broadly speaking agency theory is concerned with the study of contractual relationships that involve the delegation of some degree of decision-making autonomy to one or more parties to the contract. The simplest instance of an agency relationship is one in which one party (known as the principal) hires another party (known as the agent) to undertake certain activities on behalf of the principal.

Several real-life situations lend themselves to agency-theoretic analysis: for example, owner/manager, insurer/insuree, client/lawyer, patient/doctor. Consider, for example, a contract between an insurance company and an insuree. Suppose, in return for an annual premium, the insurance company agrees to indemnify the insuree against personal accident. The trouble with such a contract from the insurer's point of view is that it imposes no restrictions on the activities of the insuree. In particular the insuree may have a reduced incentive to avoid dangerous pastimes. Because of this possibility the insurer may place restrictions on the observable circumstances under which it will pay compensation to the insuree.

The insurer/insuree relationship is an example of the general agency relationship with the principal identified as the insurer and the agent as the insuree. The insurance relationship involves a contract under which the insurer pays out compensation only if certain observable events occur. The relationship is an agency relationship because the probability of the insured event occurring is, at least partially, dependent on the actions of the agent.

From an economic point of view probably the most important agency relationships are the contractual relationships between the managers and the various classes of outside investors in large public companies. One purpose of this chapter is to examine these relationships using the concepts of agency theory.

Our discussion of agency theory will be divided into two main parts. This division reflects the fact that the agency literature itself has developed along two fairly distinct lines. On the one hand there is a body of literature that is largely concerned with the design of optimal incentive contracts in situations involving uncertainty. We will refer to this literature as the *principal–agent literature*. On the other hand there is a second agency literature which is non-mathematical and positively oriented. We will refer to this literature as the *positive agency literature*.

The first part of this chapter presents an overview of the principal–agent literature. It begins by providing an example of the model underlying the principal–agent literature. This example is followed by a more formal statement of the model and a brief section on multiperiod versions of the model. The next section considers the effects of information in an agency context. Part 1 concludes with a discussion of some recent attempts to integrate the principal–agent model with the mainstream theory of finance.

The second part of the chapter provides an introduction to the main concepts and themes of the positive agency literature.

PART 1
The Principal–Agent Literature

8.2 AN EXAMPLE OF THE PRINCIPAL–AGENT MODEL

The model underlying the principal–agent literature considers a situation where one person (the principal) hires another person (the agent) to perform some activity. All such models have two common features. First the agent has some degree of decision-making autonomy; that is, there are certain decision variables over which the agent exercises choice which influence the welfare of both the principal and the agent. Second the principal and the agent differ in their preferences over the alternative possible levels of the agent's decision variables; that is, there is a degree of conflict between the objectives of the principal and the agent. For example, it is often assumed in agency models that the total monetary

Table 8.1   Example of the principal-agent model

	States probabilities			
Effort level	s_1 0.3	s_2 0.3	s_3 0.2	s_4 0.2
$e_1 = 6$	55,000	55,000	55,000	40,000
$e_2 = 5$	55,000	55,000	40,000	40,000
$e_3 = 4$	55,000	40,000	40,000	40,000

payoff to the agency depends partly on the state of the world and partly on the amount of effort exerted by the agent. The principal is assumed to prefer more money to less and to be indifferent to the level of effort exerted by the agent. The agent also prefers more money to less but derives disutility from the exercise of effort.

Table 8.1 provides a simple numerical example of the agency model. In this example the agent can choose one of three alternative effort levels. The total monetary payoff to the agency is influenced by both the agent's effort level and the state of the world. If state 1 occurs the payoff is 55,000 whatever the effort level. If state 2 occurs the payoff is 40,000 if e_3 is selected or 55,000 otherwise, and so on. The reader should be able to see that increasing effort shifts the cumulative probability distribution of payoff to the right. This is illustrated in figure 8.1. The cumulative density function (CDF) under effort level e_3 is zero up to 40,000 when it jumps to 0.7 and then there

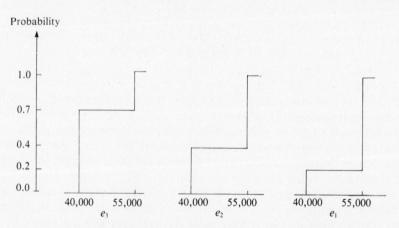

Figure 8.1   Cumulative density functions for three effort levels

is a further jump to 1.0 at 55,000. Under effort level e_2 the CDF jumps from 0.4 to 1.0 at 55,555, and so on. In effect increasing effort increases the probability of the higher payoffs.

The simplest agency model assumes that the principal is risk-neutral and that he prefers more money to less. Let X denote the total realized payoff and X_p denote the principal's share of the payoff. Let X_a be the agent's share of the payoff, that is, X less X_p. Let us assume that the agent has a utility function of the following form:

$$\text{agent's utility} = X_a^{1/2} - e^2$$

The agent derives utility from money and disutility from effort. The utility derived from money is equal to the square root of the agent's monetary payoff. Among other things this ensures that the agent is risk-averse with respect to monetary payoffs. The agent's disutility from effort is equal to the effort level squared.

To see some of the implications of the conflict of interest between the principal and the agent, suppose first that the agent is guaranteed a fixed reward of 13,456. Since the principal receives the residual payoff he will want the agent to select effort level 1. However since the agent is guaranteed 13,456 whatever the realized payoff, it would be irrational for her to select effort level 1. She will maximize her utility by adopting effort level 3 (our examples assume a male principal and a female agent).

Because of this conflict of interest it may be sensible for the principal to design a contract that provides the agent with an incentive to exert greater effort. Such a contract will be acceptable to the agent so long as her expected utility under the new contract is at least as great as it was under the old contract, namely, $(13,456)^{1/2} - 4^2 = 100$. Suppose, for example, that the principal can directly observe the agent's effort level. Then the principal will be able to offer a contract whereby the agent is paid 18,496 if and only if the agent selects effort level e_1. If the agent selects e_1 her expected utility will be the same as it was under the original contract so she would have no reason to reject the principal's proposal. The principal, on the other hand, will be better off under the new contract than he was under the original contract because his expected payoff under the new contract will be 33,504, whilst it was only 31,044 under the original contract. This type of contract is referred to as a 'forcing' contract because its terms effectively force the agent to adopt the effort level specified by the principal.

Whilst a forcing contract is an attractive solution to the agency problem, in many real-life situations it may not be feasible if the principal cannot observe the agent's effort level. Under these more realistic circumstances the reward function of the agent must be related to variables that are

Table 8.2 Expected utility of the agent when the principal is guaranteed a fixed payoff of 32,750

Effort level	Expected utility of the agent
e_1	$(55000 - 32750)^{1/2}.(0.8) + (40000 - 32750)^{1/2}.(0.2) - 36 = 100.36$
e_2	$(55000 - 32750)^{1/2}.(0.6) + (40000 - 32750)^{1/2}.(0.4) - 25 = 98.56$
e_3	$(55000 - 32750)^{1/2}.(0.3) + (40000 - 32750)^{1/2}.(0.7) - 16 = 88.35$

observable by both parties. Suppose, for example, that the principal can only observe the realized payoff. Is there any way that the principal can supply the agent with an incentive to exert effort whilst maintaining the agent's utility at 100? One possibility would be for the principal to offer a contract under which the principal receives a fixed payoff with the agent receiving the residual payoff. The guaranteed payoff to the principal must be chosen so as to maintain the expected payoff of the agent at 100. In fact it is not difficult to show that the agent can maintain her expected utility of 100 if the principal is guaranteed a payoff of 32,750. This is illustrated in table 8.2, which shows that the agent's expected utility will be 100 if she adopts the effort level e_1. Under this new contract the principal has an expected payoff of 32,750 which is better than his payoff under the original contract but not as much as it was under the 'ideal' forcing contract.

The question we now need to consider is whether this new contract is Pareto efficient within the limitations imposed by the fact that the principal can only observe the realized payoff. In particular we need to consider whether any other contractual arrangement would yield a higher utility for the principal whilst maintaining the agent's expected utility at 100. To examine this question let R_{55} be the amount paid to the agent if the payoff is 55,000 and R_{40} be the agent's reward if 40,000 is realized. Let $\phi_{55}(e)$ be the probability of a payoff of 55,000 as a function of the agent's effort level. Thus $\phi_{55}(e_1)$ equals 0.8, and so on. To achieve the effort level e_1 the values R_{55} and R_{40} will have to satisfy the following constraints:

$$R_{55}^{1/2}\phi_{55}(e_1) + R_{40}^{1/2}\phi_{40}(e_1) - e_1^2 = 100 \qquad (8.1)$$

$$R_{55}^{1/2}\phi_{55}(e_1) + R_{40}^{1/2}\phi_{40}(e_1) - e_1^2 \geq R_{55}^{1/2}\phi_{55}(e_2) + R_{40}^{1/2}\phi_{40}(e_2) - e_2^2 \qquad (8.2a)$$

$$R_{55}^{1/2}\phi_{55}(e_1) + R_{40}^{1/2}\phi_{40}(e_1) - e_1^2 \geq R_{55}^{1/2}\phi_{55}(e_3) + R_{40}^{1/2}\phi_{40}(e_3) - e_3^2 \qquad (8.2b)$$

The expression on the left hand side of (8.1) is the agent's expected utility if she adopts e_1. This is to be maintained at 100. The constraints (8.2a) and (8.2b) are referred to as the *incentive compatibility constraints*. These ensure that the agent will be motivated to select e_1 by requiring the agent's expected utility under e_1 to be at least as great as it would be under any other effort level. For example, (8.2a) requires the agent's expected utility under e_1 to be at least as great as her expected utility under e_2.

To find the optimum way of achieving e_1 the principal must solve the following constrained optimization problem:

$$\text{maximize } (55{,}000 - R_{55})\, \phi_{55}(e_1) + (40{,}000 - R_{40})\phi_{40}(e_1) \qquad (8.3)$$

subject to (8.1), (8.2a) and (8.2b)

Here the objective function of the principal, equation (8.3), is to maximize his expected net payoff under effort level e_1. The choice variables of the principal are R_{55} and R_{40}. These must be chosen to maximize (8.3) subject to maintaining the agent's expected utility at 100 and subject to the incentive compatibility constraints. The optimum solution to this problem is to set R_{55} equal to 21,609 and R_{40} equal to 8,464. This yields an expected payoff to the principal of 33,020 which is an improvement over the contract under which the principal receives a fixed reward of 32,750. To see exactly how this improvement is achieved it is instructive to compare the payoffs of the two parties under the two alternative contracts. These are given in table 8.3.

Under contract A the principal is guaranteed 32,750 whilst the agent receives 22,250 with a probability of 0.8 and 7,250 with a probability of 0.2. Under contract B the agent receives 8,464 with a probability of 0.2 and 21,609 with a probability of 0.8. Although contract B offers the agent a lower expected payoff than contract A it is nevertheless just as attractive as contract A because its payoff structure is less risky. Hence by sharing some of the risk the principal is able to increase his own expected payoff whilst maintaining the expected utility of the agent.

This is not the end of the story. There is further scope for improving the principal's payoff whilst maintaining the agent's welfare. Notice that we have so far implicitly assumed that the Pareto efficient effort level when the principal cannot observe the agent's effort level is the same as it was

Table 8.3 Payoffs of principal and agent under alternative contracts

Realized payoff of the agency	$\phi(e_1)$	Principal's payoff		Agent's payoff	
		Contract A	Contract B	Contract A	Contract B
55,000	0.8	32,750	33,391	22,250	21,609
40,000	0.2	32,750	31,536	7,250	8,464

when the principal could use the forcing contract. In fact it is quite possible for the optimum effort level in the absence of perfect observability of effort to be different from the Pareto efficient effort level in the presence of perfect information. This can be demonstrated in the context of our present example. In particular by setting R_{55} equal to 18,769 and R_{40} equal to 11,449 the principal can induce the agent to select effort level e_2, yielding an expected utility to the agent of 100 and an expected payoff to the principal of 33,159. Within the restrictions imposed by the principal's limited observational powers this contract yields the largest expected payoff to the principal whilst maintaining the expected utility of the agent at 100. Also by subtracting the expected payoff of the principal under this optimum contract from his expected payoff under the forcing contract we arrive at his willingness to pay for perfect information, that is, the principal is willing to pay up to $33,504 - 33,159 = 345$ to observe the agent's effort level.

8.3 A FORMAL STATEMENT OF THE PRINCIPAL–AGENT MODEL

The principal–agent model involves a single agent and a single principal in a single-period context. The principal hires the agent to supply effort. As a reward for her effort the agent is given a share in the output from her labours. We adopt the following assumptions:

1 The payoff from the agent's effort is subject to uncertainty. Specifically there are V possible payoff levels labelled X_1 to X_V and, without loss of generality, $X_{v+1} > X_v$ for all $v = 1, \ldots, V$.
2 Let $\phi_v(e)$ stand for the probability of payoff X_v if the agent exerts effort level e. We assume that the principal and the agent have homogeneous beliefs. We define the cumulative payoff distribution, given effort level e, as

$$F_v(e) = \sum_{i \leq v} \phi_i(e)$$

3 The agent is productive in the sense that an increase in e shifts the cumulative payoff distribution to the right, that is, if e_2 is greater than e_1 then, for any v

$$F_v(e_1) \geq F_v(e_2) \tag{8.4}$$

and (8.4) holds with strict inequality for at least one v.
4 The effort level is assumed to be unobservable by the principal either

directly or indirectly. Consistent with this assumption we assume that $\phi_v(e)$ is strictly positive for all v and all possible e. This ensures that it is never possible to infer e from the observed payoff. In the terminology of chapter 7 the support of the payoff distribution is independent of the effort level.

5 Both the principal and the agent observe the payoff. The principal observes no other information.

6 The agent's utility if payoff X_v occurs can be expressed as

$$U_a(R_v) - D(e)$$

where $U_a(.)$ is the agent's (strictly concave) utility for money function; R_v is the reward received by the agent if payoff X_v is realized; and $D(.)$ is increasing and strictly convex in effort and represents the agent's disutility from effort.

7 The principal's utility if payoff X_v occurs can be expressed as

$$U_p(X_v - R_v)$$

where U_p is increasing and concave in money and represents the principal's utility from his net payoff, that is, the gross payoff X_v less the reward paid to the agent.

Now let $R = (R_1, \ldots, R_V)$. Then the principal's decision problem can be expressed formally as follows:

$$\text{maximize}_{R,e} \sum_v U_p(X_v - R_v) \cdot \phi_v(e) \qquad (8.5)$$

subject to

$$\sum_v U_a(R_v) \phi_v(e) - D(e) \geq EU \qquad (8.6)$$

and

$$e \in \text{argmax}_{\hat{e} \in E} \left(\sum_v U_a(R_v) \phi_v(\hat{e}) - D(\hat{e}) \right) \qquad (8.7)$$

Expression (8.5) is simply the expected utility of the principal, given R and the effort level e. The principal chooses the reward vector R and the effort level e to maximize (8.5) subject to two constraints. The first constraint, expressed by inequality (8.6), requires the expected utility of the agent (the left hand side of (8.6)) to be at least as great as the expected utility that she could get by refusing to work for the principal (represented by EU). We will refer to EU as the agent's reservation level of utility. The second constraint, represented by (8.7), captures the idea that the level of e chosen by the principal must be incentive-compatible. In particular, since it is the agent who ultimately controls the effort level, the principal must supply the agent with appropriate incentives to induce her to adopt the desired level of *e*. This is represented by (8.7) which requires *e* to be an element of the argmax of the term in brackets. The argmax is the set of *e* values that maximize the term inside the brackets. The term inside the brackets is the expected utility of the agent under the reward vector *R* and effort level *e*. Hence the effect of (8.7) is to require the desired level of effort to be a utility-maximizing choice for the agent when faced by the reward vector *R*.

A Useful Simplification

The presence of (8.7) in the principal's problem makes it difficult to analyse. Fortunately there exists a simplification of the model which is valid in a wide range of circumstances. This simplification is known as the 'first-order approach' and involves the replacement of (8.7) by the following first-order condition:

$$\sum_s U_a(R_v)\phi_v'(e) - D'(e) = 0 \tag{8.8}$$

Equation (8.8) follows if one assumes that the agent's optimum effort choice can be represented as a stationary point of her effort choice problem. In general the agent's effort choice problem involves choosing *e* so as to maximize her expected utility, that is,

$$\max_e \sum_v U_a(R_v)\phi_v(e) - D(e) \tag{8.9}$$

By differentiating (8.9) with respect to *e* and setting the result equal to zero we get equation (8.8). Under certain conditions (8.8) will be both necessary and sufficient for an optimum solution to the agent's choice problem. When these conditions hold we can replace (8.7) by the more tractable (8.8). In fact the precise conditions under which (8.7) can be safely replaced by (8.8) is a subject of ongoing research. Rogerson (1985), following earlier work by Mirlees (1975), has shown that the following additional assumptions are sufficient to justify the first-order approach:

8 The functions $\phi_v(e)$ satisfy the *monotone likelihood ratio condition* (MLRC): if $\hat{e} < \hat{\hat{e}}$ then $\phi_v(\hat{e})/\phi_v(\hat{\hat{e}})$ must be non-increasing in *v*.
9 The functions $\phi_v(e)$ satisfy the *convexity of the distribution function condition* (CDFC): $F_v''(e)$ must be non-negative for every *v* and every possible value of *e*.

The MLRC strengthens assumption 3. For any two payoff levels *v* and *v'* such that $v' > v$ it requires the relative probability of *v'* to *v* to increase with the level of effort. In a world where the functions $\phi_v(e)$ are differentiable in e this condition is equivalent to the requirement that $\phi_v'(e)/\phi_v(e)$ be non-decreasing in v for every possible effort level.

The CDFC further strengthens assumption 3 which requires $F_v(e)$ to be decreasing in e. In particular the CDFC requires $F_v''(e)$ to be non-negative. In other words $F_v(e)$ should decrease *at a decreasing rate* as e increases. The CDFC can be interpreted as a kind of stochastic diminishing returns to scale.

Analysis of the Simplified Model

Given assumptions 1 to 9 the model can be expressed as follows:

$$\text{maximize}_{\substack{R,e}} \sum_v U_p(X_v - R_v)\phi_v(e) \tag{8.5}$$

subject to

$$\sum_v U_a(R_v)\phi_v(e) - D(e) \geq EU \tag{8.6}$$

and

$$\sum_v U_a(R_v)\phi_v'(e) - D'(e) = 0 \tag{8.8}$$

This problem can be solved by introducing Lagrange multipliers on (8.6) and (8.8) and differentiating the resultant expression with respect to R and e to yield the following first-order conditions: (8.6) and (8.8) plus

$$U_p'(X_v - R_v)/U_a'(R_v) = \lambda + \mu \ \phi_v'(e)/\phi_v(e) \qquad \text{for all } v \tag{8.10}$$

$$\sum_v U_p(X_v - R_v) \ \phi_v'(e) + \mu (\sum_v U_a(R_v) \ \phi_v''(e) - D''(e)) = 0 \tag{8.11}$$

where λ is the Lagrange multiplier on (8.6), μ is the Lagrange multiplier on (8.8), and the double primes represent second-order derivatives.

In discussing these conditions it is interesting to compare them with the analogous conditions that hold when (8.8) is not a binding constraint, that is, when observational limitations can be ignored. In this case the first-order condition analogous to (8.10) becomes

$$U_p'(X_v - R_v)/U_a'(R_v) = \lambda \qquad \text{for all } v \tag{8.12}$$

Condition (8.12) is the first-order condition for full Pareto efficient risk sharing familiar from chapter 2. It is instructive to consider the implications of (8.12) in some detail. In particular suppose that the principal is risk-neutral so that U_p' is a constant. Then (8.12) implies that U_a' and hence R_v must also be constant. In other words for first best risk sharing, given a risk-neutral principal and a risk-averse agent, the principal should bear all the risk of the stochastic cash flow and the agent should receive a fixed reward independent of the realized payoff.

In contrast, when (8.8) is a binding constraint the optimum reward as a function of the realized payoff will no longer be constant. Holmstrom (1979) has shown that both λ and μ will be strictly positive in the optimum solution to the principal's problem. Given assumptions 1 and 9 this in turn implies that R_v will increase with v. To see this note that the MLRC implies that $\phi_v'(e)/\phi_v(e)$ is increasing in v. Hence as v increases the right hand side of (8.10) increases. Hence, given assumptions 6 and 7, it follows that R_v must be an increasing function of v.

Once incentive compatibility considerations are admitted into the model the optimum reward vector will no longer satisfy the conditions for full Pareto efficient risk sharing. This is because the agent has an inadequate incentive to supply effort if she is fully insured against any variation in the payoff. In order to induce the agent to supply effort the principal has to impose a greater burden of risk on the agent than would be optimal if the effort level was observable or if the agent could costlessly precommit herself to the first best effort level. This breakdown in the optimality of the risk-sharing arrangement is referred to as the *moral hazard problem* in the agency literature.

8.4 MULTIPERIOD EXTENSIONS OF THE PRINCIPAL–AGENT MODEL

By extending the principal–agent model to incorporate multiple time periods one can examine several important new questions such as:

1 Will the optimum reward function for any period depend on the payoff realized in any earlier period?
2 Will the optimum reward function for each period differ from the optimum reward function in a single-period context?
3 Will the optimum effort level in any period depend on the payoff realized in any earlier period?
4 Will the optimum effort level in any period differ from the optimum effort level in a single-period context?
5 In a model where the same agency relationship is repeated over time does the expected utility of the principal per time period increase with T (the number of repetitions)?
6 In a repeated situation will first best Pareto efficiency be approached as T tends to infinity?

Lambert (1983) has presented a multiperiod agency model which helps to shed some light on questions 1 to 5. The model adopts the following assumptions:

(a) The agency relationship is repeated over T periods.
(b) The effort level in period t affects the payoff in period t only.

(c) The states of nature that influence the payoff of each period are distributed independently over time.

(d) The agent has no borrowing or lending opportunities.

(e) Both the agent and the principal precommit to a long-term contract under which the principal agrees to employ the agent for all T periods and the agent agrees not to leave the firm.[1]

Given these assumptions Lambert shows that the optimum reward function for each period will normally depend on the payoff realized in earlier periods, that is, affirmative answers are given to questions 1 and 2. He also shows for the special case in which exactly the same agency relationship is repeated over time, that the expected utility of the principal per time period increases with the number of repetitions, that is, an affirmative answer is given to question 5.

In a later contribution Lambert (1984) presents a special case of his model which he uses to examine questions 3 and 4. For this special case he shows that the effort level of one period will be a decreasing function of the payoff realized in the previous period.

Papers by Radner (1980), and Rubinstein and Yaari (1983) have examined the implications of models in which the same agency relationship is repeated an infinite number of times.[2] The Rubinstein and Yaari paper assumes a risk-neutral principal, that the agent has no lending or borrowing opportunities, and that both the agent and principal have zero rates of time preference. They show that, given these assumptions, it is possible to sustain the first best[3] effort level and the first best level of expected utility by a form of 'trigger' contract under which the agent is given the first best reward in period t so long as the average payoff in the periods prior to t is not 'significantly' less than the expected payoff under the first best effort level. If the average payoff for the periods prior to t falls 'significantly' below the first best expected payoff the agent is given a lower (penal) reward until the average payoff returns to a satisfactory level.

The tricky feature of this reward structure is the determination of what constitutes a 'significant' deviation from the expected payoff level. The problem here is that if the allowable deviation is set too large then the agent will be able to get away with a lower effort level without being detected, whilst if the allowable deviation is set too small the agent will suffer penalties when they are not deserved. Rubinstein and Yaari make use of advanced probability theory to show how this problem can be overcome.

For present purposes the importance of the papers reviewed in this section is the finding that the losses from moral hazard can be significantly reduced by long-term contracts. However, such losses disappear entirely only when the parties to the contract have infinite lives and zero rates of time preference. A major limitation of these papers is the assumption that the agent has no access to borrowing and lending opportunities. Moreover, according to Lambert (1983), it will be difficult to incorporate a capital market into the analysis, principally because the agent's effort strategy cannot then be assumed to be independent of her saving decision. For the finance theorist the inability to incorporate saving and lending decisions is currently a major limitation of the principal–agent approach which will have to be overcome if successful integration with mainstream finance theory is to be achieved.

8.5   INFORMATION IN THE PRINCIPAL–AGENT MODEL

Alternative Information Scenarios

In discussing the effects of information in an agency context it is helpful to distinguish different types of information according to its timing and according to its distribution between the principal and the agent. The main distinctions of interest are set out in table 8.4.

Table 8.4   Types of information

	Distribution	
Timing	Private to the agent	Public
Pre-contract	A	B
Pre-effort	C	D
Post-effort, pre-payoff	E	F (Formally equivalent to category H)
Post-payoff – *ex post* information	G	H

The table distinguishes eight information scenarios according to two criteria. The first criterion distinguishes information that is received privately by the agent from information that is observed by both parties. The second criterion refers to the time at which the information is received relative to certain critical events in the agency contract. These critical events are illustrated in figure 8.2 which shows the time line of a typical agency contract.

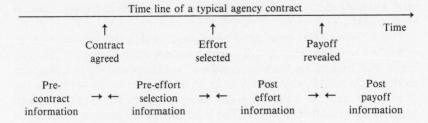

Figure 8.2 Time line of a typical agency contract

Figure 8.2 illustrates three critical events in an agency contract: the agreement of the contract, the selection of the effort level by the agent, and the realization of the payoff. With reference to these three events there are four possible time periods during which information might be received: before a contract has been agreed, before effort selection, after effort selection but before the payoff is observed, and after the realization of the payoff.

With regard to the eight categories identified by table 8.4 very little has been written on categories A and B. Readers interested in these categories should find Sappington (1984) to be a useful starting point. Dye (1983) has explored category E. He has shown that such information can be of value to the agency, in the sense that it can be used to achieve a Pareto improvement if the agent can communicate with the principal. Most of the available literature has focused on categories C, D and H. The remainder of this section provides an overview of this literature beginning with category H. It will also be shown why category G information has no value.

Public Post-Payoff (Ex-Post) Information (Category H)

This category has proved to be the one most amenable to formal analysis. Two normative issues have been the main object of inquiry:

1 Under what conditions will the introduction of *ex post* information yield a strict Pareto improvement?
2 Under what conditions will one *ex post* information function Pareto dominate another?

In both cases attention has been directed towards discovering general results which do not depend on the details of the beliefs or preferences of the principal and the agent. The rest of this subsection focuses on the first issue. Readers interested in the second issue should consult Gjesdal (1981, 1982).

Holmstrom (1979) gives conditions under which the introduction of public *ex post* information will yield a strict Pareto improvement. The basic idea behind his findings can best be understood by recalling the example discussed in section 8.2. In that example we showed that the principal's expected utility if he can observe the agent's effort level will typically be greater than it would be if he could only observe the realized payoff. Intuitively, therefore, it seems reasonable to expect that any information function that contains information about the agent's effort level over and above that contained in the realized payoff will be of potential value to a principal who only observes the realized payoff. This intuition is confirmed by Holmstrom (1979) who also provides a formal characterization of the idea that an information function contains information about the effort level over and above that contained in the realized payoff.

We shall now present Holmstrom's findings formally. Let η be an *ex post* information function with possible signals y_i, $i = 1, \ldots, Y$. Let $\phi_{vi}(e)$ denote the probability of signal y_i and payoff X_v, given effort level e. Since the principal observes both X_v and y_i it is legitimate to express the reward paid to the agent as a function of both X_v and y_i. Therefore let R_{vi} denote the reward paid to the agent if both payoff X_v and signal y_i occur.

In the presence of *ex post* information, the first-order condition for a Pareto efficient reward function corresponding to (8.10) above becomes:

$$U_p'(X_v - R_{vi})/ U_a'(R_{vi}) = \lambda + \mu \quad \phi_{vi}'(e)/\phi_{vi}(e) \quad \text{for all } v \text{ and all } i \quad (8.13)$$

Comparing (8.13) with (8.10) it seems reasonable to suggest that the information function will be of no value if $\phi_{vi}'(e)/\phi_{vi}(e)$ is independent of i for all v and all e since it will then be possible to satisfy (8.13) with a reward function that is independent of i. Indeed Holmstrom (1979) proves exactly this; an information function will be of no value if $\phi_{vi}'(e)/\phi_{vi}(e)$ is independent of i for all v and e. Moreover Holmstrom also shows that if $\phi_{vi}'(e)/\phi_{vi}(e)$ is not independent of i for all v and e then the information function will be of value to the principal. In other words he shows that a necessary and sufficient condition for an information function to be of no value is that $\phi_{vi}'(e)/\phi_{vi}(e)$ be independent of i for all v and all e.

Holmstrom also derives the following equivalent condition for an *ex post* information function to be of no value. He shows that $\phi_{vi}'(e)/\phi_{vi}(e)$

will be independent of i for all v and all e if and only if the probability function $\phi_{vi}(e)$ can be expressed as follows:[4]

$$\phi_{vi}(e) = g(v, i)h(v, e) \tag{8.14}$$

Equation (8.14) expresses the probability function $\phi_{vi}(e)$ as a product of two other functions, one of which depends only on v and i, the other of which depends only on e and v. If (8.14) holds, *ex post* information will be of no value to the principal. On the other hand if (8.14) does not hold then *ex post* information will be of value to the principal.

To see the intuition behind (8.14) it is instructive to view the principal as a statistician who is attempting to infer the effort level of the agent from the observed values of v and i. He knows that the joint probability distribution of v and i depends on the level of e. In statistical theory v is said to be a sufficient statistic for i with respect to e if and only if the conditional distribution of i given v is independent of e for all values of v.[5] Moreover one can show that v will be a sufficient statistic for i with respect to e if and only if (8.14) holds. In statistical theory (8.14) is known as the factorization criterion for a sufficient statistic. Hence, in terms of the language of statistical theory, equation (8.14) states that an information function will be of no value to the principal if and only if the observed payoff is a sufficient statistic for the payoff and the realized signal with respect to e.

Further insight into (8.14) is supplied by the numerical example below which assumes that all six states are equally likely:

	s_1	s_2	s_3	s_4	s_5	s_6
$e_1 = 10$	2	3	3	4	5	5
$e_2 = 5$	2	2	3	4	4	5

Consider the following information function:

$$\{s_1\} \mapsto y_1$$
$$\{s_2, s_3\} \mapsto y_2$$
$$\{s_4, s_5, s_6\} \mapsto y_3$$

This information function is valuable because the realized payoff is not a sufficient statistic for the signal. In particular consider signal 2. The probability of signal 2 given a payoff of 2 and effort level 1 is equal to zero. The probability of signal 2 given a payoff of 2 and effort level 2 is equal to $\frac{1}{2}$. Notice also that the principal would be able to use a forcing contract to enforce effort level 1 if he had access to this information function since he could write a contract under which the agent agrees to pay a severe penalty if signal 2 is observed simultaneously with a realized payoff of 2.

Now consider the following information function:

$$\{s_1, s_2, s_3\} \mapsto y_1$$
$$\{s_4, s_5, s_6\} \mapsto y_2$$

This information function is of no value because it provides no information over and above that provided by the payoff. The conditional probability of y_1 given X_v for both levels of e is given below:

$$\phi(y_1/X_v = 2, \ e = 10) = 1 \qquad \phi(y_1/X_v = 2, \ e = 5) = 1$$
$$\phi(y_1/X_v = 3, \ e = 10) = 1 \qquad \phi(y_1/X_v = 3, \ e = 5) = 1$$
$$\phi(y_1/X_v = 4, \ e = 10) = 0 \qquad \phi(y_1/X_v = 4, \ e = 5) = 0$$
$$\phi(y_1/X_v = 5, \ e = 10) = 0 \qquad \phi(y_1/X_v = 5, \ e = 5) = 0$$

Clearly the distribution of the two signals is independent of e for each possible value of X_v, that is, the payoff is a sufficient statistic for X_v and i with respect to e.

Private Information Received Prior to
Effort Selection (Category C)

Suppose that a private information function can be made available to the agent with the signals received before she makes her effort selection. Will the introduction of such information always allow the principal to effect a Pareto improvement? Perhaps surprisingly the answer to this question is *no*. It is possible to construct examples in which the introduction of private pre-effort information results in a deterioration in the principal's welfare. It is also possible to construct examples in which the principal's welfare improves as a result of giving the agent access to private information.

To illustrate these possibilities consider the following example which draws on the work of Christensen (1981, 1982).

As in the examples of section 8.1 we assume that the principal is risk-neutral and that the agent's utility function can be expressed as $U_a = R^{1/2} - e^2$. We also assume that the agent's reservation level of utility is 100. The payoff matrix is as below (all states are equally likely):

	s_1	s_2	s_3	s_4
$e_1 = 0$	0	0	0	0
$e_2 = 5$	20,000	20,000	25,000	30,000
$e_3 = 6$	20,000	30,000	30,000	35,000

If the principal can observe the agent's effort level the Pareto efficient effort level will be e_3 with the agent receiving a reward of 18,496 if and only if she supplies the agreed level of effort. The principal's expected payoff will be 10,254.

If the principal can only observe the realized payoff he will be able to enforce the effort level e_3 by paying the agent 18,496 if a payoff of 20,000, 30,000, or 35,000 is observed and zero if any other payoff is observed. To see that this will induce the agent to select e_3 note that the agent's expected utility will be zero if she adopts effort level 1 and 77 (that is, $(0.75) 18,496^{1/2} - 25$) if she adopts e_2. Hence the best the agent can do for herself is to select effort level 3 giving an expected utility of 100. Note that in this example the principal is able to achieve the first best outcome even though he only observes the realized payoff.

To see the effect of allowing the agent access to private information suppose the agent is supplied with the following information function:

$$\{s_1, s_2\} \mapsto y_1$$
$$\{s_3, s_4\} \mapsto y_2$$

In this case the payoff function which was optimal in the absence of private information will no longer induce the agent to select e_3 in all states of the world. In particular the agent will be able to reduce her effort level to e_2 without penalty whenever she observes signal 1. In this situation the Pareto efficient reward function can be shown to be $R_{20} = 14,722$, $R_{30} = 20,544$ and $R_{35} = 18,496$ and zero otherwise where, for example, R_{20} denotes the reward paid to the agent if a payoff of 20,000 is realized. The Pareto efficient effort strategy is for the agent to adopt e_3 under both signals. This new reward function yields an expected payoff of 10,173 to the principal, less than his expected reward when the agent received no private information.[6]

For an example in which private information leads to a Pareto improvement consider the example below which is almost the same as the previous one except for row 2 of the payoff matrix.

	s_1	s_2	s_3	s_4
$e_1 = 0$	0	0	0	0
$e_2 = 5$	20,000	25,000	25,000	30,000
$e_3 = 6$	20,000	30,000	30,000	35,000

As in the previous example the optimum effort level if the agent has no private information is e_3. This can be achieved by a contract under which the agent receives 18,496 if a payoff of 20,000, 30,000, or 35,000 is realized and zero if any other payoff is realized. The principal's expected payoff will be 10,254 as before.

Now consider the implications of introducing the same information function considered in the previous example. In this case it will still be possible to induce the effort level e_3 under both signals without changing the reward contract. However this will no longer be a Pareto efficient reward contract. The principal can do even better by introducing the following reward contract: pay the agent 15,170 if the payoff is 20,000 or 25,000, pay 17,030 if the payoff is 30,000, and pay 21,074 if the payoff is 35,000.

To see how this reward structure would affect the behaviour of the agent first consider how the agent will react if she receives signal 1. In this case her expected utility if she adopts e_2 will be 98.17 ($= 15,170^{1/2} - 25$). If she adopts e_3 her expected utility will be 90.8 (that is, $15,170^{1/2}(0.5) + 17,030^{1/2}(0.5) - 36$). Hence she will adopt e_2 if she receives signal 1. If she receives signal 2 she will adopt effort level e_3 yielding an expected utility of 101.83. Her overall expected utility averaged over the two signals will be 100 as required. The average gross payoff will be 27,500 and the average reward paid to the agent will be 17,111. Hence the principal's expected payoff will be 10,389 which represents an improvement over the situation where the agent receives no private information.

These two examples clearly illustrate why it is that the introduction of private information can sometimes improve the principal's welfare and sometimes reduce the principal's welfare. In the first example the principal was able to achieve the first best position, in the absence of private information, by using a kind of forcing contract. The agent could not risk adopting e_2 for fear of a payoff occurring under which she would receive no reward. However, once she has access to private information she no longer runs any risk of incurring a zero reward if she adopts e_2 when she observes signal 1. Hence the agent is able to 'shirk' without penalty because the shirking remains undetected by the principal.

The possibility that the agent may use her private information to shirk is a potential cost of allowing the agent access to private information. Our second example illustrated a potential advantage from the provision of such information. In this example the marginal productivity of moving from e_2 to e_3 differs substantially according to whether signal 1 or signal 2 is received. If signal 1 is received the increase in the gross expected payoff associated with an increase in effort from e_2 to e_3 is only 2,500. On the other hand when signal 2 is received the increase in the gross expected payoff is 5,000. It therefore makes sense for the agent to adopt e_2 when the marginal productivity of effort is low and to adopt e_3 when the marginal productivity of effort is high.

To summarize, there are two possible effects associated with the provision of private information to the agent prior to effort selection. On the one hand there is a danger that the agent may use the information to shirk. On the other hand potential benefits arise from the possibility of the agent adjusting her effort level in line with the marginal productivity of effort signalled by the private information. Whether or not the principal becomes better or worse off depends on which of these two effects is the more important.

Finally the reader should now be able to appreciate why it is that category G information has no value. Since category G information is received privately it cannot be used as a basis for contract enforcement and, since the information is received ex post it cannot influence the agent's effort choice. Hence, since it can have no effect, it must have no value.

Public Information Received Prior to Effort Selection (Category D)

As in the case of category C information there is no guarantee that the introduction of public information prior to effort selection will result in a Pareto improvement. In particular it is possible for the principal's expected utility to decline as a result of introducing such information.

To see this possibility consider again the first example from the previous subsection but now suppose that the information is observed by both the principal and the agent. In comparison with the case where the information was only observed by the agent the principal has one crucial extra degree of freedom in designing the reward function. He can now allow the reward function to depend on the publicly observed signal as well as the observed payoff. In particular when a payoff of 30,000 is observed the principal can vary the reward paid to the agent depending on whether signal 1 or signal 2 is observed. In this case the optimum reward function can be shown to be the following:

> pay the agent 15,625 if 20,000 is observed
> pay the agent 21,609 if 30,000 *and* signal 1 is observed
> pay the agent 18,496 if 30,000 *and* signal 2 is observed
> pay the agent 18,496 if 35,000 is observed

The reader can check that this reward function will induce the agent to adopt effort level 3 whichever signal is observed. Also her expected utility is maintained at 100. The expected payoff to the principal is 10,193.5 which is better than his expected payoff when the agent received the information privately but not as much as he received when neither party received information.

In general there are two, sometimes counteracting, forces involved when public pre-effort information is introduced into the agency relationship. On the one hand the introduction of public information, whilst holding the agent's information constant, can never result in a Pareto loss and will often result in a Pareto improvement. On the other hand an increase in the information available to the agent at the time she selects her effort can sometimes result in a Pareto loss due to the shirking problem. The previous example has shown that situations can arise where the loss due to shirking exceeds the gain from public information.

Communication in Agencies and the Revelation Principle

The analysis of category C information which we developed above ignored the possibility that the agent may be able to communicate with the principal after receiving her private information. Several articles in the agency literature have shown that it may be possible to increase the principal's welfare if such communication is possible (see, for example, Christensen, 1981, 1982; Baiman and Evans, 1983; Dye, 1983; Penno, 1984). These articles make use of an important result known as the *revelation principle* (due to Myerson, 1979).

The revelation principle provides a convenient theoretical device for handling the possibility that the agent may be tempted to communicate false information to the principal. The revelation principle states that for any optimum solution to the agency problem that involves the communication of false information by the agent, there exists an alternative solution in which the agent is provided with sufficient incentives to tell the truth and that yields the same levels of utility to the principal and the agent. Hence in searching for an optimum solution to any agency problem where communication is allowed the analyst can safely confine attention to the subclass of all possible solutions in which the agent is motivated to tell the truth.

To illustrate the revelation principle consider again the first example of the subsection on category C information but now suppose that the agent can communicate with the principal prior to effort selection by announcing whether she has received signal 1 or signal 2. Suppose also that the contract enforcement system is such that any message sent by the agent can be used as a basis for contracting. Let $R_{v,m}$ denote the reward received by the agent if payoff X_v is observed and if she sends message

m where m can be (signal) 1 or (signal) 2. For example $R_{20,1}$ is the reward received by the agent if a payoff of 20,000 is realized when she sends message 1. The principal's problem for enforcing effort level 3 can be expressed as follows:

Maximize $(20,000 - R_{20,1})(0.25) + (30,000 - R_{30,1})(0.25) +$
$$(30,000 - R_{30,2})(0.25) + (35,000 - R_{35,2})(0.25)$$

subject to

$$R_{20,1}^{1/2}(0.25) + R_{30,1}^{1/2}(0.25) + R_{30,2}^{1/2}(0.25) + R_{35,2}^{1/2}(0.25) - 36 = 100$$

$$R_{20,1}^{1/2}(0.5) + R_{30,1}^{1/2}(0.5) - 36 \geq R_{20,1}^{1/2}(1.0) - 25$$

$$R_{30,2}^{1/2}(0.5) + R_{35,2}^{1/2}(0.5) - 36 \geq R_{25,1}^{1/2}(0.5) + R_{30,2}^{1/2}(0.5) - 25$$

$$R_{20,1}^{1/2}(0.5) + R_{30,1}^{1/2}(0.5) \geq R_{20,2}^{1/2}(0.5) + R_{30,2}^{1/2}(0.5)$$

$$R_{30,2}^{1/2}(0.5) + R_{35,2}^{1/2}(0.5) \geq R_{30,1}^{1/2}(0.5) + R_{35,1}^{1/2}(0.5)$$

Here the objective function is the expected payoff to the principal if the agent adopts effort level 3 and communicates truthfully. The first constraint requires the agent's expected utility to be maintained at 100. The next two constraints are the incentive compatibility constraints. There is one constraint for each signal. Both constraints require the agent's expected utility conditional on the observed signal to be at least as great under effort level 3 as it would be under effort level 2. The final two constraints are called the *truth telling* constraints. For example, the first of these two constraints requires the expected utility of the agent if she receives signal 1 and sends message 1 to be at least as great as her expected utility if she sends message 2 when she receives signal 1.

For this particular example it turns out that the optimum reward function is the same as it would have been if the information was publicly observed. This is the case because if the agent lies she runs the risk of her lie being detected when the payoff is realized. Thus, for example, if she sends message 2 when she receives signal 1 she runs the risk of a payoff of 20,000 occurring which will clearly indicate that she must have lied. In this particular example, therefore, the principal's expected payoff if communication is possible is the same as it was when the information was observed publicly. It is, however, possible to construct examples in which the expected payoff to the principal in the presence of private information and communication falls between his expected payoff when the information is observed publicly and his expected payoff when the information is observed privately but no communication is possible. Of course the expected payoff of the principal when communication is possible is never less than his expected utility when communication is not possible and never more than his expected utility when the pre-effort information is observed publicly.

8.6 THE PRINCIPAL–AGENT MODEL WITH SEVERAL AGENTS

In assessing the performance of an agent it may often be quite sensible to pay some regard to the performance of other agents faced with similar production conditions. For example, in assessing the performance of the management of a firm it may be sensible to compare the performance of the firm with the performances of other firms in the same industry.

There are a number of papers in the principal–agent literature which extend the basic agency model to incorporate several agents. The novel feature of these models is that the reward of each agent now depends not only on the agent's own absolute performance but also on her performance *relative* to the performances of agents faced with similar production conditions.

Holmstrom (1982) and Mookherjee (1984) extend the basic agency model to incorporate several agents. Green and Stokey (1983), Lazear and Ronen (1981) and Nalebluff and Stiglitz (1983) have examined the possibility of rewarding multiple agents according to an ordinal ranking of the performances of the individual agents. However, Holmstrom (1982) has shown that such *rank-order tournaments* may be informationally wasteful if performance levels can be measured cardinally rather than ordinally. More recently a number of papers have examined models with multiple agents in which the agents have access to private pre-effort information (see, for example, Demski and Sappington, 1984).

For present purposes the paper by Holmstrom (1982) is particularly interesting. This paper considers a model involving several agents and a single principal. The output of the ith agent is expressed as

$$x_i = x_i(e_i, z_i) \qquad i = 1, \ldots, I$$

where x_i is the output of agent i; e_i is the effort exerted by agent i; and z_i is some random, non-controllable, and unobservable influence over the output of agent i.

In this model the role of the principal is to choose an I-vector of effort levels $(e_1, \ldots, e_I)$ and I reward functions of the form $R_i(X)$ where $X = (x_1, \ldots, x_I)$. Writing the reward function as a function of the vector X captures the possibility that the reward of the ith agent may depend on the performances of other agents as well as on her own performance. The model also assumes that the agents select their effort levels non-cooperatively, that is, in selecting their own effort levels they treat the actions of the other agents as being beyond their control.

Given the assumptions of his analysis Holmstrom is able to derive conditions under which relative performance evaluation will be valuable. In particular he proves that the reward function of the ith agent will be independent of the performances of the other agents if and only if z_i is, statistically speaking, independent of the random factors that influence the performances of the other agents. In other words, the output of the other agents will be useful for evaluating the performance of agent i if and only if there are common factors that influence the performance of other agents as well as the performance of agent i.

It is important to emphasize the necessary and sufficient nature of Holmstrom's findings. If there is some common underlying uncertainty that influences the performances of the agents then some form of relative performance evaluation will be valuable. On the other hand if there are no common uncertainties then there is no value in relative performance evaluation; inducing competition among agents by tying their rewards to each other's performance has no intrinsic value. What is of value is the information that can be gained from relative performance evaluation.

As an example of his general model Holmstrom considers a special case in which the stochastic relationship between effort and output for each agent can be expressed as follows:

$$x_i = e_i + \theta + \epsilon_i \qquad i = 1, \ldots, I$$

Here both θ and ϵ_i are random factors that influence the output of agent i. The factor θ influences the performance of all agents whilst the factor ϵ_i is assumed to affect the output of agent i only. In other words the ϵ_i are assumed to be cross-sectionally independent. For this special case Holmstrom shows that for very large values of I (strictly speaking, as I approaches infinity) the optimum reward function of the ith agent can be expressed as a function of x minus an estimate of θ, where the estimate of θ is derived according to the following formula:

$$\hat{\theta}_i = \sum_{j \neq i} (x_j - e_j)/(I - 1)$$

Here $\hat{\theta}_i$ is the estimate of θ used to assess the performance of agent i and e_j is the optimum effort level of agent j. In effect, as the number of agents increases towards infinity, the factor θ can be inferred from the performance levels of the $I - 1$ agents other than agent i. The reward of the ith agent can then be related directly to $x_i - \theta$.

8.7   IMPLICATIONS OF THE PRINCIPAL–AGENT MODEL
FOR INVESTMENT POLICY

Most leading textbooks on corporate finance base their discussions of investment policy on a variant of the two-parameter capital asset pricing model (see, for example, Fama and Miller, 1972; Copeland and Weston, 1983; Brealey and Myers, 1984).

According to this model the equilibrium expected rate of return on any asset can be calculated as follows:

$$E(\tilde{r}_i) = r_f + \lambda \text{cov}(\tilde{r}_i, \tilde{r}_m) \qquad (8.15)$$

where $\tilde{r}_i$ is the rate of return on asset i; r_f is the rate of return on a risk-free asset; $\tilde{r}_m$ is the rate of return on the value-weighted market portfolio; $E(\tilde{r}_i)$ is the equilibrium expected rate of return on asset i; $E(\tilde{r}_m)$ is the equilibrium expected rate of return on the value-weighted market portfolio; $\text{cov}(\tilde{r}_i, \tilde{r}_m)$ is the covariance of $\tilde{r}_i$ with $\tilde{r}_m$; and λ is the 'market price of risk' calculated as follows:

$$\lambda = (E(\tilde{r}_m) - r_f)/\sigma^2(\tilde{r}_m)$$

where $\sigma^2(\tilde{r}_m)$ is the variance of $\tilde{r}_m$.

Equation (8.15) is known as the security market line (SML). In words, it states that the equilibrium return on asset i is equal to the risk-free rate plus a premium for risk where the risk premium is calculated as the covariance of $\tilde{r}_i$ with the return on the market portfolio multiplied by the market price of risk.

The SML implies the following formula for valuing a risky cash flow, $\tilde{X}$, where the cash flow is to be received at the end of one period.[7]

$$V(\tilde{X}) = (E(\tilde{X}) - \lambda \text{cov}(\tilde{X}, \tilde{r}_m))/(1 + r_f) \qquad (8.16)$$

The formula (8.16) is known as the certainty-equivalent valuation formula. It sets the value of an uncertain cash flow equal to the certainty equivalent value of the cash flow discounted for one period at the risk-free rate. The certainty equivalent of the cash flow is calculated by deducting a risk premium from the expected value of the cash flow. The key feature of (8.16) is the use of the covariance of X with the return on the market portfolio as the appropriate measure of risk. This is multiplied by the market price of risk in calculating the risk premium. According to this formula it is only the risk that is correlated with the market portfolio that is relevant for valuation. Risk that is uncorrelated with the return on the market portfolio is irrelevant for valuation. Capital market theorists refer to risk that is correlated with the market portfolio as 'systematic risk'. Risk that is uncorrelated with the market portfolio is known as 'unsystematic risk'. Formula (8.16) states that only systematic risk is relevant for valuation.

Formula (8.16) yields a straightforward approach for appraising investment projects involving an immediate (and certain) cash outflow followed by a single cash inflow at the end of one period. According to (8.16) such a project should be implemented if and only if the value of the uncertain end-of-period cash flow given by (8.16) is greater than or equal to the required initial outlay. Similarly in comparing two or more mutually exclusive investment alternatives the firm should select the alternative yielding the largest (positive) difference between the value of its end-of-period cash flow and its initial outlay, that is, the firm should select the alternative with the largest net present value.

Recent papers by Holmstrom (1982), Diamond and Verrecchia (1982) and Ramakrishnan and Thakor (1984) have investigated the implications of principal–agent theory for this popular investment appraisal rule. The basic point of these papers can be demonstrated by considering an economy in which assets are valued according to (8.16) and where the end-of-period cash flows of all investment projects, *prior* to the payment of the project manager's reward, are generated according to a formula of the following form:

$$\tilde{X}_p = e_p + \beta_p \tilde{r}_m + \tilde{\theta}_p \qquad (8.17)$$

where $\tilde{X}_p$ is the end-of-period cash flow gross of the manager's reward; β_p is the sensitivity of the gross cash flow to the return on the market portfolio; e_p is the effort supplied by the project manager; and $\tilde{\theta}_p$ is a random variable which is uncorrelated with the market portfolio and which has an expected value of zero and variance of $\sigma^2(\tilde{\theta}_p)$.

Now suppose that $\sigma^2(\tilde{\theta}_p)$ can be reduced by the expenditure of resources paid out of the end-of-period cash flow. Let σ^2_{max} be the level of $\sigma^2(\tilde{\theta}_p)$ that will apply if nothing is spent on reducing it. Let y_p be the reduction in $\sigma^2(\tilde{\theta}_p)$ achieved by the expenditure of resources and let $C(y_p)$ be the cost of achieving the reduction. We assume that $C(.)$ is increasing and strictly convex in y_p. By definition $\sigma^2(\tilde{\theta}_p)$ will be equal to σ^2_{max} less y_p.

Let R_p be the reward paid to the manager out of the end-of-period cash flow. Hence the cash flow received by investors is equal to $X_p - R_p$. By using (8.16) the value of the project net of the project manager's reward can be expressed as follows:

$$V_p = (E(\tilde{X}_p) - E(\tilde{R}_p) - C(y_p) - \lambda \text{cov}(\tilde{X}_p, \tilde{r}_m) + \lambda \text{cov}(\tilde{R}_p, \tilde{r}_m))/(1 + r_f)$$

$$(8.18)$$

Now if e_p is observable the reward of the manager will be some guaranteed amount, $\bar{R}_p$. Moreover one can show that the level of $\bar{R}_p$ will be an increasing and strictly convex function of the desired level of effort.[8] So (8.18) will become[9]

$$V_p = (e_p + \beta_p E(\tilde{r}_m) - \bar{R}_p(e_p) - C(y_p) - \lambda \beta_p \sigma^2(\tilde{r}_m))/(1 + r_f)$$

$$(8.19)$$

From (8.19) one can easily see that, whatever the desired level of e_p, one should always set y_p equal to zero so as to maximize (8.19). Hence in the absence of moral hazard it is impossible to increase the value of the project by expending resources to reduce the project's unsystematic risk.

Now suppose that $\tilde{X}_p$ and $\tilde{r}_m$ are observable (or effectively so, as in Holmstrom, 1982) but that e_p is not observable. Given $\tilde{X}_p$ and $\tilde{r}_m$ the owners can derive an estimate of e_p by subtracting β_p times $\tilde{r}_m$ from $\tilde{X}_p$. Let $\hat{e}_p$ be this estimate and suppose that the owners reward the manager according to some function of $\hat{e}_p$. Denote this function by $R_p(\hat{e}_p)$. Given the statistical independence of $\tilde{\theta}_p$ and $\tilde{r}_m$ the reward paid to the manager will in turn be independent of $\tilde{r}_m$, hence the final term in the numerator of (8.18) will still be zero, as above. Hence (8.18) becomes

$$V_p = (e_p + \beta_p E(\tilde{r}_m) - E(\bar{R}_p(\hat{e}_p)) - C(y_p) - \lambda \beta_p \sigma^2(\tilde{r}_m))/(1 + r_f)$$

$$(8.20)$$

The third term in (8.20) is the expected reward of the manager. Now the reward of the manager depends directly on the observed payoff. Moreover one can show that, for a given desired level of e_p, the variability of the manager's reward increases as $\sigma^2(\tilde{\theta}_p)$ increases. Because of this increased variation the manager must be given a higher expected reward to compensate her for the increased risk. Hence, in general $E(R_p(e_p))$ increases as $\sigma^2(\tilde{\theta}_p)$ increases.

In this case it may be possible to increase the market value of the project by expending resources to reduce unsystematic risk. Such costs should be incurred up to the point where $C(y_p)$ is equal to the marginal reduction in the expected reward of the manager induced by the marginal reduction in unsystematic risk.

In terms of implications for investment policy we can see that the introduction of moral hazard leaves the basic certainty equivalent valuation formula intact provided the expected cash flows are expressed *net* of the expected reward paid to the project manager and provided one takes into account the dependence of the expected reward of the manager on the unsystematic risk associated with the project.

PART 2
The Positive Agency Literature

8.8   INTRODUCTION AND OVERVIEW OF BASIC CONCEPTS

The introduction to this chapter mentioned that the agency literature divides into two fairly distinct lines of intellectual activity: the principal-agent literature and the positive agency literature. The purpose now is to review the main features of the positive agency literature and to discuss its major implications for the modern theory of finance.

This section provides an overview of the main theoretical concepts associated with the positive agency school. Sections 8.9 and 8.10 discuss two major applications of the positive agency approach: the separation of ownership from control and the agency costs of debt.

Basic Concepts of the Positive Agency Literature

To appreciate the novelty of the positive agency approach it is important to understand that the approach is first and foremost a theory of alternative organizational forms. The central theoretical purpose of positive agency theory is to explain why certain types of organizational form tend to dominate certain areas of economic activity. For example, why is it that open corporations tend to dominate the manufacturing sector whilst sole proprietorships and partnerships dominate important parts of the service sector such as accountancy and law?

At the core of the positive agency literature is the idea that most organizations can be viewed as legal fictions that serve as a nexus for a set of contracting relationships between several individuals. In particular the positive approach calls into question the normal theoretical practice of attempting to model an organization as an individual with a single well-defined objective function. Rather the positive agency literature models the behaviour of an organization as the outcome of a complex process in which the conflicting interests of various 'contributors' to the organization are brought into equilibrium. In general terms an organization is viewed as a set of contracts that, in effect, define the rules of an economic game played by the contributors to the organization. The equilibrium conditions for a solution to the game defined by the organization characterize the equilibrium behaviour of the organization.

In modelling any particular organization it is necessary to specify the key contributors whose behaviour is to be modelled. In game-theoretic terminology it is necessary to specify the active players in the organizational game. In general the positive agency literature focuses on two main classes of contributors: the top level decision makers and the residual claimants. In addition, when discussing the corporate form of organization, the bondholders of the firm are sometimes included as a third class of key contributors.

The contractual structures of most organizations limit the risks of most contributors to the organization either by guaranteeing some fixed reward or by tying rewards explicitly to some contractually defined measure of performance. The residual claimants are those who guarantee payment of the fixed contractual rewards. The residual claimants bear the risk of the difference between the stochastic cash inflows and the promised payments to other participants. Fama and Jensen (1983a, 1983b, 1985) argue that different organizational forms can be distinguished primarily by the characteristics of their residual claimants. For example, the open corporation is distinguished by the fact that its residual claimants, the ordinary shareholders, are entirely unrestricted in the sense that (a) shareholders are not required to have any other role in the organization (in particular they are not required to be decision makers), (b) their claims are freely tradable, (c) their claims are rights in the net cash flows of the corporation for the life of the corporation.

Alternative organizational forms compete for survival in the economic sphere just as alternative species do in nature. Fama and Jensen argue that the form of organization that survives in a particular activity is the one that can deliver the product to consumers at the lowest price whilst covering costs. Moreover the costs of an organization include the costs of monitoring and enforcing the contracts between its key contributors. These costs are referred to generically as the 'agency costs' of the organization. Agency costs include the costs of structuring, monitoring and bonding a set of contracts between contributors with conflicting interests. Agency costs also include the value of output lost because the costs of full enforcement of contracts exceed the benefits. This particular agency cost is referred to as 'the residual loss'.

A core assumption of the approach is that all contributors behave rationally and as if they expect all other contributors to behave rationally. Thus, for example, if a debt contract leaves some scope for equity holders to transfer wealth from the bondholders to themselves this possibility will be fully anticipated by the bondholders at the time the debt is issued and the debt will be priced accordingly. Jensen and Meckling (1976) show that this rationality assumption implies that the agency costs of a contractual relationship will be incorporated explicitly into the decision calculus of the contracting parties at the time the contract is made. Hence sufficient incentives always exist to write contracts that provide monitoring and bonding activities to the point where their marginal cost equals the marginal gain from reducing the residual loss.

Jensen and Meckling (1976) present a straightforward illustration of the agency costs that can arise between an owner–manager of a firm and the outside shareholders of the firm. The illustration assumes that the owner–manager has access to a number of on-the-job consumption opportunities or perquisites (perks). In the absence of outside shareholders the marginal costs of perk consumption is borne entirely by the owner–manager, that is, every pound spent on perks results in a loss of one pound in the owner–manager's personal wealth. However, if a proportion, α, of the firm is owned by outsiders the marginal cost to the owner–manager of one pound of perks will be the fraction $(1-\alpha)$ of a pound. This will lead to excessive expenditure on perks by the owner–manager. However, under the strong rationality assumption, the losses from excessive perk consumption will be fully anticipated by the outsiders at the time of issue of the outside equity. Hence the amount the outsiders will be willing to pay for their shares will be the fraction α of the value they expect the firm to have in the presence of the excessive expenditure on perks induced by the issue of outside equity. This in turn implies that the decline in the value of the firm resulting from excessive perk expenditure will be borne entirely by the owner–manager. In this illustration the gross agency cost is simply the difference between the value that the firm would have if the owner–manager could costlessly precommit to an agreed level of perk expenditure and the value of the firm when she cannot so precommit. The net agency cost is equal to the gross agency cost minus the owner-manager's willingness to pay for the extra perk consumption she enjoys in the presence of outside shareholders. Since the net agency costs are borne entirely by the owner-manager the rationality assumption implies that she will adopt whatever actions are necessary to minimize such costs. Jensen and Meckling refer to these particular agency costs as 'the agency costs of outside equity'.

8.9   THE SEPARATION OF OWNERSHIP FROM CONTROL

The separation of ownership from control has been a recurrent theme of the positive agency literature. In particular the literature has been concerned to explain the survival of organizations in which the important decisions are made by contributors who do not bear a substantial share of the wealth effects of those decisions. Of special concern in this regard are the reasons for the dominance enjoyed by the open corporation in many areas of large-scale economic activity.

Fama and Jensen's (1983a, 1983b) explanation for the success of the open corporation turns on the unrestricted nature of the residual claims of such organizations and on the existence of sophisticated multifaceted decision control mechanisms which help to mitigate the agency costs arising from the separation of ownership and control.

On the one hand the unrestricted nature of ordinary equity combined with limited liability allows specialist risk bearing by the shareholders who advance wealth which is used to bond the payments promised to the other contributors. Since shareholders are not required to fill any decision-making role in the corporation the residual risk can be shared among a large number of individuals who in turn can choose to hold well-diversified portfolios of securities. Also, since decision makers are not required to be residual claimants, they can be selected purely by reference to their decision-making skills without regard to their personal wealth (of course, in some market regimes an individual's personal wealth may help to signal her decision-making ability).

Against the benefits of specialized risk bearing and specialized decision skills must be offset any agency costs arising from the conflicts of interest between the decision makers and the residual claimants. Fama and Jensen argue that such costs can be mitigated by complex hierarchical decision control mechanisms which separate decision management (initiation and implementation) from decision control (ratification and monitoring). They also make an important distinction between 'complex' and 'non-complex' organizations. Complex organizations are those in which specific knowledge relevant to different decisions is dispersed throughout the organization. In such organizations, because of the costs of transmitting information to the centre, decision-making rights tend to be decentralized to those in possession of the relevant information; devices that separate decision management from decision control are introduced to control any ensuing agency problems. In such complex organizations the net additional costs of achieving a complete separation of ownership and control are relatively small. Thus the survival rate of corporations tends to be highest in large-scale activities involving widely dispersed information and large risks.

Hierarchical control systems such as those described by Fama and Jensen mitigate the agency costs associated with the separation of ownership and control by separating decision management from decision control at all levels of the organizational hierarchy. What happens though when one reaches the top of the hierarchy? What mechanism controls the decisions initiated by the top-level decision makers in the open corporation? Fama and Jensen point to five mutually supportive mechanisms that help to bring the interests of the senior management of open corporations into line with the interests of their shareholders. First, the contracts of top executives often tie their rewards explicitly to measures of firm performance (managerial stock options, for example, link the manager's reward to the firm's share price performance). Second, the so-called 'market for corporate control' (Manne, 1965) provides an arena in which alternative management teams compete for rights to manage company resources (see Jensen and Ruback, 1983, for further discussion and empirical evidence). Third, the managerial labour market, at least in the long term (see Fama, 1980), tends to ensure that managers are penalized for actions that run counter to the interests of their shareholders. Fourth, it is possible that mutual monitoring and competition for positions within the firm may impose some discipline on managers. Finally, the inclusion of expert outsiders on the board of directors with powers of access to inside information may further limit the powers of inside directors.

8.10 CAPITAL STRUCTURE AND THE AGENCY COSTS OF DEBT

Finding a convincing explanation for the observed time series and cross-sectional variation in the debt/equity ratios of corporations has been a topic of sustained academic enquiry ever since the seminal contribution of Modigliani and Miller (1958).

The purpose of this section is to focus on one particular aspect of the capital structure puzzle, namely, the agency costs of debt. In practice a financial manager in choosing an optimal capital structure will have to weigh the agency costs of debt against other factors that influence the relative attractiveness of debt and equity of which the most important are:

(a) corporate and personal tax considerations (Modigliani and Miller, 1963; Farrar and Selwyn, 1967; Miller, 1977; and DeAngelo and Masulis, 1980);
(b) the agency costs of equity (see section 8.8 above);

(c)   signalling considerations (see chapter 7 above);
(d)   bankruptcy costs (Baxter, 1967; Stiglitz, 1972; Kraus and Litzenberger, 1973; Warner, 1977a,b; and Kim, 1978).

Factors (a), (b) and (c) are often cited as the main potential sources of benefit associated with increased leverage. In determining the optimal debt/equity ratio these factors must be weighed against any possible bankruptcy costs and the agency costs of debt. An optimal debt/equity ratio is one for which the marginal benefits of increased leverage is equal to the marginal cost.

To understand the agency costs of debt it simplifies the presentation to consider a world where none of the other factors in the capital structure trade-off are operative. Hence, following Fama (1978), we assume:

1   Perfect markets: zero transaction costs, zero taxes, zero agency costs of equity, and zero bankruptcy costs.
2   Equal access: individuals and firms have equal access to capital markets.
3   Homogeneous information: any information is costlessly available to all market participants.
4   Only wealth counts: aside from the effects on security holder wealth, the financing decisions of a firm do not affect the characteristics of the portfolio opportunities available to investors.
5   Given investment strategies: the decision rules that firms use to make investment decisions are given and, in particular, are independent of how the firm is financed.

According to Fama (1978) these five assumptions are sufficient for the validity of Proposition I of Modigliani and Miller (1958), that is, the market value of the firm is independent of its financial structure. However, even though the total market value of the firm is independent of how it is financed this need not imply that a firm's financing decisions will be a matter of indifference to its security holders. In particular, in a multiperiod context, it may be possible to increase the wealth of the existing shareholders at the expense of the current debtholders by issuing additional debt with a claim to the firm's assets equal to or superior to the claim of the existing debt. The following additional assumption rules out this possibility:

6   A firm's debtholders and shareholders protect themselves with costlessly enforceable 'me-first' rules that ensure that the payoff characteristics of the firm's outstanding debt are unaffected by any changes in the firm's capital structure.

When assumption 6 holds as well as assumptions 1 to 5 not only will the firm's market value be independent of its capital structure but also the firm's capital structure will be a matter of indifference to all its existing security holders. Moreover, since assumptions 1 to 6 are sufficient for the irrelevance of capital structure it follows that at least one of these assumptions must be relaxed if the choice of capital structure is to have any effect on the firm's market value.

The literature on the agency costs of debt focuses on the implications of relaxing assumption 5. It argues that conflicts of interest between shareholders and debtholders can arise if the firm is unable to precommit itself to a value-maximizing investment policy at the time of issue of the debt. In particular two main areas of potential conflict have been identified. First, the shareholders may be able to increase their own wealth at the expense of debtholders by shifting the risk profile of the firm's assets in favour of riskier assets (Galai and Masulis, 1976; Jensen and Meckling, 1976). Second, the shareholders may be able to increase their own wealth at the expense of debtholders by rejecting all projects with a net present value less than the face value of the outstanding debt (Myers, 1977).

To understand the first type of conflict and to see its effect on the firm's market value consider the example below:

State	Probability	Plan A	Plan B
1	1/6	0	0
2	1/6	100	0
3	1/6	100	0
4	1/6	100	100
5	1/6	100	250
6	1/6	250	250
Required initial outlay		100	100

For simplicity assume that all individuals are risk-neutral with zero rates of time preference and homogeneous beliefs. Then the net present value of plan A will be 50/6 and the net present value of plan B will be zero. If the firm can precommit to plan A it will be able to finance the plan by issuing debt with a face value of 200. The debt will sell for 100 and the equity will be valued at 50/6.

Now suppose that the firm cannot precommit to plan A. Suppose that, after receiving the debt finance it is able to switch to plan B. Consider the case where the firm issues debt with a face value of 200. In this case the payoff to the firm's shareholders under plans A and B will be as below:

State	Plan A	Plan B
1	0	0
2	0	0
3	0	0
4	0	0
5	0	50
6	50	50

Clearly the shareholders will prefer the riskier plan B to plan A. However if the debtholders are rational, which is the usual assumption of the positive agency approach, they will anticipate the adoption of plan B and value the debt issue according to its payoff structure under plan B. Hence the debt will be valued at 500/6 and the firm as a whole will be valued at 100. The difference between the value of the firm when it can precommit to plan A and its value when it cannot so precommit is referred to as an agency cost of debt.

The second area of conflict is illustrated in the following example which is based on the work of Myers (1977). The example involves two main time points. At time point 0 the firm issues zero coupon debt (that is, debt that pays no interest) with a face value of 50 which matures at time point 1. The proceeds of the debt issue are paid out at time point 0 as a dividend to the firm's original shareholders. The only asset of the firm is an option to undertake an investment at time point 1. The project requires an initial outlay of 100 to be financed entirely by the issue of new equity. Table 8.5 provides information relating to the value of the project at time point 1. Here the prices in the second column are those ruling at time point 0. V_{DA} is the value of the debt if the project is accepted; V_{EA} is the value of the old equity if the project is accepted; V_{DR} is the value of the debt if the project is rejected; V_{ER} is the value of the old equity if the project is rejected. Columns three to eight refer to values at time point 1

Table 8.5 Project values

State of the world	Simple state claim price	Value of project	Net value of project	V_{DA}	V_{EA}	V_{DR}	V_{ER}
s_1	1/3	90	−10	50	−60	0	0
s_2	1/3	140	40	50	−10	0	0
s_3	1/3	200	100	50	50	0	0

conditional on the state at time point 1. We assume that the management knows the state at the time the investment decision is made.

If state 1 occurs the project has a negative net present value and the total value of the firm would be maximized by rejecting the project. If state 2 occurs the project has a positive net present value and the value of the firm would be maximized by accepting the project. However, the original shareholders will prefer to reject the project if state 2 occurs because the present value of the project net of the amount owed to debtholders is less than the required outlay of 100. In state 3 the project has a positive net present value and the shareholders will accept the project. Hence the debtholders will receive a zero payoff in states 1 and 2 and a payoff of 50 in state 3. Under the usual assumption that debtholders fully anticipate the shareholders' decision strategy the debt will be valued at 50/3 when it is issued at time point 0. Also the equity will be valued at 50/3 making the total value of the firm 100/3. Now if the shareholders had been able to costlessly precommit to accept all projects with positive net present values the debtholders would have received 50 in both state 2 and state 3 and the debt issue would have been valued at 100/3. The equity of the firm would have been valued at 40/3 giving a total firm value of 140/3. The difference between the value of the firm with precommitment and the value without precommitment is one of the potential agency costs of debt.

Leading finance theorists differ in the importance they attach to such agency costs. Fama (1978) argues that market forces will prevent firms from deviating too far from value-maximizing policies. In particular firms that deviate significantly from value-maximizing policies leave themselves open to the threat of a take-over. Also firms have clear-cut incentives to evolve mechanisms that allow them to precommit to value-maximizing policies especially in a multiperiod context. Finally Galai and Masulis (1976) point out that the incentives for a firm's shareholders to deviate from value-maximizing policies will be reduced to the extent that they also hold the firm's debt securities. Advocates of the importance of agency costs argue that deviations from value maximization may be very difficult to detect. For example, it is not obvious how outsiders could detect a decision to reject a project with positive net present value.

Ultimately the question of how important are the agency costs of debt must be settled empirically. For some preliminary findings the reader is encouraged to consult Smith and Warner (1979) and Jensen and Smith (1985b).

8.11 CONCLUDING REMARKS

The principal–agent literature reviewed in sections 8.2 to 8.7 offers mathematically precise prescriptions for the design of optimum incentive schemes in the presence of uncertainty, risk aversion and information asymmetry. It has also contributed a great deal towards our understanding of incentive structures and the value of information in contractual situations involving uncertainty. Unfortunately it is rather difficult to integrate this approach with the more traditional theories of finance.

This point is worth bearing in mind when assessing the contributions of the positive agency literature to the modern theory of finance. As compared to the principal–agent paradigm the positive agency approach appears somewhat lacking in logical rigour. In particular the positive agency literature on the separation of ownership and control makes use of terms such as 'complexity' and 'diffuse information' which play a crucial role in the analysis but which are never precisely defined. At times this particular part of the literature seems like apologetics for corporate capitalism. Nevertheless the approach does offer the advantage that its insights are more readily integrated with the mainstream theory of finance. In particular the literature on the agency costs of debt seems destined to play a major role in any future attempts to explain the capital structures of large corporations.

Notes

INTRODUCTION

1 Throughout the text we adopt the convention of using the masculine form 'him' or 'his', but no sexist implication is intended.
2 Throughout the text the *ex ante/ex post* distinction is made with reference to the time at which actions and/or trading decisions are made.

CHAPTER 1

1 $V(.)$ is a positive linear transformation of $U(.)$ if $V(.) = e + fU(.)$ where e and f are constants with $f > 0$. The reader can check that if a_1 is ranked above a_2 under $U(.)$, then it will also be ranked above a_2 under $V(.)$.
2 Mention should be made here of the pioneering contributions of Simon (see, for example, Simon, 1978). Simon has argued that individuals exhibit a degree of similarity in the way they go about simplifying complex problems. There may be sufficient material here for the development of a theory of suboptimal behaviour.
3 In the previous example we had $a(y_1) = a_2$ and $a(y_2) = a_3$.
4 To avoid confusion recall that an element of the partition G is a subset of S.
5 N is the number of signals associated with $\eta(.)$. N' is the number of signals associated with $\eta'(.)$. A Markov matrix is one with all non-negative elements and with the sum of the elements of each row equal to 1.

CHAPTER 2

1 To avoid cumbersome notation in this and subsequent chapters we use an s subscript to denote dependence on state s. Also the symbol C will be used henceforth to denote a consumption level.
2 Some further consideration of the assumption of additive separability of the utility function over time is contained in chapters 3 and 4.

3   These terms are explained more fully in the following sections.
4   The process of short selling (or going short in) a security may be more easily
    understood with reference to borrowing and lending in a risk-free security. In
    this case short selling is equivalent to borrowing; short sellers effectively issue
    their own risk-free security, receiving funds now in return for a promise to
    repay principal plus interest in the future. Similarly in the text, short selling
    one unit of C_2 means that the seller receives a payoff of 3.15 now (the current
    market value of C_3) and promises in return to pay 3, 5 or 5 in the future
    depending upon which state of the world actually occurs.

CHAPTER 3

1   A (European) call option, $C(X, E)$, on the primary security X, with exercise
    price E, gives the owner the right to acquire security X on the payoff date of
    the security for a price equal to E. Since this right will only be exercised if
    it is valuable, the payoff from the call option is the greater of zero and $X(s) - E$,
    where $X(s)$ is the payoff from X in state s.
2   A (European) put option on the primary security X, with exercise price E, gives
    the owner the right to sell security X on the payoff date for the exercise price
    E. Since this right will only be exercised if it is valuable, the payoff from the
    put option will be the greater of zero and $E - X(s)$. The writer of the put is
    in the opposite position to the buyer and effectively has to pay out the maximum
    of zero and $E - X(s)$ on the payoff date.
3   More extensive consideration of the role of information in improving allocative
    efficiency can be found in chapter 4.
4   And assuming in addition that the set of firm securities cannot be rendered
    incomplete by the actions of any one firm.
5   Necessarily here, firms' production plans must result in output only in those
    states for which consumption claims can be traded. Otherwise firms' net market
    values are not defined.
6   There has been separate consideration in the literature of unanimity results that
    apply to a firm's ex post shareholders and those that apply to a firm's ex ante
    shareholders. The distinction arises because in a stock market economy, shares
    are traded and so the owners of the firm change through time. Unfortunately,
    the distinction itself is not clearly addressed in the literature which remains
    rather confusing in this area. One way of addressing (avoiding?) the problem
    is to assume that initial shareholders choose from those plans that will not
    subsequently be unanimously overturned to their disadvantage by future
    shareholders (and similarly for future shareholders and 'further into the future'
    shareholders in a multiperiod economy). To some extent then we are justified
    in focusing on unanimity among initial shareholders.

CHAPTER 4

1   Some authors equate social value with an actual Pareto improvement. We find
    it useful to distinguish between these two concepts.

2 To avoid excessive use of subscript notation the notation for time 0 and time 1 utility differs slightly from the notation used in chapter 2.

3 Strictly speaking we do not even require homogeneous beliefs for proposition 2 to hold. As can be seen from (4.5) the crucial requirement is homogeneous signal beliefs; i.e., $\phi_i(y) = \phi_j(y)$.

4 This additional requirement returns us to the setting of complex contingent claims or stock market economies of chapter 2.

CHAPTER 5

1 The issue of what constitutes the set of tradable securities is an important consideration here. The issue is discussed in section 5.2.

2 In a stock market economy, traders would be constrained to proportional ownership of the two firms X and Y. For this example, with two (linearly independent) firms and five states, individuals would be able to vary independently the payoffs from only two states (and excluding the independent variation of s_1 and s_2 payoffs and also of s_3 and s_4 payoffs).

3 Note that we have invoked the artificial restriction here that short-selling is precluded.

4 The expressions ψ_A and ψ_B are as defined in equations (3.2) of chapter 3.

5 For the particular functional form of the model which Verrecchia employs to make his analysis tractable, all traders of the same risk tolerance acquire an identical amount of information. This amount (generally) increases as traders become more risk-tolerant due to the fact that more risk-tolerant traders demand more information to protect their riskier positions.

6 The partition defined by event-contingent homogeneity of beliefs can be derived using the method given in chapter 3 (see equations (3.1) and (3.2) with the expressions ϕ and ψ_i now calculated with respect to the revised beliefs of the individuals.

CHAPTER 6

1 Recent theoretical work has questioned the validity of the assumption of a constant discount rate when individuals are risk-averse. Leroy (1973) shows that the time series of asset prices follows a martingale (see text following) if and only if there is no risk in the economy or investors are risk-neutral.

2 For additional examples of this approach see Fama (1970).

3 This special result holds because of the homogeneous conditional beliefs and because of our assumption of logarithmic utilities (see chapters 2 and 3).

CHAPTER 7

1 This labelling of informed insiders and uninformed outsiders often corresponds in the wider literature on screening and signalling to an informed selling group and an uninformed buying group respectively. This labelling is not always

appropriate; in insurance markets the companies who sell insurance are assumed to be uninformed about the attributes of the applicants. However, for the examples to be discussed in this chapter, our labelling of outsiders or buyers as being the uninformed group and of insiders or sellers as being the informed group holds true.

2 In a general model the cost would have to be derived endogenously, but the example illustrates the idea behind a signalling equilibrium.

3 Unlike the simple example in the introductory remarks to this chapter the Leland and Pyle paper derives the signalling cost endogenously.

4 That is, assuming there are no institutional restrictions on the form of contract that can be entered into.

5 That is, with normally distributed project payoffs, the range of possible payoffs extends from minus infinity to plus infinity regardless of the parameters of the distribution.

CHAPTER 8

1 Lambert subsequently relaxes this assumption to exclude precommitment by the agent.

2 Fama (1980) has derived similar results and has coined the term '*ex post* settling up' to describe the phenomenon.

3 By 'first best' here we are referring to the optimum solution to the principal's problem in a single-period context where the principal can directly observe e.

4 Note that $\phi_{vi}(e)$ is a function of X_v, y_i and e.

5 If the conditional distribution of y_i given X_v is independent of e one cannot learn anything further about e from y_i given X_v. This discussion parallels the previous discussion on an FRREE (see p. 111). For an introduction to the sufficient statistic concept see Mood, Graybill and Boes (1974, chapter 7).

6 The principal's problem can be expressed in abbreviated form as follows:

Maximize $(20{,}000 - R_{20}).(0.25) + (30{,}000 - R_{30}).(0.5) + (35{,}000 - R_{35}).(0.25)$ (1)

subject to $R_{20}^{\frac{1}{2}}.(0.25) + R_{30}^{\frac{1}{2}}.(0.5) + R_{35}^{\frac{1}{2}}.(0.25) - e_3^2 = 100$ and (2)

$R_{20}^{\frac{1}{2}}.(0.5) + R_{30}^{\frac{1}{2}}.(0.5) - e_3^2 > R_{20}^{\frac{1}{2}} - e_2^2$ (3)

where

(1) is the expected payoff to the principal under e_3;

(2) requires the agent's expected utility under e_3 to be maintained at 100; and

(3) requires the agent's expected utility if she selects e_3 on receipt of y_1 to be at least as great as her expected utility if she selects e_2.

7 Equation (8.16) can be derived as follows:
by equation (8.15)

$$E((\tilde{X} - V(\tilde{X}))/V(\tilde{X})) = r_f + \lambda.\text{cov}((\tilde{X} - V(\tilde{X}))/V(\tilde{X}), \tilde{r}_m)$$ (1)

Multiplying both sides of (1) by $V(\tilde{X})$ yields

$$E(\tilde{X}) - V(\tilde{X}) = r_f V(\tilde{X}) + \lambda \text{cov}(\tilde{X} - V(\tilde{X}), \tilde{r}_m)$$ (2)

Now, since $V(\tilde{X})$ is not a random variable, $\text{cov}(\tilde{X} - V(\tilde{X}), \tilde{r}_m) = \text{cov}(\tilde{X}, \tilde{r}_m)$. Hence, by rearranging (2) we get (8.16).

8 To maintain the agent's utility at EU we require

$$U_a(\bar{R}) - D(e) = EU$$

Differentiating this equation with respect to e we get

$$\frac{dU}{d\bar{R}} \frac{d\bar{R}}{de} - \frac{dD}{de} = 0$$

Hence since dV/de is positive and $dU/d\bar{R}$ is positive it follows that $d\bar{R}/de$ must also be positive. Differentiating again we get

$$\frac{d^2U}{d\bar{R}^2} \left(\frac{d\bar{R}}{de}\right)^2 + \frac{dU}{d\bar{R}} \frac{d^2\bar{R}}{de^2} - \frac{d^2D}{de^2} = 0$$

Since $d^2U/d\bar{R}^2$ is negative, $dU/d\bar{R}$ is positive, and d^2D/de^2 is positive. It follows that d^2R/de^2 must be positive.

9 (8.19) can be derived from (8.18) as follows:
Since $R(e)$ is certain, $\text{cov}(R_p, r_m)$ in (8.18) will be zero.
Also

$$\text{cov}(\tilde{X}_p, \tilde{r}_m) = \beta_p . \sigma^2(\tilde{r}_m), \quad E(\tilde{X}_p) = e_p + \beta_p E(\tilde{r}_m) \quad \text{and} \quad E(\tilde{R}_p) = \bar{R}_p(e_p).$$

(8.19) follows immediately.

References

Ackley, G. 1983: Commodities and capital. *American Economic Review*, 1–16.

Akerlof, G. 1970: The market for lemons: quantitative uncertainty and the market mechanism. *Quarterly Journal of Economics*, 488–500.

Allais, M. 1953: Le comportement d'homme rational devant le risque. *Econometrica*, 503–46.

Allen, B. 1981: Generic existence of completely revealing equilibria for economies when prices convey information. *Econometrica*, 1173–99.

Amershi, A. H. 1981: Social value of information, spot-trading and rational expectations equilibria in informationally incomplete exchange markets. Working Paper, Graduate School of Business, Stanford University. Stanford Calif.

—— 1985: A complete analysis of full pareto efficiency in financial markets for arbitrary preferences. *Journal of Finance*, 1235–43.

Arrow, K. J. 1964: The role of securities in the optimal allocation of risk bearing. *Review of Economic Studies*, 91–6.

—— 1971: *Essays on the Theory of Risk Bearing*. Amsterdam. North Holland.

Baiman, S. 1982: Agency theory research in managerial accounting: a survey. *Journal of Accounting Literature*, 154–213.

Baiman, S. and Evans, J. H. 1983: Decentralization and pre-decision information. *Journal of Accounting Research*, 371–95.

Baxter, N. D. 1967: Leverage, risk of ruin, and cost of capital. *Journal of Finance*, 395–403.

Beaver, W. H. 1981a: Market efficiency. *Accounting Review*, 23–37.

—— 1981b: *Financial Reporting: an accounting revolution*. Englewood Cliffs, NJ: Prentice-Hall.

Begg, D. K. H. 1982: *The Rational Expectations Revolution in Macroeconomics*. Deddington, Oxon.: Philip Allan.

Bhattacharya, S. 1979: Imperfect information, dividend policy, and the bird in the hand fallacy. *Bell Journal of Economics and Management Science*, 259–70.

—— 1980: Nondissipative signalling structures and dividend policy. *Quarterly Journal of Economics*, 1–24.

Black, F. and Scholes, M. 1973: The pricing of options and corporate liabilities. *Journal of Political Economy*, 637–54.

Blackwell, D. 1951: Comparison of experiments. In J. Neyman (ed.), *Proceedings of the Second Berkeley Symposium on Mathematical Statistics and Probability*. Berkeley: University of California Press.

—— 1953: Equivalent comparisons of experiments. *Annals of Mathematical Statistics*, 265–73.

Borch, K. 1962: Equilibrium in a reinsurance market. *Econometrica*, 424–44.

—— 1967: Economics and game theory. *Swedish Journal of Economics*, 215–28.

Brealey, R. and Myers, S. 1984: *Principles of Corporate Finance*, 2nd edn. New York. McGraw-Hill.

Cass, D. and Stiglitz, J. E. 1970: The structure of investors' preferences and asset returns, and separability in portfolio allocation: a contribution to the pure theory of mutual funds. *Journal of Economic Theory*, 122–60.

Christensen, J. 1981: Communications in agencies. *Bell Journal of Economics and Management Science*, 661–74.

—— 1982: The determination of performance standards and participation. *Journal of Accounting Research*, 589–603.

Copeland, T. E. and Weston, J. F. 1983: *Financial Theory and Corporate Policy*, 2nd edn. Reading, Mass.: Addison-Wesley.

DeAngelo, H. 1981: Competition and unanimity. *American Economic Review*, 18–27.

DeAngelo, H. and Masulis, R. 1980: Optimal capital structure under corporate and personal taxation. *Journal of Financial Economics*, 3–30.

Debreu G. 1959: *Theory of Value*. New Haven and London. Yale University Press.

Demski, J. S. and Sappington, D. 1984: Optimal incentives with multiple agents. *Journal of Economic Theory*, 152–71.

Diamond, D. W. and Verrecchia, R. E. 1981: Information aggregation in a noisy rational expectations economy. *Journal of Financial Economics*, 221–35.

—— 1982: Optimal managerial contracts and equilibrium security prices. *Journal of Finance*, 275–87.

Dixit, A. K. 1976: *Optimization in Economic Theory*. Oxford: Oxford University Press.

Dreze, J. H. 1974: Axiomatic theories of choice, cardinal utility and subjective probability: a review. Chapter 1 of J. H. Dreze (ed.), *Allocation under uncertainty: equilibrium and optimality*. London: Macmillan.

Duffie, D. and Huang, C-F. 1985: Implementing Arrow–Debreu equilibria by continuous trading of few long-lived securities. *Econometrica*, 1337–65.

Dyckman, T. R., and Morse, R. D. 1986: *Efficient capital markets and accounting: a critical analysis*, 2nd edn. Englewood Cliffs, New Jersey, Prentice-Hall.

Dye, R. A. 1983: Communication and post-decision information. *Journal of Accounting Research*, 514–33.

Fama, E. F. 1970: Efficient capital markets: a review of theoretical and empirical work. *Journal of Finance*, 383–417.

—— 1976a: Reply to efficient capital markets: comments. *Journal of Finance*, 143–5.

—— 1976b: *Foundations of Finance*. New York: Basic Books.

—— 1978: The effects of a firm's investment and financing decisions on the welfare of its security holders. *American Economic Review*, 272–84.

Fama, E. F. 1980: Agency problems and the theory of the firm. *Journal of Political Economy*, 288–307.

Fama, E. F. and Jensen, M. C. 1983a: Separation of ownership and control. *Journal of Law and Economics*, 301–26.

—— 1983b: Agency problems and residual claims. *Journal of Law and Economics*, 327–50.

√ —— 1985: Organizational forms and investment decisions. *Journal of Financial Economics*, 101–20.

Fama, E. F. and Laffer, A. 1971: Information and capital markets. *Journal of Business*, 289–98.

Fama, E. F. and Miller, M. H. 1972: *Theory of Finance*. New York: Holt, Rinehart and Winston.

Farrar, D. E. and Selwyn, L. 1967: Taxes, corporate financial policy and returns to investors. *National Tax Journal*, 444–54.

√ Firth, M. 1986: Efficient markets theory. Chapter 1 of M. Firth and S. M. Keane, *Issues in Finance*. Deddington, Oxon.: Philip Allan.

? Flavin, M. A. 1983: Excess volatility in the financial markets: a reassessment of the empirical evidence. *Journal of Political Economy*, 929–56.

Galai, D. and Masulis, R. W. 1976. The option pricing model and the risk factor of stock. *Journal of Financial Economics*, 53–82.

Gjesdal, F. 1981: Accounting for stewardship. *Journal of Accounting Research*, 208–231.

—— 1982: Information and incentives: the agency information problem. *Review of Economic Studies*, 373–90.

Green, J. R. 1973: Information, efficiency, and equilibrium. Discussion paper no. 284, Harvard Institute of Economic Research. Cambridge Mass.

Green, J. R. and Stokey, N. 1983: A comparison of tournaments and contracts. *Journal of Political Economy*, 349–64.

Grossman, S. J. 1976: On the efficiency of competitive stock markets when investors have diverse information. *Journal of Finance*, 573–85.

—— 1978: Further results on the informational efficiency of competitive stock markets. *Journal of Economic Theory*, 81–101.

—— 1981: An introduction to the theory of rational expectations under asymmetric information. *Review of Economic Studies*, 541–59.

√ Grossman, S. J. and Hart, O. D. 1983: An analysis of the principal-agent problem. *Econometrica*, 7–45.

Grossman, S. J. and Shiller, R. J. 1981: The determinants of the variability of stock market prices. *American Economic Review*, 222–7.

Grossman, S. J. and Stiglitz, J. E. 1976: Information and competitive price systems. *American Economic Review*, 246–53.

Hahn, F. H. 1973: *On the Notion of Equilibrium in Economics*. Cambridge: Cambridge University Press.

—— 1984: *Equilibrium and Macroeconomics*. Oxford: Basil Blackwell.

Hakansson, N. H. 1977: The superfund: efficient paths toward efficient capital markets in large and small countries. Part IV of H. Levy and M. Sarnat (eds), *Financial Decision Making under Uncertainty*. New York: Academic Press.

Hakansson, N. H., Ohlson, J. A. and Kunkel, G. 1982: Sufficient and necessary conditions for information to have social value in pure exchange. *Journal of Finance*, 1169–81.

Harris, M. and Raviv, A. 1979: Optimal incentive contracts with imperfect information. *Journal of Economic Theory*, 231–59.

Harsanyi, J. C. 1968: Games of incomplete information played by Bayesian players. Parts I, II, and III. *Management Science*, 159–89, 320–34, 486–502.

⌀ Hellwig, M. F. 1980: On the aggregation of information in competitive markets. *Journal of economic Theory*, 477–98.

✓ Hirshleifer, J. 1971: The private and social value of information and the reward to inventive activity. *American Economic Review*, 561–74.

⚡ Holmstrom, B. 1979. Moral hazard and observability. *Bell Journal of Economics and Management Science*, 74–91.

✓—— 1982: Moral hazard in teams. *Bell Journal of Economics and Management Science*, 324–40.

Jaffe, J. F. 1975: On the use of information in financial markets. *Journal of Finance*, 831–40.

Jensen, M. C. and Meckling, W. 1976: Theory of the firm: managerial behaviour, agency costs, and ownership structure. *Journal of Financial Economics*, 305–60.

Jensen, M. C. and Ruback, R. C. 1983: The market for corporate control: the scientific evidence. *Journal of Financial Economics*, 5–50.

Jensen, M. C. and Smith, C. W. 1985a: The theory of corporate finance: an historical overview. Introduction to *The Modern Theory of Corporate Finance*. New York: McGraw-Hill.

—— 1985b: Stockholder, manager, and creditor interests: applications of agency theory. Chapter 4 of E. I. Altman and M. G. Subrahmanyam (eds), *Recent Advances in Corporate Finance*. Homewood Illinois: Irwin.

✓ John, K. and Kalay, A. 1985: Informational content of optimal contracts. Chapter 5 of E. I. Altman and M. G. Subrahmanyam (eds), *Recent Advances in Corporate Finance*. Homewood Illinois: Irwin

Jordan, J. S. 1982: The generic existence of rational expectations equilibria in the higher dimensional case. *Journal of Economic Theory*, 224–43.

✓ Jordan, J. S. and Radner, R. 1982: Rational expectations in microeconomic models: an overview. *Journal of Economic Theory*, 201–23.

Kahneman, D. and Tversky, A. 1979: Prospect theory: an analysis of decision making under risk. *Econometrica*, 263–91.

Keane, S. M. 1983: *Stock Market Efficiency*. Deddington, Oxon.: Philip Allan.

Kendall, M. G. 1953: The analysis of economic time-series, Part 1: Prices. *Journal of the Royal Statistical Society*, 11–25.

Kim, E. H. 1978: A mean-variance theory of optimal capital structure and corporate debt capacity. *Journal of Finance*, 45–64.

Kleidon, A. W. 1983: Variance bounds tests and stock price valuation models, Working paper, Stanford University, Graduate School of Business. Stanford Calif.

—— 1985: Variance bounds tests and stock price valuation models, Working paper, Stanford University, Graduate School of Business. Stanford Calif.

Kleidon, A. W. 1986: Bias in small sample tests of stock price rationality. *Journal of Business*, 237–61.

Kraus, A. and Litzenberger, R. 1973: A state preference model of optimal financial leverage. *Journal of Finance*, 911–22.

* Kreps, D. M. 1982: Multiperiod securities and the efficient allocation of risk: a comment on the Black–Scholes option pricing model. Chapter 6 in J. J. McCall (ed.), *The Economics of Uncertainty and Information*. Chicago: University of Chicago Press.

Kunkel, J. G. 1982: Sufficient conditions for public information to have social value in a production and exchange economy. *Journal of Finance*, 1005–73.

√ Lambert, R. A. 1983: Long-term contracts and moral hazard. *Bell Journal of Economics and Management Science*, 441–52.

—— 1984: Income smoothing as rational equilibrium behavior. *Accounting Review*, 604–17.

√ Latham, M. 1986: Informational efficiency and information subsets. *Journal of Finance*, 39–52.

Lazear, E. P. and Rosen, S. 1981: Rank-order tournaments as optimum labor contracts. *Journal of Political Economy*, 841–64.

* Leland, H. and Pyle, D. H. 1977: Informational asymmetries, financial structure, and financial intermediation. *Journal of Finance*, 371–87.

Leroy, S. F. 1973: Risk aversion and the martingale property of stock prices. *International Economic Review*, 136–46.

—— 1976: Efficient capital markets: comment *Journal of Finance*, 139–41.

Leroy, S. F. and LaCivita C. J. 1981: Risk aversion and the dispersion of asset prices. *Journal of Business*, 535–47.

? Leroy, S. F. and Porter, R. D. 1981 The present-value relation: tests based on implied variance bounds. *Econometrica*, 555–74.

Lintner, J. 1956: The distribution of incomes of corporations among dividends, retained earnings, and taxes. *American Economic Review*, 97–113.

—— 1965: The valuation of risky assets and the selection of risky investments in stock portfolios and capital budgets. *Review of Economics and Statistics*, 13–37.

Lucas, R. E. 1972: Expectations and the neutrality of money. *Journal of Economic Theory*, 103–24.

Makowski, L. 1983: Competition and unanimity revisited. *American Economic Review*, 329–39.

Mankiw, N. G., Romer, D. and Shapiro, M. D. 1985: An unbiased reexamination of stock market volatility. *Journal of Finance*, 677–87.

Manne, H. 1965: Mergers and the market for corporate control. *Journal of Political Economy*, 110–20.

Markovitz, H. M. 1959: *Portfolio Selection: efficient diversification of investments*. New York: Wiley.

Marschak, J. and Radner, R. 1972: Economic theory of teams. Cowles foundation monograph. New Haven and London. Yale University Press.

√ Marsh, T. A. and Merton, R. C. 1986: Dividend variability and variance bounds tests for the rationality of stock market prices. *American Economic Review*, 483–98.

Marshall, J. M. 1974: Private incentives and public information. *American Economic Review*, 373–90.

Merton, R. C. 1985: On the current state of the stock market rationality hypothesis. MIT working paper. Cambridge Mass.

Milgrom, P. and Stokey, N. 1982: Information, trade and common knowledge. *Journal of Economic Theory*, 17–27.

Miller, M. H. 1977: Debt and taxes. *Journal of Finance*, 261–75.

——— 1983: Can management use dividends to influence the value of the firm? in *Issues in Corporate Finance*. New York. Stern, Stewart, Putnam and Macklis.

Miller, M. H. and Modigliani, F. 1961: Dividend policy, growth and the valuation of shares. *Journal of Business*, 411–33.

Miller, M. H. and Rock, K. 1985: Dividend policy under asymmetric information. *Journal of Finance*, 1031–51.

Minford, P. and Peel, D. 1983: *Rational Expectations and the New Macroeconomics*. Oxford: Martin Robertson.

Mirlees, J. 1975: The theory of moral hazard and unobservable behaviour – Part 1. Mimeo, Nuffield College, Oxford.

Modigliani, F. and Miller, M. H. 1958: The cost of capital, corporation finance, and the theory of investment. *American Economic Review*, 261–97.

——— 1963: Corporate income taxes and the cost of capital. *American Economic Review*, 261–97.

Mood, A. M., Graybill, F. A. and Boes, D. C. 1974: *Introduction to the Theory of Statistics*, 3rd edn. New York: McGraw-Hill.

Mookherjee, A. 1984: Optimal incentive schemes with many agents. *Review of Economic Studies*, 433–46.

Mossin, J. 1977: *The Economic Efficiency of Financial Markets*. Lexington, Mass.: D. C. Heath.

Myers, S. C. 1977: The determinants of corporate borrowing. *Journal of Financial Economics*, 147–76.

Myerson, R. B. 1979: Incentive compatibility and the bargaining problem. *Econometrica*, 61–73.

Nalebluff, B. and Stiglitz, J. 1983: Prizes and incentives: towards a general theory of compensation and competition. *Bell Journal of Economics and Management Science*, 21–43.

Ohlson, J. A. and Buckman, G. 1981: Towards a theory of financial accounting: welfare and public information. *Journal of Accounting Research*, 399–433.

Osborne, M. F. M. 1959: Brownian motion and the stock market. *Operations Research*, 145–73.

——— 1962: Periodical structure in the Brownian motion of stock prices. *Operational Research*, 345–79.

Penno, M. 1984: The asymmetry of pre-decision information and managerial accounting. *Journal of Accounting Research*, 177–91.

Pratt, J. W. 1964: Risk aversion in the small and in the large *Econometrica*, 122–36.

Radner, R. 1968: Competitive equilibrium under uncertainty. *Econometrica*, 31–58.

——— 1979: Rational expectations equilibrium: generic existence and the information revealed by prices. *Econometrica*, 655–78.

Radner R. 1980: Does decentralization promote wasteful conflict? Bell Laboratories Economic Discussion Paper. Murray Hill. New Jersey.

—— 1981: Monitoring cooperative agreements in a repeated principal–agent relationship. *Econometrica*, 1127–48.

—— 1982: Equilibrium under uncertainty. Chapter 20 of K. J. Arrow and M. D. Intriligator (eds), *Handbook of Mathematical Economics*. Amsterdam, North Holland.

Ramakrishnan, R. T. S. and Thakor, A. V. 1984: The valuation of assets under moral hazard. *Journal of Finance*, 229–38.

Rogerson, W. P. 1985: The first-order approach to principal–agent problems. *Econometrica*, 1357–67.

Ross, S. A. 1973: The economic theory of agency: the principal's problem. *American Economic Review*, 134–9.

—— 1976: Options and efficiency. *Quarterly Journal of Economics*, 75–89.

—— 1977: The determination of financial structure: the incentive signalling approach. *Bell Journal of Economics and Management Science*, 373–90.

Rubinstein, A. and Yaari, M. 1983: Repeated insurance contracts and moral hazard. *Journal of Economic Theory*, 74–97.

Rubinstein, M. 1975: Securities market efficiency in an Arrow–Debreu economy. *American Economic Review*, 812–24.

Samuelson, P. A. 1965: Proof that properly anticipated prices fluctuate randomly. *Industrial Management Review*, 41–9.

—— 1973: Proof that properly discounted present values of assets vibrate randomly. *Bell Journal of Economics and Management Science*, 369–74.

Sappington, D. 1984: Incentive contracting with asymmetric and imperfect precontractual knowledge. *Journal of Economic Theory*, 52–70.

Sharpe, W. F. 1964: Capital asset prices: a theory of market equilibrium under risk. *Journal of Finance*, 425–42.

Shavell, S. 1979: Risk sharing and incentives in the principal and agent relationship. *Bell Journal of Economics and Management Science*, 55–73.

Sheffrin, S. M. 1983: *Rational Expectations*. Cambridge: Cambridge University Press.

Shiller, R. J. 1981a: Do stock prices move too much to be justified by subsequent changes in dividends. *American Economic Review*, 421–36.

—— 1981b: The use of volatility measures in assessing market efficiency. *Journal of Finance*, 291–304.

—— 1984: Stock prices and social dynamics. *Brookings Papers on Economic Activity*, part 2. Washington D.C. The Brookings Institution.

Simon, H. A. 1978: Rationality as process and product of thought. *American Economic Review*, 1–16.

Smith, C. W. and Warner, J. B. 1979: On financial contracting: an analysis of bond covenants. *Journal of Financial Economics*, 117–61.

Spence, A. M. 1976: Informational aspects of market structures: an introduction. *Quarterly Journal of Economics*, 591–7.

Stiglitz, J. E. 1972: Some aspects of the pure theory of corporate finance: bankruptcies and takeovers. *Bell Journal of Economics and Management Science*, 458–82.

Stiglitz, J. E. and Weiss, A. 1981: Credit rationing in markets with imperfect information. *American Economic Review*, 393–410.

—— 1983: Sorting out the differences between screening and signalling models. Princeton University working paper, Princeton, NJ.

Tobin, J. 1958: Liquidity preference as behavior towards risk. *Review of Economic Studies*, 65–85.

Varian, H. R. 1984: *Microeconomic Analysis*, 2nd edn. New York: Norton.

Verrecchia, R. E. 1982: Information acquisition in a noisy rational expectations economy. *Econometrica*, 1415–30.

Warner, J. 1977a: Bankruptcy costs: some evidence. *Journal of Finance*, 337–47.

—— 1977b: Bankruptcy, absolute priority, and the pricing of risky debt claims. *Journal of Finance*, 239–76.

Working, H. 1934: A random difference series for use in the analysis of time series. *Journal of the American Statistical Association*, 11–24.

Index

Index

Indexed by J.B. McDermott

✓ Journal of accounting research